MEDIA, FEMINIS

The Sacred Cinema of Andrei Tarkovsky
by Jeremy Mark Robinson

Jean-Luc Godard: The Passion of Cinema / Le Passion de Cinéma
by Jeremy Mark Robinson

Liv Tyler
by Thomas A. Christie

Disney Business, Disney Films, Disney Lands
The Wonderful World of the Walt Disney Company
Daniel Cerruti

Steven Spielberg: God-light
by Jeremy Mark Robinson

Stepping Forward: Essays, Lectures and Interviews
by Wolfgang Iser

Wild Zones: Pornography, Art and Feminism
by Kelly Ives

'Cosmo Woman': The World of Women's Magazines
by Oliver Whitehorne

Walerian Borowczyk
by Jeremy Mark Robinson

Andrea Dworkin
by Jeremy Mark Robinson

Cixous, Irigaray, Kristeva: The Jouissance of French Feminism
by Kelly Ives

Sex in Art: Pornography and Pleasure in Painting and Sculpture
by Cassidy Hughes

The Erotic Object: Sexuality in Sculpture
From Prehistory to the Present Day
by Susan Quinnell

Women in Pop Music
by Helen Challis

Detonation Britain: Nuclear War in the UK
by Jeremy Mark Robinson

Julia Kristeva: Art, Love, Melancholy, Philosophy, Semiotics
by Kelly Ives

Luce Irigaray: Lips, Kissing, and the Politics of Sexual Difference
by Kelly Ives

Helene Cixous I Love You: The **Jouissance** *of Writing*
by Kelly Ives

Feminism and Shakespeare
by B.D. Barnacle

About the Author

Thomas Christie has a life-long fascination with films and the
people who make them. Currently reading for a PhD in Scottish
literature, he lives in Scotland with his family.
He holds a first-class Honours degree in Literature and a
Masters degree in Humanities, specialising with distinction in
British Cinema History, from the Open University in Milton
Keynes.
Books by Thomas Christie include *Liv Tyler, Star in Ascendance: Her First
Decade in Film* (2007), *John Hughes and Eighties Cinema* (2009),
Ferris Bueller's Day Off: Pocket Movie Guide (2010) and *The Cinema of
Richard Linklater* (2011). Available from Crescent Moon Publishing.
For more information about Tom and his books, visit his
website at: http://www.tomchristiebooks.co.uk

The Cinema
of
Richard Linklater

The Cinema
of
Richard Linklater

Thomas A. Christie

Crescent Moon

Second edition 2011.
© Thomas A. Christie 2008, 2011.

Printed and bound in the U.S.A.
Set in Book Antiqua 10 on 14pt and Gill Sans.
Designed by Radiance Graphics.

British Library Cataloguing in Publication data available for this title.

Christie, Thomas A.
The Cinema of Richard Linklater
I. Title
791.4'33

ISBN-13 9781861712486

Crescent Moon Publishing
P.O. Box 393
Maidstone
Kent
ME14 5XU, U.K.

Contents

Acknowledgements

If there's one thing that can be said about Richard Linklater, it's that his films are never dull, and this was certainly also true when it came to writing about them. It was Thomas Edison who so memorably said – and here I paraphrase – that authorship is one percent inspiration and ninety-nine percent perspiration. (Indeed, in my experience this ratio may in fact have been a conservative estimate with regard to the perspiration side of things – one might have thought that Edison of all people would have realised this, living with all those electric lightbulbs that he had invented.) Anyway, one thing is indisputable: the fact that neither motivation or effort is of much use without encouragement, and in this respect I have undeniably been fortunate beyond measure.

First of all I'd like to thank my wonderful, long-suffering family – my mum Sandra, sister Julie, aunt Mary and Molly the Wonder Westie – for their endless support, their patience, and their tolerance of a certain computer keyboard chattering into the wee small hours on more than a few occasions.

Thanks once again are due to my mentor and good friend Douglas J. Allen, for his kind and much appreciated input into the project. His wisdom and experience, as well as his enthusiasm for films from all around the globe and across the decades, remain as valuable as always. My gratitude also goes to my many friends from the Borders and Northumberland, whose eagerness and fervour for this project has been a great encouragement. First of all, thanks to one of my oldest friends, Ivy Lannon, for our always-valued discussions about film, fiction, politics, society, culture, and everything and anything else besides. (If there's anyone who I know I can set the world to rights with, it's Ivy.) Appreciation is also due to Alistair McGregor Dalrymple, another incredibly supportive pal, for providing all sorts of input and insight which were to assist in the creation of this book.

Thanks too to Denham and Stella Hardwick, two people whose appreciation for the arts and live performance knows no limits, as well as my old pals Bill and Sue Wood for all their interest and kind words. And not forgetting, of course, the lovely Cheryl Redpath, a good friend and a fascinating person whose endless enthusiasm for life and travel just can't fail to inspire. I would also like to thank the Department of English Studies at the University of Stirling, in particular Professor Roderick Watson and Dr Scott Hames. A friendlier and more supportive learning environment one couldn't hope to ask for, and studying there has proven to me that Confucius was undeniably right in his assertion that, if you choose to apply yourself wholeheartedly to the furtherance of something that you love, you'll never really work a day in your life (deadlines notwithstanding).

Appreciation is due to all of my friends at the Rotary Club of Carse of Stirling for all of their interest and fellowship, particularly to Eddy Bryan, Ian McNeish, John Adamson, Hector McLennan and Charles Shields. Additional greetings also to my former Club, the Rotary Club of Berwick-upon-Tweed, for the continued friendship of their members.

I'd also like to voice gratitude to my many supportive friends at the Stirling Smith Art Gallery and Museum, one of the great cultural hubs of Central Scotland. Specific thanks are due to Dr Elspeth King, Michael Donnelly, Michael McGinnes, Margaret Job, and to artist Peter Russell.

Thanks also must go to journalist and poetry expert Lesley Duncan for her advice and interest in the project. I would also like to add a special word of thanks to Kirsten McMurray of Detour Filmproduction for all of her kind co-operation with Crescent Moon Publishing which has been invaluable in the process of compiling the second edition of this book.

The last word is reserved for the man who allowed this project to take form, and without him the book in your hands would not exist. The person that I mention is Jeremy Mark Robinson of Crescent Moon Publishing, and I would like to thank him most sincerely for his supportive encouragement at all points in the development of this book, as well as the stimulating correspondence that we have maintained about film in all of its multitudinous forms.

Thank you, one and all. What a long, strange trip it's been!

This book is dedicated to my father

Gilbert Christie
(1945-1981)

"Art is but a vision of reality."

W.B. Yeats
(*Ego Dominus Tuus*, 1917.)

"The meaning doesn't matter if it's only idle chatter of a transcendental kind."

Sir W.S. Gilbert
(*Patience*, Act 1, 1881.)

Richard Linklater

Richard Linklater with Kris Kristofferson

(Warner Independent)

(Top to bottom: Universal. Detour.
Warner Independent)

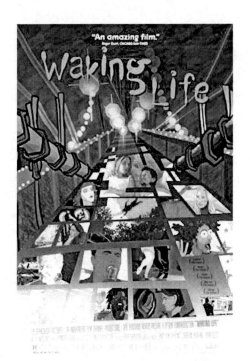

(Top to bottom: Fox Searchlight.
Lions Gate. Paramount)

(Warner Independent)

(Paramount)

FOREWORD

Welcome to the world of Richard Linklater, the extraordinary US movie director from Austin, Texas, whose broad range of films – from indie (*Slacker*) to mainstream (*School of Rock*) – makes it impossible to pigeonhole him. What is not open to debate is the quality of his output – his films are original, entertaining, intelligent, philosophical, innovative, adventurous, unpredictable, eclectic... to be honest, the adjectives could go on ad infinitum.

Welcome also to the world of Thomas A. Christie, whose pioneering attempt to pin down the elusive nature of the maverick *auteur* makes for an impressive follow-up to his recent volume on Liv Tyler. This new work bears all the hallmarks of the earlier book – wide-ranging and meticulous research, detailed intelligent commentaries on each film, backed up by well informed and even-handed opinions. In every chapter Christie demonstrates his encyclopaedic knowledge of Linklater, his films and movieland in general – you feel safe in his cinematic hands.

His opinions are authoritative – you know instinctively that Christie's judgements are the result of detailed viewing and analysis of Linklater's oeuvre, filtered through a sharp and perceptive mind. Christie proves once again that he is master of fine detail and well formulated opinion, expressed in the clearest narrative prose. We couldn't ask for a better guide to the world of Linklater.

If you don't know Linklater's films, this book will make you want to see them. If you feel you know them all already, think again – you'll want to re-view them again and again after reading Christie's thought-provoking volume.

Douglas J. Allen
Lecturer in Social Sciences
Motherwell College

INTRODUCTION

Richard Stuart Linklater (1960-) is one of the most interesting, original and exciting independent film-makers active in America today. He has become known as the high priest of slacker culture, a persuasive and distinctive proponent of complex philosophical issues, a socio-political filmic polymath, and one of the most expressive articulators of the Generation X ethos. But in truth, his body of work presents a far wider remit than even these fashionable appellations would suggest, and the intricate range of themes with which he has engaged over the past two decades has proven to be both extensive and comprehensive.

Linklater came to prominence in the early 1990s, a time when major new American film-making talent was emerging in the form of pioneering directors including Whit Stillman, Kevin Smith, Hal Hartley and Quentin Tarantino. Even more than these others, Linklater's output would quickly transcend simple generic categorisation, and the density and thematic intricacy of his films have come to establish him as one of the most innovative and imaginative directors currently working in the United States.

A majority of his films contain the robust ability to connect the viewer with multifaceted philosophical, social and political deliberation, in a manner which is as engaging as it is thought-provoking. Sharp, intelligent dialogue, keenly-drawn characterisation and an occasional tendency to contain the narrative of an entire film within the time-span of a single day have all become hallmarks of a typical Richard Linklater film. But then, Linklater's films are usually anything but typical.

This book discusses Richard Linklater's canon of full-length motion pictures to date, from his low-budget debut *It's Impossible to Learn to Plow by Reading Books* (1988) to his recent, acclaimed *Me and Orson Welles* (2008). Linklater has worked on a number of other features throughout the course of his career, including nontheatrical releases (*Heads I Win/ Tails You Lose*, 1991), short features (*Woodshock*, 1985), *Live From Shiva's Dance Floor*, 2003), and work for television (*$5.15/ Hr*, 2004). However, as the purpose of this text is to explore the style and themes of Linklater's feature-length cinematic output, works which were not intended for the big screen will not be discussed here.

Although the flair and richness of his works has variously been compared with the styles of numerous great directors over the years, ranging from Luis Buñuel to Robert Altman and from Jim Jarmusch to Eric Rohmer, there is no doubt that Linklater is an entirely unique talent in his own right, irresolutely creative and persistently inventive. Like any true master of his craft, he is disinclined to accommodate easy answers in a world of ever increasing moral and philosophical complexity, and consequently he never shies away from presenting difficult or unpalatable truths along the way.

Richard Linklater is very much a voice of reason in uncertain times, a film-maker of distinction in an unpredictable and complicated world. From highly individualistic cult success to global mainstream achievements, there are few who would deny that Linklater has become one of the most respected, influential and accomplished directorial talents of twenty-first century America.

1

IT'S IMPOSSIBLE TO LEARN TO PLOW BY READING BOOKS (1988)

Detour Filmproduction

Director: Richard Linklater
Producer: Richard Linklater
Screenwriter: Richard Linklater

Main Cast
Richard Linklater
James Goodwin
Dan Kratochvil
Linda Finney
Tracy Crabtree
Linda Levine
Lisa Schiebold
Erin McAfee

It's Impossible to Learn to Plow by Reading Books was Richard Linklater's first full-length motion picture. It was the production of this film, along with other features, which led to him establishing his now-famous Detour Filmproduction company, following time spent at Sam Houston State University and, later, working on an oil rig as well as in other areas of employment.[1] *It's Impossible to Learn to Plow* presents one of his most unconventional narratives, layered with many subtle thematic undercurrents and shrewd character observations. Although it has been overshadowed by his later successes, and is dwarfed in particular by the massive significance of his breakthrough success with *Slacker*, this early micro-budget presentation reveals many of Linklater's cultural and philosophical concerns by complex implication, some years before he would come to state them more explicitly in later films. Shot on Super-8 film with a meagre budget of $3000,[2] an analysis of this first film remains valuable in that it provides early proof not only of the potency of Linklater's ongoing thematic preoccupations, but also his unwavering professional seriousness as an artist.

This most offbeat of road movies features the various journeys of a young man (Richard Linklater) as he treks across America via bus, train, car and, at one point, ferry. A student in further education, we join him as he travels through different areas of America, spends time with friends, family and occasionally strangers… and, indeed, a straightforward breakdown of the plot more or less ends there. The film is simply one long unending journey, with no particularly apparent beginning and no readily definable conclusion, and there is little incident along the way. And yet there is no doubt from the very deliberate nature of the film's structure that Linklater always intended it to be this way; a narrative which employs the message that there is no destination without first undergoing a journey to get there, and consequently examining the nature of just what such a journey entails. Are the destinations, in fact, merely temporary stopping points, part of the trip rather than any one of them forming a conclusion in and of itself? Linklater posits no easy answers. The fact that so little noteworthy action takes place during the protagonist's transit underscores Linklater's point that, in travel as in life, there is only a hair's breadth between the serene and the banal – and during the film's long journey, *It's Impossible to Learn to Plow* deliberately crosses over that boundary, and back again, with considerable regularity to prove exactly this point.

Given that it was his feature film debut, it is remarkable just how assured Linklater's directorial presentation is – particularly considering its severe budgetary restraints. *It's Impossible to Learn to Plow* is, of course, uncompromisingly raw film-making; from the grainy, dimly-lit domestic interiors to the grimy utilitarianism of the protagonist's voyage through America's public transport system, the audience is left in no doubt that this is a real slice-of-life depiction of eighties' culture in Ronald Reagan's America. Relying entirely on his own skill as a film-maker to bring the feature to life, with no extensive crew behind him, Linklater articulates well the central theme of the film – that of the essential isolation of life in the society of the time, and the problems entailed in overcoming it given the multifaceted and often difficult nature of communication between people in the modern world. Yet it would be overly straightforward to assign an explicitly solipsistic agenda to Linklater's film. Indeed, while Linklater appears to be very much concerned with communication (not only the content of what people have to say, but the manner in which they choose to say it), he seems to be just as determined to examine the characteristics of interpersonal connections between individuals – however mundane – as much as he ponders the nature of the self. However, unlike the almost entirely dialogue driven *Slacker* which was to follow it, *It's Impossible to Learn to Plow* contains very little spoken discourse, and although the quality of the sound tends to be muffled throughout (perhaps by design, reinforcing the film's grittiness, but more likely due to the limitations of the film's budget), the rare instances of verbal intercourse do focus the viewer's attention as being specifically significant, largely because of the general dearth of speech from the majority of the film. Given the near-absence of the spoken word, it is just as noteworthy to observe the way in which Linklater fuses verbal and nonverbal communication into a combined dialogic strategy. This is evident, for instance, in the beautifully rendered sequence where the protagonist meets a stranger in a train station during the course of his journey. He exchanges small-talk with her for a while, albeit indistinctly and rather uneasily, before they both fall asleep in the station's waiting area. No particular connection between them is suggested until the protagonist awakens, realises that the young woman is still asleep, and leaves a hastily scribbled note on top of her luggage before departing. Here, even by saying very little in verbal terms, Linklater suggests a fragile and oddly touching temporary bond between the two strangers which foreshadows one of the most prominent themes that would come to develop throughout his career; a fascination with the way in which ordinary people are influenced by the ebb and flow of society around them, and the importance of the connections forged between people even in spite of the multifarious cultural currents which affect and ultimately shape their individual lives. This particular encounter is also significant in the way in which it subtly foreshadows the meeting between two other young travellers which was to come a number of years later in Linklater's *Before Sunrise*.

It's Impossible to Learn to Plow was, for many years, a difficult feature to track down, with only occasional sporadic screenings at film festivals. However, it has justly enjoyed a revival of interest following its inclusion on the 2004 Criterion Collection edition of *Slacker*, where it features on a supplementary DVD along with Linklater's even earlier short feature *Woodshock* (1985). (There is actually an interesting link between *Woodshock* and *It's Impossible to Learn to Plow* – the affable stranger who offers Linklater a copy of his recorded cassette tape near the conclusion of the film is strongly reminiscent of a similar character in *Woodshock*, and inadvertently also reveals the reasoning behind *It's Impossible to Learn to Plow*'s enigmatic title.)

Largely due to the nature of its highly unconventional structure, *It's Impossible to Learn to Plow* did not fare particularly well with the critical community at the time, though its recent release on DVD has led to some modern reviewers re-examining its qualities more favourably in retrospect.[3] Today, the film remains almost certainly Linklater's most obscure and least watched feature, and although there is undoubted interest to be gained from its relaxed, strangely melancholic take on the banality of an everyman's travels across the United States of the eighties, perhaps its principal function has now become as a wistful but insightful prelude to Linklater's vastly more significant next feature, *Slacker*.

2

SLACKER (1991)

Detour Filmproduction

Director: Richard Linklater
Producer: Richard Linklater
Screenwriter: Richard Linklater

Main Cast
Richard Linklater – 'Should Have Stayed at Bus Station'
Mark James – Hit-and-Run Son
Jerry Delony – 'Been on the Moon Since the 50s'
Teresa Taylor – Papsmear Pusher
John Slate – Conspiracy A-Go-Go Author
Louis Mackey – Old Anarchist
R. Malice – Scooby Doo Philosopher
Wammo – Anti-Artist

Slacker was undoubtedly the breakthrough feature in Richard Linklater's directorial career. It is difficult to overstate just how significant and influential the film has become, not only in terms of Linklater's own filmography, but in the wider context of American independent cinema from the early nineties. Although only his second film, *Slacker* was to make Linklater one of the most distinctive voices of the independent film world, and along with films like Gus Van Sant's *My Own Private Idaho* (1991), Kevin Smith's *Clerks* (1994) and Ben Stiller's *Reality Bites* (1994), it is no exaggeration to say that Linklater was a major factor in helping to define the sometimes chaotic voice of Generation X during that period in time.[4] Indeed, so profound was the impact of *Slacker* that it is still, in many eyes, the work most associated with Richard Linklater's name even today, and the film's distinctly American take on Generation X encapsulated the offbeat youth attitudes of the time so successfully that for a number of commentators, Linklater's narrative approach would remain entwined with the key concepts behind the Generation X appellation for many years to come.

Slacker's potency as a fixture in nineties' popular culture is more or less assured, for its synonymy with Generation X has made it something of a cult legend amongst certain audiences. The term 'Generation X' has acquired many connotations and conflicting definitions over the years,[5] and indeed even the date boundaries which demarcate it from other generations are somewhat hazy.[6] However, there is general agreement that most members of Generation X would have lived through their teen-age years in the 1980s, and reached their twenties by the time of the 1990s. The term itself actually originated from research dating back to the mid-sixties, but entered the public lexicon with considerably greater prominence thanks to the publication of Canadian author Douglas Coupland's novel *Generation X: Tales for an Accelerated Culture* (1991).[7] This remains today almost certainly the foremost literary manifestation of what it meant to belong to Generation X at the time[8] and – like Linklater's film – clearly acknowledged the fact that this age group was complicated, multifaceted and above all difficult to explicitly categorise.[9] With *Slacker*, Linklater would not only deal with the social and philosophical makeup of Generation X, but was also to actively challenge the negative connotations that had come to surround it throughout the eighties, questioning whether the term's often-attributed qualities of nihilism and socio-political insecurity could in fact be counterbalanced by far more positive characteristics.

As a feature film, *Slacker* is notoriously awkward to define in even the broadest terms, with no apparent dominant plotline and no clear driving force to guide the film's narrative (some commentators have actually termed it an 'anti-narrative').[10] Many critics have ventured the opinion that to even attempt to pigeonhole the film is to miss the point entirely[11] -when asked what *Slacker* is about, the only really meaningful answer in narrative terms is that it's about an hour and a half long. More than most films, its unorthodox structure means that it has to be seen to be experienced. And that, perhaps, is Linklater's whole point; like the lives of its characters, the film has an organic, lackadaisical quality, where the unpredictable almost becomes the norm and enlightenment can be found in anomalous, brief and unexpected moments of offbeat illumination.

In an opening sequence that would be familiar to any viewer of *It's Impossible to Learn to Plow by Reading Books*, *Slacker* begins with an unnamed character – played by Richard Linklater – travelling on a bus. He arrives at his destination in Austin, Texas, gets into a taxi... and from thereon in, *Slacker* diverges from its predecessor in almost every conceivable way. Linklater's character utters more dialogue in his protracted, one-sided conversation with the taciturn taxi driver than had been contained in more or less the entirety of *It's Impossible to Learn to Plow*. Even from this early point in the film, we are left in no doubt that *Slacker* is a film about discussion, interaction and the nature of relationships – however brief – between different people, with a diverse multiplicity of communication methods examined throughout the course of the film. As Linklater's contemplative character reflects on the notion of parallel universes and the possibility that every choice we make has unseen but consequential ramifications, the audience is being prepared for a journey that will be just as meandering and offbeat as that of *It's Impossible to Learn to Plow*, but with colourful characters and thought-provoking concepts replacing the stark, vaguely bleak destinations of *Slacker*'s predecessor. Linklater's reflective philosopher expounds the theory that many distinct realities may simultaneously be existing parallel to his own, and – to obliquely prove his point – we quickly switch from the taxi to a car accident on a nearby street. This accident, we soon discover, may in fact be far from unintentional. We then shift from the victim in order to follow the culprit, who is arrested soon after. The focus is then transferred to another individual. This cycle continues over and over until the film reaches its abrupt conclusion when, in a strikingly symbolic gesture, a Super-8 camera is thrown over the top of a cliff by the last character to appear (Greg Ward).

Slacker is a fascinating travelogue through the city of Austin, journeying not just around the lives of people of a largely similar age, but also through the concepts and notions which were coming to characterise that age group. The majority of the characters are in their twenties, but Linklater does not marginalise others who fall outside of this age bracket. Anyone given cause to doubt this fact by the film's early hit-and-run incident, where a middle-aged lady (Jean Caffeine) is struck by a speeding car before her character can be established in even the vaguest terms, need only compare it to the fascinating, rambling 'Old Anarchist' (Louis Mackey), whose long-winded reminiscences with a strangely personable burglar who has broken into his house (Michael Laird) reveal that he has not allowed his advancing years to dilute his revolutionary fervour or zeal for political issues. Yet it is admittedly when the film is centring on its twenty-something cast, as it mostly does, that Linklater's theories on life and all of its manifold nuances are coaxed out of the characters in the most gratifying and faintly mesmerizing ways. We bear witness to faltering romances, religious rumination, political postulation, the hithertounknown spiritual function of the Smurfs, and – just as memorably – the attempted sale of the results of a cervical smear test carried out on a world-famous pop star, which raises all manner of questions about the cult of celebrity (as the 'Pap Smear Pusher' (Teresa Taylor) points out, it's the kind of item that has more immediate consequence to a 'true fan' than just a straightforward, commonplace album or poster). Other characters have equally compelling motivations, such as the 'Video Backpacker' (Kalman Spelletich) whose motivations suggest an interesting dichotomy between the temptations of materialism and that of simple capital gain – a topic of particular importance following the West's emergence from the avarice and acquisitiveness of the eighties. There are many, many such intriguing characters scattered throughout *Slacker*, and almost all of them have something to say (indeed, more often than not, several things).

Slacker is a film where there are no boundaries, and where no rules are set. The film is part satire, part social commentary, and as Linklater has noted, deals mostly with individuals who are on the periphery of any consequential involvement in the mainstream social order, and who have taken the initiative to abstain from that society rather than willingly offering it the opportunity to discard them on its own terms.[12] This duality of purpose is especially evident in many of the characters' inclination towards wild conspiracy theories – encapsulating everything from the assassination of John F. Kennedy to alien beings, UFOs and the Moon landings. These qualities of deep suspicion regarding authority and the establishment are most prominently manifest in the characters 'Been on the Moon Since the '50s' (Jerry Delony) and 'Conspiracy A-Go-Go Author' (John Slate), and the rich stratum of distrust and wariness of authority which is woven throughout the film was to mirror the speculative paranoia on display in many of the decade's most successful mainstays of popular culture, particularly evident in acclaimed television shows such as David Lynch's *Twin Peaks* (1990-91) and Chris Carter's *The X-Files* (1994-2002). This implicitly fantastic element is further compounded by the film's sometimes dreamlike quality, bolstered by the frequent, surrealistic discussions of the nature of reality which occur throughout.

Of course, the term 'slacker' is not interchangeable with Generation X,[13] and this is a fact that Linklater communicates most succinctly. As one character points out, retreating from society in disdain is not the same as being indifferent to it,[14] and throughout the film even the most disaffected and feckless characters are demonstrably unique and, in their own way, self-motivated – even if those motivations are oblique or ambiguous. One does not need to be a member of Generation X to demonstrate Slacker credentials, we soon learn. Take, for instance, the 'Old Man Recording Thoughts' (Joseph Jones), an elderly gent with a tape recorder making a spontaneous audio chronicle of his opinions and feelings in a way that might, strangely enough, have appealed to Leopold Bloom in James Joyce's *Ulysses*, for that novel's stream-of-consciousness style has been acknowledged by Linklater as a profound influence on his approach to art.[15] Significantly, the passage read almost ceremonially by 'Guy Who Tosses Typewriter' (Steven Anderson), in an attempt to conciliate the romantic woes of his compatriot 'Jilted Boyfriend' (Kevin Whitley), is itself drawn from *Ulysses*. Thus Linklater makes the point that, just as every individual in the film is perceptibly distinctive, there is likewise no 'one' Generation X which can be easily categorised, labelled or branded. Furthermore, there is the tangential fact that in Joyce's *Ulysses*, the entire narrative takes place – famously – within the timeframe of a single day; an effective technique that was most certainly not lost on Linklater's subsequent approach to film-making, for *Slacker* was to be his first feature to exercise the technique of confining the film's narrative to within a roughly twenty-four hour period. This was a convention which he would subsequently utilise to such effect that it has become one of his directorial trademarks, certainly with regard to his early career.

Linklater cleverly posits the theory that, just because the rationale behind a slacker's existence is hazy, they may nonetheless be driven by an impetus known only to themselves, which is no less legitimate than an agenda ascribed to them by wider society. As Charles Gunning's 'Hitchhiker Awaiting "True Call"' memorably expresses it, although he may exist imperfectly in the eyes of mainstream social conventions, at least he doesn't have to be toiling in nine-to-five employment in order to earn the privilege of said existence.[16] It is this contempt for the rat-race, the refusal to conform to standardised, homogenous social norms, which so gracefully underpins *Slacker*'s agenda of eccentric but authentic freedom.

Slacker met with near-unanimous critical approval on its release, and in terms of formal qualities was to be variously compared with Luis Buñuel's *The Phantom of Liberty* (1974),[17] Max Ophuls's *La Ronde* (1950)[18] and even a kind of highly mobile variation on Louis Malle's *My Dinner with Andre* (1981).[19] Even Linklater himself has voiced some surprise in media interviews at the influence, prominence and high regard that has come to surround the film, given its quirky, oblique narrative, lack of famous performers and deficiency of conventional action.[20] Yet for all its frequently-mentioned lack of traditional onscreen exploits, *Slacker* is actually a very vibrant and spontaneous film, a patchwork of unpredictable character sketches and rewarding moments of genuine, if rather eccentric, humanity. By changing its focus so rapidly from character to character, aspects of each individual's personality and worldview are conveyed to the audience without the viewer ever becoming closely involved with any one person as the film continues its easygoing but nonetheless persistent drive forward. And this, perhaps, is why the film became such a successful collage of social realities (and, to a degree, non-realities) in that rarefied transitional stage between the eighties and nineties – many aspects of human life are allowed an allotted few minutes in the spotlight to be examined and acknowledged before another takes centre stage.

While the film's fractured structure and transitional, conversational style of storytelling were not new in and of themselves, Linklater was able to reinvigorate the method and successfully reinvent it for a new audience and a new generation. The fact that he was able to do this with a cast of unknowns and a minuscule budget of $24,000 (though a king's ransom in comparison with *It's Impossible to Learn to Plow*),[21] says much for his professionalism and single-mindedness of purpose. As some critics noted, perhaps Linklater's single greatest achievement with *Slacker* was to project an air of casual improvisation throughout the film when, in fact, the whole is painstakingly engineered to create a very specific and deliberately calculated effect.[22] The film also proved to be very influential amongst other directors of the time, including (perhaps most famously) Kevin Smith, who frequently cited it as a major inspiration for his own Generation X classic *Clerks* (1994).[23]

Slacker was nominated for the Grand Jury Prize for a Dramatic Presentation at the 1991 Sundance Film Festival, and Linklater was also to be nominated for Best Director and Best First Feature at the Independent Spirit Awards in 1992. The film's critical success had brought Linklater to the attention of some of the most eminent film commentators in America, and paved the way for his later, larger-scale features. There was no doubt now that Richard Linklater had truly arrived on the scene, and that with *Slacker* a major contribution to independent film had been made.

3

DAZED AND CONFUSED (1993)

Detour Filmproduction / Alphaville Films

Director: Richard Linklater
Producers: Sean Daniel, James Jacks and Richard Linklater
Screenwriter: Richard Linklater

Main Cast
Jason London – Randall 'Pink' Floyd
Rory Cochrane – Ron Slater
Wiley Wiggins – Mitch Kramer
Sasha Jenson – Don Dawson
Michelle Burke – Jodi Kramer
Adam Goldberg – Mike Newhouse
Anthony Rapp – Tony Olson
Matthew McConaughey – David Wooderson

Dazed and Confused marked an interesting shift in gear for Richard Linklater's directorial career. A spiky, nostalgic take on high school culture in Gerald Ford's America of the mid-seventies, the film exchanged *Slacker*'s rough-and-ready style of mock improvisation for glossier production values and a painstakingly accurate period setting. Yet as had been the case in his previous feature, Linklater's highly proficient command of characterisation would be seen to remain very much in evidence, as was his increasingly dextrous narrative playfulness. Still fresh from the critical acclaim of *Slacker*, and with an expansive cast of talented young actors to employ, the stage was set for Linklater's grandest creative project thus far.

It's late in the afternoon on the 28th of May 1976 – the last day of term at Lee High School. For senior students, the raucous festivity is mixed with reflection as they consider the road that lies ahead of them. For freshmen about to leave junior high, there is the more pressing issue of trying to avoid the punishing initiation rites concocted by the seniors. Over the course of a roughly 24-hour period during the long hot summer of America's Bicentennial year, we witness the exploits of a wide array of teenagers as they undergo celebration, contemplation, ritual induction, and an admirable amount of partying.

One of Linklater's most estimable achievements in *Dazed and Confused* was his irresolute refusal to offer up any lazy character stereotypes or a clichéd, formulaic plot. Indeed, much like *Slacker* before it, there is a sense that there is little need to impress a rigorously enforced storyline upon the viewer when the main thrust of the film's ethos is one of a lackadaisical drift through a short but intense period of time – the euphoric liberation that can only come from leaving school (for some, for the summer vacation; for others, for life). Yet for all the jubilation and excitement of that life-affirming moment when the school bell rings for the final time, Linklater seems determined to emphasise the fact that this is no golden age for these characters; there are uncertainties ahead, with difficulties to face and tough choices to make.[24] Just because the film's seventies setting suggests an affectionate nostalgia at times, there is a strong awareness that the setting should not be perceived as idealised, and that the past should not be presented as either romanticised or somehow more innocent than the present day.

Like its predecessor, the whole filmic experience of *Dazed and Confused* is made up of a complex mosaic of individual, well-observed occurrences all the way throughout. The film is at its best when gleefully subverting well-worn teen movie truisms, including the illicit purchase of alcohol from convenience stores by kids too young to legally buy it – quirkily, the whole process of procuring liquor comes off entirely without incident, in contrast to almost every other high school movie in living memory, perhaps the most famous example being Rod Daniel's *Teen Wolf* (1985). There is also the requisite wild house party which, against all tradition, fizzles out before it has a chance to begin, thanks to the inopportune early arrival of the beer-keg delivery man (a memorably tongue-in-cheek performance from John Swasey). Much entertainment is later derived from the discomfort of the hapless would-be party host, Kevin Pickford (Shawn Andrews), at his father's calculated thwarting of his plans, and the older man's subsequent spirited repulsion of the prospective partygoers as soon as they arrive throughout the evening.

Notably, *Dazed and Confused* is at its most interesting when it is presenting us not just with clever and astutely-drawn situations (though they are there in abundance nonetheless), but rather when it draws the viewer into the minds of its colourful and skilfully created characters. As a number of critics have noted, Linklater's characters are never ciphers, and are always presented as living, breathing people with complicated and sometimes weighty concerns which seem to extend beyond the confines of the film.[25] Most of the characters are motivating and entertaining in equal measure. Take, for example, the permanently-stoned Ron Slater (Rory Cochrane), who seems largely oblivious to anything going on around him (and if he could notice it, one senses that he probably wouldn't care all that much), but who is only too happy to share his engagingly crackpot theories about George and Martha Washington's alleged marijuana-imbibing habits. There's also Fred O'Bannion (Ben Affleck), a testosterone-fuelled class jock who – it is hinted – has deliberately failed his end-of-year exams in order to live through his senior year of high school all over again. His bizarrely obsessive focus on freshmen initiation rituals (basically, walloping their rear-ends repeatedly with a makeshift wooden paddle) glaringly highlights the fact that his life is sadly lacking in purpose, almost as though his rapidly-fading school days mark a kind of high water mark which he feels he will be unable to match in later life. Equally unable to separate himself from the past is David Wooderson (Matthew McConaughey), a tragicomic figure now in his mid-twenties who is still hanging out with people almost a decade younger than him. He intriguingly describes his motivations in terms of the fact that although he grows older with every passing year, the senior girls in high school always seem to remain the same age.

Amongst the weird and wonderful characters is a scattering of subdued, more contemplative individuals. Foremost among them is freshman Mitch Kramer (Wiley Wiggins), a relative newcomer to the seniors' way of life who watches the day's memorable goings-on with a strangely wistful, distant air of introspection that belies his youth. Linklater also demonstrates a characteristic unwillingness to present simplified moral answers with the long-running battle of wills between star baseball player Randall 'Pink' Floyd (Jason London) and the patriarchal, authoritarian Coach Conrad (Terry Mross). Conrad wants Floyd to sign a pledge abrogating bad living; Floyd resents the repression that this oath represents, but his rebellion in turn sparks friction with his friends on the team, who fear that his mutiny will jeopardise their own sporting futures. But what ultimately matters more to Floyd – his perceived freedom and principles, peer pressure, or compliance with the establishment in order to secure his ambitions? In lesser hands, this kind of ethical tug-of-war may have been handed so blandly that it would have been resolved with merely insipid mediocrity, but Linklater presents the issues so strikingly – and with such maturity on the part of the characters – that the conclusion feels both valid and compelling.

One of the most prominent factors of the film, of course, was that in place of *Slacker*'s extensive cast of unknowns, *Dazed and Confused* featured a dizzying array of up-and-coming young talent occupying many of the central roles. Principal among them was Ben Affleck as Fred O'Bannion, who would go on to become one of the best-known acting names of his generation due to prominent appearances in films as diverse as *Good Will Hunting* (1997), *Armageddon* (1998) and *Pearl Harbor* (2001). Today an Academy Award winner, Affleck has also featured in many successful collaborations with director Kevin Smith, including *Mallrats* (1995), *Chasing Amy* (1997), *Dogma* (1998) and *Jersey Girl* (2004) amongst others. The Kevin Smith connection is shared with Joey Lauren Adams, who played Simone Kerr in *Dazed and Confused* and who would also come to appear in Smith's *Mallrats* and *Chasing Amy* as well as the anarchic *Jay and Silent Bob Strike Back* (2001). Other famous appearances included Cole Hauser as Benny O'Donnell, who would later appear in *Pitch Black* (2000), *White Oleander* (2002) and *2 Fast 2 Furious* (2003), whereas Milla Jovovich – *Dazed and Confused*'s Michelle Burroughs – went on to further success with films such as *The Fifth Element* (1998), *The Million Dollar Hotel* (2000) and *Resident Evil* (2002).

Notably, many of the film's young cast of actors would work with Linklater again in the years ahead. *Dazed and Confused*'s Darla Marks was played by Parker Posey, generally considered to be one of the most sophisticated acting talents in American independent film,[26] who would later appear in Linklater's *subUrbia* in 1996. She was to continue her varied and prolific performance career with distinctive films such as *Waiting For Guffman* (1996), *The House of Yes* (1997), *You've Got Mail* (1998) and the hugely successful box-office hit *Superman Returns* (2006). Matthew McConaughey, virtually unknown before appearing in the role of David Wooderson in *Dazed and Confused*, went on to appear in many famous features, among them being *A Time to Kill* (1996) and *Amistad* (1997), before his appearance in Linklater's *The Newton Boys* (1998). Rory Cochrane, who had played the genial but addled Ron Slater, would appear again in many films including *Empire Records* (1995), *Dogtown* (1997) and *Hart's War* (2002), as well as reuniting with Linklater for *A Scanner Darkly* in 2006. And Wiley Wiggins, the actor behind Mitch Kramer, would appear in films such as *Plastic Utopia* (1997) and *The Faculty* (1998) before also working with Linklater again – this time as the central character in *Waking Life* (2001).

Linklater's departure from the intense, calculatedly disjointed style of *Slacker* was readily apparent. As it made a break from its predecessor's famous grainy tracking shots and long, lingering takes, *Dazed and Confused* found itself compared less with the directorial style of Max Ophuls and more with the kind of freewheeling storytelling approach that has been associated with Robert Altman,[27] crossed with other admired American coming-of-age dramas including the likes of George Lucas's *American Graffiti* (1973) and Barry Levinson's *Diner* (1982). (Interestingly, Linklater was to disavow any purported similarity to *American Graffiti*, stating that the well-loved Lucas film had focused on an idealised form of nostalgia which *Dazed and Confused* explicitly rejects.)[28]

Dazed and Confused was vastly more refined in technical terms than had been the case with the ultra low-budget *Slacker*, and Linklater makes the most of his enhanced production values by ensuring that the period setting is portrayed with unerring accuracy. A glance at the products on display at the local convenience store or the diverse pop culture paraphernalia in Pickford's bedroom, for instance, is as telling an evocation of the age as are the faithfully reproduced fashions and ostentatious hairstyles. As Linklater has observed in interviews, the film depicts not so much the seventies America that people wanted to live through, but rather the decade that people actually did live through.[29]

Dazed and Confused did not have the same immediate impact with critics as had been the case with *Slacker*, but in general it was favourably received by those reviewing it at the time.[30] Linklater gained particular praise for his steadfast refusal to offer a comfortably moralistic standpoint on the film's action, including (controversially) the depiction of the casual use of soft drugs which was essential to the social and historical accuracy of the narrative.[31] Significantly, the film has acquired a greater reputation in recent years, becoming regular cult viewing amongst audiences, while a number of its iconic scenes and lines of sharp dialogue have penetrated the cultural consciousness. Likewise, the film's marvellous rock soundtrack has become the stuff of legend, due to Linklater's carefully chosen selections drawn from prominent artists of the time including Alice Cooper, Kiss, Deep Purple, Black Sabbath and Aerosmith (the latter being particularly significant given the characters' repeated desire throughout the film to get their hands on Aerosmith concert tickets).

Dazed and Confused gained Richard Linklater a nomination for the Golden Leopard Award at the 1993 Locarno International Film Festival, and would also see Jason London nominated for Best Youth Actor Co-Starring in a Motion Picture Drama for his role as 'Pink' Floyd at the Young Artist Awards in 1994. Just as importantly, it further established Linklater's unique and articulate voice, proving that his distinctive directorial imprimatur had survived the transition from its roots in low-budget filmmaking unscathed.[32] Critical expectation grew as to where he would next turn his artistic attentions and, as usual, when the time came Linklater was not to fail in surprising everyone.

4

BEFORE SUNRISE (1995)

Detour Filmproduction / Castle Rock Entertainment / Filmhaus Wien Universa Filmpro / Sunrise Production / Columbia Pictures

Director: Richard Linklater
Producer: Anne Walker-McBay
Screenwriters: Richard Linklater and Kim Krizan

Main Cast
Ethan Hawke – Jesse
Julie Delpy – Celine
Andrea Eckert – Wife on Train
Hänno Poschl – Husband on Train
Karl Bruckschweaiger – Guy on Bridge #1
Tex Rubinowitz – Guy on Bridge #2
Erni Mangold – Palm Reader
Dominik Castell – Street Poet

Before Sunrise was to mark something of a change of pace for Linklater's filmography. An immaculately observed character study centring around a developing romance between two complete strangers, the film's intimate atmosphere was a world away from the vast ensemble casts of *Slacker* and *Dazed and Confused*, and seemed almost a return – albeit an infinitely more refined one – to the personal and highly detailed character analysis witnessed in *It's Impossible to Learn to Plow by Reading Books*.

Before Sunrise is an immediately striking film because, like *Slacker* before it, it proves almost impossible to pigeonhole into any one straightforward genre category. Although the film has the theme of romance positioned squarely as its central locus, Linklater was to use the film's highly discursive narrative as a springboard to explore many other issues including international relations, gender equality and – most significantly – the nature of interpersonal communication. The film's multi-layered screenplay also marked a highly successful collaboration between Linklater and Kim Krizan, a writer and actress who had previously appeared in *Slacker* in the role of 'Questions Happiness', and later in *Dazed and Confused* as teacher Ginny Stroud.

One summer's day in the mid-nineties, a young American man named Jesse (Ethan Hawke) is travelling on a train through Europe on his way to catch a return flight to the States from Austria. Having just suffered an acrimonious split from his girlfriend, whom he had flown out to Madrid to spend time with, he feels discontented and jaded, and thus decides to travel alone for a few weeks across the continent. Shifting seats to avoid being caught in an angry crossfire which is taking place between a bickering married couple, he meets Celine (Julie Delpy), a French woman in her early twenties who has been visiting her grandmother in Budapest and is now returning to Paris to continue her studies at the Sorbonne. The pair begin to talk and decide to move to the buffet carriage, where they can enjoy a more leisurely conversation. They immediately strike up a friendly rapport and, as the train nears Vienna, Jesse makes a bold suggestion: as he has the better part of a day to kill before his flight leaves for America, why doesn't Celine store her baggage at the station and join him – a complete stranger – for a day in the city? Intrigued by his off-the-cuff proposal, Celine decides to take a risk and follow this mysterious new acquaintance into the sunshine of a warm Viennese afternoon.

What is perhaps most immediately apparent about the captivating relationship between Jesse and Celine is the very naturalistic manner in which the connection between them is established. Although the audience is certainly made aware of an instant, subtle attraction between the two characters, Linklater and Krizan are careful to remove the pair about as far as is humanly possible from an anodyne, hackneyed tale of love at first sight. Both Celine and Jesse are pragmatic and yet also idealistic, even a little world-weary for all of their relative youth. They alternate between cynicism and optimism with regularity as their relationship develops. Sometimes they take positions of diametric opposition in an argument, whereas at other times they find themselves discovering shared commonality on the least likely of subjects. These alternating conflicts and harmonies are perhaps most obviously demonstrated in their relatively frequent discuss-ions of gender-related issues, where Jesse's rawness and despond-ency over his recent relationship breakdown is interestingly contrasted with Celine's distinctively feminine self-confidence and sharp observation of male behaviour patterns.

Jesse and Celine have a memorable trip through Vienna, sometimes partaking in typical tourist activities (such as their visit to the famous Wiener Prater ferris wheel which had featured so memorably in Carol Reed's *The Third Man* (1949)), but more often forging their own path away from the well-worn sightseeing destinations. As Vienna is a city that neither of the two is intimately acquainted with, their unearthing of its attractions and eccentricities subtly mirrors their gradual discovery of each other. The spontaneous bond which was established between them on the train grows as the day progresses, and as they embark upon their relaxed, mildly inquisitive trek through Vienna – never staying in one place for any length of time as they traverse its restaurants and backstreets, its historic graveyards, churches and amusement parks – their understanding of each other is progressively developed further and ever deeper.

Their encounters with some of Vienna's fascinating denizens reveal much about Jesse and Celine's characters, including the differences and similarities between them. When a street poet (Dominik Castell) composes a verse especially for the pair, his spontaneous artistry delights Celine but instils Jesse with the lingering suspicion that the man basically recycles the same poem with minor cosmetic changes to suit any passer-by that happens to cross his path. In true Linklater style, it is left entirely up to the individual viewer to decide whose outlook they sympathise with. Yet the couple also gradually realise that there are more factors to unite them than to divide them; although the cultural disparity between the pair is sometimes apparent, it does not cause friction between them, but rather is the catalyst for the drawing of telling contrasts between their own individual world views. This is particularly telling in the restaurant sequence, where they take turns at making imaginary telephone calls to friends back home, discussing the impressions that they have built of each other thus far.

Before Sunrise is filled with many memorable sequences and affecting moments. Amongst them are Jesse and Celine's silent observation of a harpsichord player (Wolfgang Glüxam), oblivious to their presence as his powerfully stirring music emanates from the depths of his basement apartment. Their two-pronged attempt to politely deprive an affable bartender (Haymon Maria Buttinger) of a bottle of wine and two glasses is also touching and entertaining in equal measure, though most critics pointed to Jesse and Celine's session in a record shop's listening booth as one of the film's most poignant sequences, where they appreciate the music – and each other – with a mixture of cordiality and self-consciousness due to their close proximity to one another.[33]

At one point in the film, the pair reflect that their day together has come to resemble a dream; a fantasy that is taking place, against all odds, while the mundanity of everyday existence flows around their own bubble of rarefied reality, never fully being able to penetrate it. And indeed, they are just as aware that this waking daydream is ultimately a finite one, destined to end as soon as Jesse gets on his plane back to the States. Their appreciation of this fact grows as the film progresses, as dawn approaches and – with it – the end of their special but restricted time together. Yet as Jesse and Celine's understated but tangible sense of dread grows with the inevitable coming of sunrise, they find themselves facing difficult choices about the feasibility of whether they can ever look towards a shared future together, or whether their encounter was always destined to be simply a single perfect day spent between two strangers who may also be soul-mates.

Once again, Linklater's film was to take place within a roughly 24-hour period, and contains another subtle allusion to James Joyce – as *Los Angeles Times* critic Peter Rainer noted in his review of the film, the date that Jesse and Celine spend together is the 16th of June, or Bloomsday, the day that Joyce's Leopold Bloom lives through in Dublin during *Ulysses*.[34] Just as Celine and Jesse find their philosophical and spiritual discussions drawing towards an unwelcome but unavoidable curtailment, the viewer becomes ever more aware of the fact that their dreamlike day of getting to know each other may in fact be the entirety of their relationship rather than the prelude to a long-term love affair. Yet by that same token, we are perhaps led to believe that such a short but beautiful encounter between two kindred spirits may be worth any number of bland and ill-starred relationships such as the one from which Jesse has so recently escaped.[35]

The most remarkable thing about *Before Sunrise* is the fact that, for all that the film is entirely comprised of two strangers talking, the narrative is never dull and the pace does not drag.

Although we can credit much of this to Linklater and Krizan's lively script, full of witty, on-the-ball dialogue and an accordingly broad range of conversational profundity, the film is brought to life by the unerringly honest performances of Ethan Hawke and Julie Delpy. Through their detailed portrayals of Jesse and Celine, we slowly come to experience all of their characters' hopes and fears, from their earliest childhood memories to their concerns and ruminations about their individual futures. Although both actors were comparatively young when *Before Sunrise* was filmed, they were already established performers who had built impressive careers for themselves. Hawke had been active in film since his screen debut as Ben Crandall in Joe Dante's *Explorers* (1985), for which he was nominated for the Best Starring Performance by a Young Actor prize at the 1986 Young Artist Awards. He would go on to appear in a number of high profile features including Peter Weir's *Dead Poets Society* (1989), Frank Marshall's *Alive* (1993) and Bruce Beresford's *Rich in Love* (1993), as well as demonstrating some potent Generation X credentials with a prominent appearance in Ben Stiller's *Reality Bites* (1994).[36] He would go on to collaborate with Linklater many times in the years following *Before Sunrise*.

Julie Delpy had been active in film-making as early as 1978 with a debut role in *Guerres Civiles en France*, directed by François Barat, Joël Farges and Vincent Nordon. She had appeared in many European films including Agnieszka Holland's *Europa Europa* (1990) and Volker Schlöndorff's *Homo Faber* (1991), as well as a number of English-language features such as Stephen Herek's *The Three Musketeers* (1993) and Roger Avary's *Killing Zoe* (1994).[37] Her polished performances had won her nominations for France's César Awards in 1987 and 1988. Perhaps her most famous role up to this point had been as the estranged wife of the protagonist in Krzysztof Kieslowski's *Trois Couleurs: Blanc* (1993), followed by a beautifully-realised cameo appearance in the triumphant conclusion to Kieslowski's *Three Colours* trilogy, *Trois Couleurs: Rouge* (1994).

Before Sunrise's freshness and lack of pretension played well with critics, who were generally receptive to the film on its release. Some noted that the pace of the film was considerably more measured and leisurely than had been the case with *Slacker* and *Dazed and Confused*,[38] whereas others drew interesting comparisons between the contemplative, chatty style of the film and the work of French film-maker Eric Rohmer.[39] Mick LaSalle of the *San Francisco Chronicle* also made the particularly memorable point that the film plays like a European-based version of Louis Malle's *My Dinner with Andre*, with one noteworthy exception – there's no Andre.[40] Others noted the way in which Linklater had made good use of his elegant choice of Viennese locales, which seemed quite literally a world away from the warm and hazy American summer of *Dazed and Confused* and the modern urban austerity of *Slacker*. Generally, however, much of the praise was reserved for the central performances of Hawke and Delpy who – given that they are the exclusive focus of the film throughout its entire duration – were considered to handle their roles with faultless sincerity of emotion and commendable frankness right the way through.

Before Sunrise was to win Linklater the 1995 Silver Berlin Bear Award at the Berlin International Film Festival, and also earned him a nomination for the Golden Berlin Bear at the same ceremony. The film reinforced his reputation as an inventive and artistically resourceful film-maker who was continuing to augment the scope of his thematic objectives: if *Slacker* had been an exploration of the nature of communication, then *Before Sunrise* was instead a careful study of the interaction between two specific people, examining how ideas and feelings are transmitted between the two of them and the manner in which their process of interaction deepens as trust is gradually built between Celine and Jesse on the fateful, beautiful day that they spend together. So skilfully concluded was the film, with its slow, melancholic revisiting of the now-deserted places where the protagonists had spent time during their Viennese rendezvous, that few could ever have suspected that Linklater would one day be returning to the story of Jesse and Celine, or that the characters' next meeting would not take place for almost a decade to come.

5

subUrbia (1996)

Detour Filmproduction / Castle Rock Entertainment

Director: Richard Linklater
Producer: Anne Walker-McBay
Screenwriter: Eric Bogosian, from the play by Eric Bogosian

Main Cast
Jayce Bartok – Pony
Amie Carey – Sooze
Nicky Katt – Tim
Ajay Naidu – Nazeer Choudhury
Parker Posey – Erica
Giovanni Ribisi – Jeff
Samia Shoaib – Pakeesa Choudhury
Dina Spybey – Bee-Bee

subUrbia was Richard Linklater's first cinematic adaptation of a theatrical work, and – true to form – he was to blaze a new trail by opting to film a challenging stage play written by the acclaimed actor, novelist and playwright Eric Bogosian. *subUrbia* was an interesting choice of material for Linklater, for although the hard-edged and essentially nihilistic outlook of the film's main characters was undoubtedly very different from the introspective but generally upbeat and life-affirming attitudes of *Slacker*, *Dazed and Confused* and (especially) the contemplative hopefulness of *Before Sunrise*, there were also a number of thematic similarities which would emerge in unusual and satisfying ways. As we will discover, although *subUrbia*'s characters are highly complex and psychologically intricate, there is precious little optimism within their reach, much less real hope, and certainly no easy answers.

The plays of Eric Bogosian have been greatly praised by critics, and he has created a number of well-regarded, dark and distinctive dramas and successful monologue performances, including *Men Inside* (1981), *FunHouse* (1983), *Drinking in America* (1986) and the highly commended *Pounding Nails in the Floor with My Forehead* (1994). Of most significance with regard to the world of film was his adaptation of one of his best-known plays, *Talk Radio* (1987), into a feature film which was directed by Oliver Stone in 1988. Bogosian also starred as the film's protagonist, Barry Champlain, and as an actor he has appeared in an extensive and eclectic range of other features including Taylor Hackford's *Dolores Claiborne* (1993) and Woody Allen's *Deconstructing Harry* (1997), as well as a significant number of television roles.

subUrbia is set in the fictional American town of Burnfield. It could be a suburb almost anywhere in the United States, for no precise geographical location is ever suggested. Over the course of one long night (and early the following morning), we join a peculiar and almost totally unsympathetic collection of acquaintances as they go through their nightly routine of hanging around outside a local convenience store. They drink, they philosophise, and more than anything, they waste time.

We are introduced to Jeff (Giovanni Ribisi), the nominal protagonist, who is in his early twenties and a fascinating mix of penetrating intellect and dreary inanity. Jeff is perceptive and darkly sarcastic, but also gloomy and utterly directionless. His resentment towards the establishment is shared by Tim (Nicky Katt), a cynical and often brutal waster who has recently engineered his own discharge from a short stint with the U.S. Air Force and is now languishing on the road to alcoholic poisoning. Tim, who is viciously aggrieved by the existence of almost everyone and everything, is staggeringly racist, unabashedly misogynistic, and hasn't the vaguest conception of mutual respect. Rounding off this unlikely trio is Buff (Steve Zahn), a vapid, hyperactive attention-seeker who tries the patience of the others with pointless macho exploits and comparatively energetic vigour. In his own way, and in spite of his apparent vivacity, Buff is no less pointless an individual than his two associates.

Jeff, Tim and Buff while away the night belittling each other, bemoaning the pointlessness of their own existence, and aggravating the hard-working Pakistani couple (Ajay Naidu and Samia Shoaib) who run the nearby convenience store. The shopowners, Nazeer and Pakeesa, are exasperated at the effect that these skulking layabouts are having on their business, but are met with a combination of apathy and outright hostility whenever they try to persuade them to leave. This tips over into out-and-out racial abuse when Tim unleashes a tirade of vile xenophobic insults at Nazeer, blaming him for having the audacity to set up shop on American soil while, it is implied, secretly resenting the Asian man's ambition and quiet, conscientious diligence. The verbal onslaught threatens to erupt into physical violence which is only halted when Pakeesa threatens Tim with a gun. However, Tim's bitterness towards the couple continues to simmer, and he vows to settle the score later.

We are also introduced to Sooze (Amie Carey), Jeff's ostensible girlfriend, and her friend Bee-Bee (Dina Spybey), a nursing assistant with a drink problem who's just been discharged from rehab. Sooze is an ambitious visual and performance artist with questionable abilities. Her street poetry – memorably demonstrated by Carey, who milks Sooze's pretension to hilarious effect – is not so much laced with profanity as it is, in fact, almost entirely composed of it. Bee-Bee is alone amongst the group in that she almost seems to have a vaguely benevolent nature at times; however, it is never less than apparent that she too is submerged in the same kind of suburban lassitude as the others and, through her alcoholism, is one of the most clearly damaged as a result of it. Although the group are all long-standing acquaintances, the tension between them seems almost excruciating at times, as though verbal or physical violence may erupt at almost any moment. And then events take an unexpected turn which ups the ante considerably.

Neil Moynihan, better known as Pony (Jayce Bartok) and remembered by the group as a geeky kid from their high school days, has hit the big time in the music industry, and word spreads that he is planning to return to Burnfield for an unscheduled visit. Sure enough, later that night Pony emerges from a stretch limo with a glamorous but essentially vacuous personal assistant called Erica (Parker Posey). His presence soon affects the others in quite drastic ways. For the artistically motivated but dubiously talented Sooze, he represents the chance of a break into the professional world of creative arts. Even the manic loafer Buff, who has dabbled in the amateur directing of short features, senses that Pony might just be his ticket out of Burnfield. But Jeff, whose personal goals in life are ambiguous enough as to be virtually non-existent, is deeply envious of Pony's success. Although far from content with his meaningless, freeloading suburban existence, Jeff sees no qualitative value in Pony's artistic output and questions why his old schoolmate's success should make him appear, in social and cultural terms, superior to the others. Pony, however, understands the reasoning behind Jeff's hostility only too well, for he is beginning to question the authenticity of the way in which his own artistic goals are communicated and bemoans the banality of his stage-managed professional existence. His concerns about the validity of the particular corner of popular culture that he populates is reflected in the bland and insecure Erica, whose ill-advised attempts to sexually entice the borderline-psychopathic Tim look set to bring an unfortunate (and possibly tragic) end to her visit to Burnfield.

By the time that dawn breaks over the suburb, every member of the group finds themselves affected to some degree by the events of the past night, and Tim's sadistic feud with Nazeer reaches a harrowing climax. Yet by the film's conclusion, perhaps the most compelling question remains whether – in spite of the film's intense events – any of the characters truly have either the capacity or the inclination to change their lives for the better in the face of such unremitting nihilism.

As Godfrey Cheshire noted in his review of the film for *Variety*, one of *subUrbia*'s most significant factors is how well its narrative harmonises with Linklater's earlier output, given that it is the first film that he had directed where he had not also been the creator of the screenplay.[41] Indeed, the theme of aimless youth so energetically engaged with in *Slacker* and *Dazed and Confused* surfaces in *subUrbia* in a much more potent, distilled form, and thus the film takes Linklater's examination of Generation X to an entirely new level. In *subUrbia*, we see a flipside to the assured indolence of the *Slacker* culture which exchanges eccentricity and individuality for lethargy and hopelessness. Roger Ebert perceptively noted at the time of *subUrbia*'s cinematic release that, for the film's characters, killing time wasn't simply a preoccupation – it was, in fact, a lifestyle choice.[42] Eric Bogosian's screenplay successfully and convincingly condenses his stage drama to suit a cinematic format, and Linklater manages to expand the canvas of the one-location play just enough to stop his film openly disclosing its stage-based roots, whilst retaining Bogosian's sense of tension and claustrophobia.

The ensemble cast of *subUrbia* was considerably more restricted in number than had been the case with the sprawling dramatis personae of *Slacker* or *Dazed and Confused*, and Linklater fully employs Bogosian's detailed characterisation to flesh out each of the group in complex and rewarding ways.[43] Although Jeff is perhaps the most complicated character, a mass of contrary personality traits who is too egotistical and insensitive for the audience to easily sympathise with, even the most callous and unfeeling of characters – such as Tim – are treated as three-dimensional characters rather than simply devices to motivate the dynamics of the plot. The unstable Tim, who has a kind of post-Nietzschian approach to nihilism, has no redeeming qualities whatsoever, but thanks to the skill of both Bogosian and Linklater, by the end of the film we come very close to understanding why he has grown into such a twisted, embittered and essentially necrotic individual. As we discover, his malevolent character has been shaped not only in spite of his comfortable lower middle-class surroundings, but quite possibly because of them too.[44] The others are treated every bit as ambivalently, with Sooze and Buff being subjected to subtle but scathing derision for their pursuit of artistic fame despite no appreciable talent in their respective disciplines, while Pony and the ineffectual Erica are both presented as dissatisfied representatives of a heavily market-driven music industry, aimless and frustrated at their apparent lack of influence over the direction of their careers. Only Nazeer and Pakeesa, both incomers to the United States, are paradoxically left to symbolise the classic American values of hard work, commitment and dedication, in opposition to the nebulous postmodern malaise in which the others persist in wallowing.

Performances throughout the film are strong, and communicate well the caustic cynicism of Bogosian's script. Steve Zahn (Buff) and Samia Shoaib (Pakeeza) had both appeared in Bogosian's stage version, including the play's world premiere at the Lincoln Center Theater in 1994.[45] Giovanni Ribisi was already a highly experienced television actor at the time of *subUrbia*'s release, and was enjoying success in Tom Hanks's directorial debut *That Thing You Do!* (1996) in cinemas in the same year. He would later go on to major success with films such as Sofia Coppola's *The Virgin Suicides* (1999), Anthony Minghella's *Cold Mountain* (2003) and John Moore's *Flight of the Phoenix* (2004). Amie Carey was to appear in films such as *Dog Park* (1998), *True Vinyl* (2000) and *The Four of Us* (2001), while Jayce Bartok's varied film career has included performances in features such as *Ropewalk* (2000), *Calling Bobcat* (2000), *The Tolbooth* (2004) and *Red Doors* (2005), with a high-profile cameo appearance as the Subway Guitarist in Sam Raimi's *Spider-Man* (2002). However, it was Ajay Naidu's performance as Nazeer Chaudry which was to lead to a nomination for an Independent Spirit Award in 1998 for Best Supporting Male. Chaudry's extraordinary turn in the film's perfectly pitched closing sequence, where Nazeer faces off against Tim one last time, vociferously berating the other man for the profligate senselessness of his disinterested complacency and casual brutality, is one of the highlights of the film.

For all its dark sarcasm and uncompromising bleakness, *subUrbia* also offers moments of wit and despondent humour, a factor which was not lost on most reviewers at the time of the film's release. However, the general critical reception was rather less even than the response that most of Linklater's previous features had enjoyed. Some considered the jaded, weary tone of Bogosian's play to be conspicuously incompatible with Linklater's generally more buoyant and wistful approach[46] to his subject matter,[47] while others instead believed that the film marked a noteworthy evolution in Linklater's stylistic methodology, appearing in narrative terms to be a kind of progression that fused elements from all of his previous films to create a bleak but irresolutely expressive indictment of suburban American youth in the mid-nineties.[48] In spite of the undeniable relevance of *subUrbia*'s raw, searing critique of modern society and its affect on youth culture (and vice versa), the film caused less of an immediate impact than Linklater's past features, and today it remains perhaps the most difficult to find of all Linklater's films. Nevertheless, occasional airings on television have made the film available to audiences in recent years, and it continues to be of special interest not only to Linklater aficionados, but also to the many admirers of Bogosian's work on the stage and screen.

6

THE NEWTON BOYS (1998)

Detour Filmproduction / Twentieth Century Fox / Newton Boys Ventures Inc.

Director: Richard Linklater
Producer: Anne Walker-McBay
Screenwriters: Richard Linklater, Claude Stanush and Clark Lee Walker, from the book by Claude Stanush.

Main Cast
Matthew McConaughey – Willis Newton
Skeet Ulrich – Joe Newton
Ethan Hawke – Jess Newton
Vincent D'Onofrio – Dock Newton
Julianna Margulies – Louise Brown
Dwight Yoakam – Brentwood Glasscock
Charles Gunning – Slim
Chloe Webb – Avis Glasscock

With *The Newton Boys*, Linklater was to surprise audiences and critics once again, by producing – after an uninterrupted string of highly distinctive and individualistic features – the most narratively conventional film of his career to date. But with Linklater at the helm, audiences would discover, even the conventional can be anything but ordinary, especially when he was to be handling such colourful true-life subject matter as that of Texas's infamous Newton brothers.

The Newton Boys was Linklater's first foray into a drama set in the recent historical past since *Dazed and Confused*, but this time he was to reach back considerably further than the warm summer of '76. The film was based on the historical account of Willis and Joe Newton, as reflected in the book by Claude I. Stanush and David Middleton (Stanush was also to share a screenwriting credit with Linklater and co-writer Clark Lee Walker),[49] which related a detailed factual description of the notorious exploits of the bankrobbing Newton brothers throughout the early 1920s. This detailed non-fictional exploration of the Newtons' criminal exploits was to create a new range of challenges for Linklater's film-making and narrative skills.[50]

In Texas's Uvalde County in 1919, two brothers – Joe and Jess Newton (Skeet Ulrich and Ethan Hawke) – are working hard at herding and tending cattle. However, they are struggling to obtain a subsistence wage to care for the rest of their family, including their middle-aged mother (Gail Cronauer). Out of the blue, their ex-convict brother Willis (Matthew McConaughey) returns to the fold – although he has been absent for some time, he still irresolutely maintains his innocence at being jailed for a crime that he swears that he had never committed. Willis has been working on the cotton fields, and in spite of a successful stint in agricultural labour he knows that there are no lasting prospects in the profession, especially given the rapid progress that has been affecting the country since the turn of the century. When a love affair with a plantation owner's daughter ends badly, he decides that the direction of his life is in need of change, and sets off to make his fortune in the least conventional way possible.

Teaming up with a shady career criminal named Slim (Charles Gunning) and a skittish but highly proficient safe-cracker named Brentwood Glasscock (Dwight Yoakam), Willis takes part in a raid on a small-town bank. The robbery is a success but, taking place in broad daylight, their getaway is a less triumphant affair – Slim is injured and captured by the local lawmen. However, Willis is undeterred by his associate's capture, and determines to continue what he considers to be a winning streak. He strikes a deal with Glasscock, now even more edgy than usual, to shift their activities under the cover of darkness. By raiding banks at night, they will no longer be reliant on the compliance of bank staff to facilitate the hold-up at gunpoint. Instead, they can simply blow open the door of the targeted safe with nitro-glycerine – a technique which Glasscock has perfected to the level of an art-form. Obtaining a list of banks which rely on square-door safes – the most vulnerable to explosives – from a corrupt banking official, the men set to work on a plan of action. But with Slim out of the picture, who can they rely on to provide backup for their intended sweep of the Midwest's banking establishments?

The answer comes in the form of Jess and Joe, who answer their brother's call for assistance without any clue of what kind of help he's looking for. On discovering Willis's plan, Jess – a carefree individual with a love for attractive women, strong liquor and fine living – is all in favour of taking high risks in order to obtain some (relatively) easy money. However, the dutiful Joe finds the prospect of his brother's criminal intent to be distinctly unpalatable, due to his strong moral convictions. Willis is eventually able to talk his younger sibling around to his way of thinking by emphasising his vehemently-held view that theirs is a kind of ethically neutral thievery: in his opinion, they will not be robbing from individuals, but only from banking institutions, as they are all protected by insurance cover and will inevitably file inflated claims to recover their losses in the event of a raid. As

Willis believes the insurance companies to be acting in a manner that is much more dishonest than their own straightforward brand of robbery, he considers – with the aid of some twisted logic – that their actions will be morally unimpeachable. Not entirely convinced, Joe agrees to join his brothers in their new career of professional crime, though Willis sets out an imperishable code of conduct which they must always adhere to: no lives are to be taken during the course of their operations, women and children are always to be left unharmed, and none of them will inform on any of their accomplices.

They are soon joined by their elder brother Dock (Vincent D'Onofrio), who has just been released from prison and who wastes no time in joining his brothers' now-highly successful run of luck in the bank-robbing trade. Making up the numbers are Avis (Chloe Webb), Glasscock's ditzy yet eminently practical wife, and Louise Brown (Julianna Margulies), a cigar saleswoman at an upmarket hotel newsstand who falls for Willis's charms and eventually agrees to follow him across the country. Louise is initially unaware of his criminal activities, believing his cover story of being a fledgling oil magnate, but remains supportive even when his deceit finally – and inevitably – unravels.

Things eventually become more complicated for the brothers when, after scores of successful robberies, the tide subtly begins to shift against them. Horrified by their monetary losses, the insurance companies levy penalties on the premiums of banks with outmoded safes, encouraging them to obtain modern, more secure models. These newer designs outfox even Glasscock's proficiency with explosives. Furthermore, Willis's leadership of the gang becomes ever more ostentatious, culminating in a particularly reckless daylight raid on a Canadian bank's assets which are being manually couriered by security guards. It is an operation from which they barely escape with their liberty.

At the urging of Louise, Willis reluctantly decides to 'go straight' and invest heavily in an oil-drilling operation. However, his venture proves to be ill-fated when their corner of the oil fields

– already heavily drilled by a number of major companies – run dry. Willis is unwilling to accept this bad fortune, and resolves to make back his money by any means necessary. To this end, he conspires with the recently-released Slim – who is now keeping company with a number of influential players in Mafia-run Chicago – to pull off the gang's most lucrative operation to date. A crooked operative within the U.S. postal service leaks vital information about a mail train which will be travelling through the state of Illinois carrying vast amounts of cash – in excess of three million dollars. If the brothers can use this information to rob the train before the authorities can track them down, they will be able to get away with more money than even Willis's wildest dreams can aspire to. But given the sheer audacity of their scheme, and the vast scale of the amount that they hope to steal, is the law about to catch up with the errant Newton brothers at last?

The Newton Boys presents an efficiently executed narrative with flawless period detail throughout. Everything from the sumptuous set design (especially noticeable in the authentic brands and periodicals on display on Louise's cigar stand, and the faithfully rendered fixtures and fittings in the many banks that the Newtons 'visit' on their travels) to the impeccable period costumes combine to make a memorably faithful 1920s setting. This is also true of the excellent musical score by Edward D. Barnes, supplemented by the lively music of the Bad Livers, which further accentuates the film's 'Roaring Twenties' flavour. There are other deft touches of historical detail, such as Erich von Stroheim's *Greed* (1924) playing at a Canadian cinema during the gang's brief trip north of the border – a potent metaphor for Willis's growing avarice as his criminal ambitions become ever more outrageous. *The Newton Boys* was also Linklater's first film since *It's Impossible to Learn to Plow by Reading Books* not to constrain the narrative within a 24-hour period – indeed, *The Newton Boys* could hardly be further from this constraint, given that the storyline encapsulates a full five years of the brothers' criminal history within a two hour running time.

In spite of its departure from the style of Linklater's previous directorial output, the film also contains many similarities. Foremost among them are his trademark suspicion of the establishment, and examining the motivations of the authorities. This is obvious from Willis's palpable contempt for banking firms and insurance companies – underpinning his entire *modus operandi* – but is made even more explicit in the behind-the-scenes chicanery employed by Federal investigator K.P. Aldrich (Bo Hopkins) as he bargains with Willis to ameliorate his brothers' sentences in exchange for a clear allegation against the crooked postal coordinator William Fahy (David Jensen). Given the Newtons' sworn oath never to inform on a co-conspirator, the solution that Willis and Aldrich arrive at is as effective as it is unorthodox. The film also maintains Linklater's inclination towards a deliberate, meticulous approach to storytelling, imbuing even the more frenetic action sequences with an attentive kind of thoughtfulness not often to be witnessed in other films of the genre.

Linklater's screenplay, written in collaboration with Claude Stanush and Clark Lee Walker, weaves together an interesting central cast of characters and provides the talented array of actors with plenty of scope to flesh out their respective portrayals. Central among them is Matthew McConaughey's outstanding, appealing and energetic performance as Willis Newton. A world away from the sleazy Gooderson of *Dazed and Confused*, McConaughey builds on previous strong performances in films such as *Lone Star* (1996), *Scorpion Spring* (1996) and *Contact* (1997) to present Willis with an easy, likeable charm which makes him accessible to the audience even in spite of his unconventional morality and hazily defined motivations. Much of the film's action hinges on Willis's persuasive magnetism, and McConaughey carries this off with great panache. Charismatic country music legend Dwight Yoakam likewise puts in a terrific turn as the deeply cautious but meticulously professional safe-cracker Brentwood Glasscock, and Charles Gunning, so memorable as

Slacker's 'Hitchhiker Awaiting "True Call"', oozes calculating menace as Slim. Of the other Newton brothers, Ethan Hawke's Jess is perhaps the most striking due to his engaging personality and complex disposition (he seems equally comfortable to be in the heat of the action during a bank robbery as he is relaxing in luxurious hotels, trying to impress beautiful women). As Joe, Skeet Ulrich communicates a great deal about the moral confusion of the gang's laissez-faire approach to the law – uncomfortable with Willis's gleeful subversiveness but equally unwilling to renege on his duty to support his brothers. Vincent D'Onofrio provides solid support as the taciturn Dock; the eldest brother is no stranger to legal transgressions and the subsequent detention that they bring but, in spite of this, seems more than happy to be along for the ride.

Although the film's cast is mostly dominated by prominent male roles, there is much to commend the female members of the cast, and this is especially true of Julianna Margulies's performance as Louise Brown, Willis's long-suffering lover and moral counterbalance. At the time best known to audiences for her performance in Bruce Beresford's *Paradise Road* (1997) and as Carol Hathaway on television's enormously popular *E.R.*, she skilfully adds as much dimension to the character as her comparatively slender amount of screen time affords her. This is also the case with Chloe Webb, who brings Avis Glasscock to life with alternating quirkiness and unwavering common sense, and Gail Cronauer for her brief but heartfelt appearance as Ma Newton.

The Newton Boys received a lukewarm reception from the critics, and was overlooked at awards ceremonies – a fact which has, in subsequent years, prompted some commentators to cite the film as one of Linklater's most under-rated features.[51] Although there was a common consensus over the film's painstakingly scrupulous recreation of its 1920s locales,[52] reviewers disagreed over the effectiveness of the film's other qualities. Comparisons abounded to films such as Arthur Penn's *Bonnie and Clyde* (1967) and George Roy Hill's *Butch Cassidy and the Sundance Kid* (1969) and *The Sting* (1973), but some critics would come to note these similarities in less favourable ways than others.[53] A number were to praise Linklater's deft evocation of the Newtons' historical accounts of their various misdeeds throughout the duration of their criminal career,[54] whereas others dismissed the film as a skilful but ultimately uninspired patchwork of other period features stemming from the same genre.[55] Although Linklater's studied, purposeful pace was rather too mannered for some tastes,[56] the generally amiable performances and offbeat tone of the film struck a chord with a number of others.[57] It was not the first time that Linklater's novel and reflective approach to his material would split the critical community, and it would not be the last.

The Newton Boys had marked yet another interesting change of pace for Linklater's directorial career, and he had employed the much larger budget at his disposal – $27 million[58] – to good effect in order to recreate not just a particular time and place, but also a distinctively offbeat story of a group of ordinary men who, through their audacious criminality, created an extraordinary chain of events. Linklater is careful not to glorify criminality – indeed, the film's epilogue explains in comprehensive detail the consequences and long-term ramifications of the brothers' actions – but he is equally judicious in putting forward Willis's side of the story too, meaningfully contrasting the brothers' polite and courteous approach towards innocent bystanders caught up in their raids with the brutal interrogation techniques of Police Chief Schoemaker (Luke Askew) and the devious bargaining of Agent Aldrich.

Yet even in spite of the fact that *The Newton Boys* presented Linklater's most straightforward narrative up to this point, the film is replete with the motivating directorial style that he had so carefully established, as were many of the themes; the importance of the individual (and the decisions that the individual makes) is at the forefront of the film, as is the relationship between personal liberty and the role of the state.[59] As we shall see, these themes – and others besides – would continue to be developed by Linklater in his next feature.

7

WAKING LIFE (2001)

Detour Filmproduction / Fox Searchlight Pictures / Independent Film Channel / Thousand Words / Flat Black Films / Line Research

Director: Richard Linklater
Producers: Tommy Pallotta, Jonah Smith, Anne Walker-McBay and Palmer West
Screenwriter: Richard Linklater

Main Cast
Wiley Wiggins – Main Character
Robert C. Solomon – Philosophy Professor
Ethan Hawke – Jesse
Julie Delpy – Celine
Charles Gunning – Angry Man in Jail
Alex Jones – Man in Car with P.A.
Steven Soderbergh – Interviewed on Television
Richard Linklater – Pinball Playing Man

After producing his most mainstream title to date in the form of *The Newton Boys*, Linklater was once again to challenge critical expectations by creating a film that was even more unconventional than his earliest features. *Waking Life* not only featured a fractured non-narrative that appeared to be a logical refinement of the technique he had cultivated in *Slacker*, but the film also featured a strikingly distinctive visual style thanks to his brave decision to use a complex rotoscoping process in order to animate the action throughout. However, whereas previous films had mostly tended to employ rotoscoping in order to enhance the realism of animated characters' movement, Linklater had an entirely contrary purpose in mind when employing the technique, for his *modus operandi* was not to create an animated milieu that was convincing in real-world terms but, instead, to present an environment that was resolutely surrealistic in nature.

Rotoscoping – the technique of superimposing animation over live-action footage – was far from a new procedure, having been pioneered in the early 1910s and developed by the film industry of the 1920s onwards, but Linklater and art director Bob Sabiston managed to put an entirely new spin on this established technique by means of innovative digital processing, employing 31 different animators to add their own unique artistic styles to the film at different times which constantly shifted the visual nature of the action from minute to minute.[60] The continuously changing perspectives and eerily fluid movement of the animation added to the deliberately disorientating method of cinematic presentation, ensuring that the technique was perfectly suited to the film's central theme – that of dreams and their strange relationship to the human perception of reality.

The film's title derives from philosopher George Santayana's assertion that 'sanity is a madness put to good uses; waking life is a dream controlled',[61] and indeed dreaming and the nature of dreams is very much at the forefront of a deeply eccentric narrative. The film opens with a couple of young children (Trevor Jack Brooks and Lorelei Linklater) playing a simple paper game which leads them to the inescapable conclusion that 'dream is destiny'. We then switch to a group of musicians practicing a piece of music before finally settling on the film's unnamed protagonist (played by Wiley Wiggins of *Dazed and Confused*) arriving at a train station in a manner vaguely reminiscent of Richard Linklater's character arriving at the bus depot in *Slacker*. Upon leaving the station, the protagonist is offered a ride in an outlandish car designed like a small boat, driven by the incongruously nautical 'Boat Car Guy' (Bill Wise). The boat-car also carries a mysterious passenger (Richard Linklater) who enigmatically gives the driver very precise instructions about where the protagonist should be dropped off. He does as he is asked, and the main character leaves their company only to find himself promptly knocked over by another car. And then he wakes up, unscathed, suggesting that everything that has taken place thus far has been nothing more than a dream.

From here, the protagonist makes his way to a university class which is being taught by a philosophy professor (Robert Solomon), lecturing on the virtues of existentialism in comparison to prevailing modes of postmodernist thought. There is then a shift to actress and screenwriter Kim Krizan delivering a concise but complex monologue on language and linguistic strategies, which suddenly leads to an passionate discussion by a 'Shape-Shifting Man' (Eamonn Healy) about the nature of evolution and recent changes in human societal development. All of these intense intellectual orations run for only a few minutes each before we once again come back to the protagonist, now returning to his home and discovering that he is unable to focus on fine details, such as the numbers on his digital alarm clock – incontrovertible proof, he later discovers, that he is still dreaming.

These early incidents clearly demonstrate the ebb and flow of the film's dense non-narrative, which echoes the rhythm of *Slacker* whilst actually providing a very different audience experience. Whereas *Slacker*'s narrative had been driven by the constant shifting from one character (or series of characters) to another,

Waking Life features a nominal central character whose story affects some – but, crucially, not all – of the film's sequence of events. By randomly interspersing the protagonist's voyage through this indistinct, unreal world with seemingly unconnected incidents, Linklater perfectly captures the nebulous ambience and hazily confused structure of a dream (and, in the process, proving the point that there is in fact no 'typical' dream, for we are never quite sure if we are watching the subconscious visions of the protagonist, or of Linklater, or someone else entirely). Indeed, although the film's constituent parts may be arranged in a manner that is purposely incoherent, its overriding message is never less than articulate.

Although the nature of dreams is indisputably the core issue of the film, Linklater deftly uses it as a launching point for many other discussions which include gun control, the subordination of art and artists to commercialisation, the relationship between society and the mass-media, and (perhaps most prominently) the nature of conscious awareness. Among the many memorable incidents intermingling throughout the film are the immolating 'Self-Burning Man' (J.C. Shakespeare), whose diatribe against two-party politics recalls the incisive wit of the late, great Bill Hicks,[62] and the ranting fury of 'Angry Man in Jail' (the inimitable Charles Gunning), indignantly raging at the perceived injustice of the authorities whilst remaining totally oblivious to the hypocrisy of his Biblical pronouncement to 'judge not lest ye be judged'. The mistily absurdist confluence of events continues with other sequences which include a lecturing chimpanzee (voice of Steve Fitch) presenting a film on 'the narrative of doubt', a rambling but oddly endearing reflection on the meaning of life by poet Timothy 'Speed' Levitch (who was also the subject of Linklater's short film *Live from Shiva's Dance Floor* (2003)), and the appearance of Alex Jones, film director and Texan talk-show host, driving a van as he projects his strongly-held political beliefs through a P.A. system mounted on the roof.

Possibly the most unexpected incident in the film is a cameo appearance by Celine and Jesse of *Before Sunrise*, who have an abstract discussion in bed together where they pick up on a few strands of the philosophical ruminations that they had mulled over in the previous film. These include both the technicalities of reincarnation and the semantic parallels between death and dreaming, and both Julie Delpy and Ethan Hawke resume their respective portrayals with consummate ease, reviving the characters with such elegance that it is easy to forget that fully five years had passed since *Before Sunrise*.

As the film progresses, it becomes ever more obvious that the protagonist is unable to awaken from this increasingly intense dream, much to his bewilderment. Not even a discussion with the director himself can resolve his predicament, although Linklater (appearing as the 'Pinball Playing Man') does attempt to illuminate things for him by relaying a complex parable which involves the writings of science fiction author Philip K. Dick. Ultimately, with Linklater's assertion that he should 'just wake up', the protagonist comes to realise that the relationship between living and dreaming is far more complicated than even he had suspected, leading the film to an emotive and characteristically ambiguous climax.

Whereas *Slacker* had featured an immense cast of talented unknowns, *Waking Life* offers up a dizzying array of intellectuals, academics, theoreticians and artists as impressive as it is eclectic. Scholars such as David Sosa, Eamonn Healy, Robert C. Solomon and *Slacker* veteran Louis Mackey rub shoulders with author Aklilu Gebrewold, poets David Jewell and 'Speed' Levitch, screenwriter Kim Krizan, independent directors Steven Soderbergh and Alex Jones, and film expert Caveh Zahedi, whose ponderings on the theories of Andre Bazin and his famous notion of the 'Holy Moment' forms one of the film's most remarkable sequences.[63] Although Bazin's concept is relevant to the film in and of itself, Linklater uses Zahedi's densely layered discussion to raise the issue of faith, of humanity's ability to shape its own collective destiny, and even to question the nature of reality itself.

Taken together, these key issues underpin much of the *Waking Life*'s wider preoccupation with the connection between dreams and life (and indeed death), and also suggest that even more than *Slacker* before it, the narrative is primarily concerned with the interplay of ideas and the characters' relations to them, rather than just between the characters themselves.[64] This is one reason why Wiley Wiggins's beguilingly mystified central performance is so important in drawing the audience into the bafflingly fast-moving range of highbrow concepts that are on display; the amicable everyman that he portrays is an impeccably well-judged rendering, a character perceptively compared by critic Todd McCarthy to the eponymous hero of Voltaire's *Candide*.[65]

Waking Life's audacious break from traditional film conventions impressed many critics, a number of whom considered it to be an interesting evolutionary development in Linklater's career which harkened back to its experimental and highly inventive origins.[66] The painstaking, innovative artistry of Linklater and Sabiston's modern updating of the rotoscoping technique also received much praise for the unique visual aspect that it lent the film, with some reviewers noting the scrupulously thorough 250 hours of work that were required to render each single minute of film action,[67] whilst others compared it favourably to other prominent films which had used the rotoscoping process in years past, such as Ralph Bakshi's *The Lord of the Rings* (1978).[68] A few reviewers criticised *Waking Life* for what they considered to be a general lack of pace and momentum,[69] or pretension in its handling of such heavyweight philosophical themes,[70] whereas others believed that even if the subject matter of the film sometimes seemed lofty and indistinct, the characters themselves were generally affable and engaging, casually talkative and possessed of a recognisable human quality even at times when the narrative defiantly progresses into ever deeper dimensions of wilfully surrealistic confusion.[71]

If *Waking Life* had met with general critical approval, it fared even better at awards ceremonies, gaining nominations for many awards and going on to win several more. The recognition gained by the film included prizes for Best Animated Feature at the New York Film Critics Circle Awards (2001) and the Ottawa International Animation Festival (2002), as well as nominations in the same category at the Broadcast Film Critics Association Awards (2002) and the Online Film Critics Society Awards (2002). The film was additionally nominated for the Golden Trailer Awards in the categories of Best Animation/ Family Film and Most Original Feature in 2002, gained a nomination for Best Picture at the Chicago Film Critics Association Awards (also in 2002), and Bob Sabiston was nominated for Digital Effects Artist of the Year at the 2002 AFI Film Awards for his work on the film. *Waking Life* won Linklater the coveted CinemAvvenire Award at the 2001 Venice Film Festival, as well as a Special Mention for the Laterna Magica Prize and a nomination for the Golden Lion Award at the same ceremony. The film also did well at the Independent Spirit Awards in 2002, gaining nominations for Best Director, Best Feature and Best Screenplay.

After a gradual drift closer to mainstream subject matter with *subUrbia* and *The Newton Boys*, *Waking Life* had once again emphasised Linklater's overriding qualities as an innovative and courageous director, infinitely more concerned with art than formula and demonstrably willing to present audiences with mind-expanding themes in the most inventive of ways, ranging from topical issues to the kind of multifaceted philosophical and theoretical concepts infrequently discussed even in the boldest of independent films. This willingness to consider weighty issues with eagerness and sincerity would extend into his next feature, which was to switch the focus firmly from dreamy contemplation into the harsher, more sharply defined ambit of emotional and psychological observation.

8

TAPE (2001)

Detour Filmproduction / IFC Productions / InDigEnt / The Independent Film Channel Productions / Tape Productions Inc.

Director: Richard Linklater
Producers: Alexis Alexanian, Anne Walker-McBay and Gary Winick
Screenwriter: Stephen Belber, from the play by Stephen Belber

Main Cast
Ethan Hawke – Vince
Robert Sean Leonard – Jon Salter
Uma Thurman – Amy Randall

Linklater was to continue *Waking Life*'s theme of questioning the reliability of memory and perception in *Tape*, an adaptation of Stephen Belber's acclaimed stage play. The film was shot entirely on digital video[72] (as *Waking Life* had been, prior to the rotoscoping process being applied), lending it the kind of immediacy that was perfectly suited to a stage production whilst ensuring, through clever cutting and skilful camera movements, that the audience is never less than aware of the fact this is fully a filmic presentation in its own right, regardless of how respectful it remains to the original source material.[73] *Tape* also provides a valuable counterpoint to Linklater's previous stage adaptation, for while Eric Bogosian had skilfully widened the canvas of his *subUrbia* screenplay to develop it beyond its stage-based origins, Belber is careful to retain his original play's sense of uncomfortable claustrophobia within the film adaptation, immersing the viewer in the edginess of the emotionally devastating situation which lies at the heart of the narrative.

A prolific and well-regarded playwright, Stephen Belber's many plays have included *Through Fred* (1997), *Love* (1997), *Steak Knife* (2000) and *Passive Belligerence* (2000) . *Tape* was first performed for an audience at the Humana Festival of New American Plays, which took place at the Actors Theatre of Louisville in 2000.[74] Like the play, the film version of *Tape* may initially appear to have a deceptively simple premise, but it quickly becomes very clear that the storyline, which appears so deceivingly straightforward at the beginning, conceals many psychological complexities and unexpected developments which are gradually revealed to startling effect as the film progresses. All of the action takes place in a slightly dingy Michigan motel room, and the intense three-strong cast made the film Linklater's most intimate character study to date (even *Before Sunrise*, principally concerned with just two characters, had featured a restricted array of brief appearances by supporting players).

In Lansing, Michigan, film-maker Jon Salter (Robert Sean Leonard) is awaiting the premiere screening of his newly-completed movie at a local film festival. Vince (Ethan Hawke), a highschool acquaintance from some years back, is also visiting town – ostensibly to see Jon's film – and invites his old friend to call in on him at the motel where he is staying. It soon becomes clear that the two do not see each other regularly, and after a short period of mutual back-slapping and catching up, cracks in their friendship start to become readily apparent. Jon is concerned at Vince's seeming lack of ambition in life. Pushing thirty, he claims to be a volunteer fire-fighter, though in actuality he makes his money from illicitly supplying narcotics to select clients (while clearly not above indulging in them himself). Vince, on the other hand, deeply resents Jon's success, considering his old school friend's accomplishments to be heavily reliant upon mealy-mouthed pretensions and slack moral convictions in the furtherance of his aspirations. That Jon is trying to point out the considerable flaws in Vince's life, in an apparent attempt to help him, results only in riling him further.

Things begin to turn ugly when Vince brings up the subject of Amy Randall (Uma Thurman), an old flame whom they had both known at high school. Vince had dated Amy for some time back then, although they had never consummated their relationship, and he has a considerable axe to grind over the fact that Jon would later go on to have a brief fling with her, which he suspects involved sexual relations. Jon is uncomfortable with this line of questioning, and vigorously attempts to brush off the discussion – he hasn't seen Amy since high school a decade previously, while Vince had only met her briefly at a mutual friend's party five years beforehand. However, Vince is unwilling to let the matter go. After much verbal coercion, he forces Jon to disclose that he and Amy had indeed been intimate together on the last night of high school. But even then Vince is not satisfied, claiming that Amy had told him that Jon had in fact date-raped her. Jon is initially horrified by this allegation, strenuously denying the fact and stressing that it was, in fact, simply rough sex to which Amy had fully consented. However, following further intense interrogation by Vince, he later admits that he had used vigorous verbal coercion to persuade Amy into intercourse. Even then Vince refuses to turn down the heat, and ultimately Jon becomes exasperated by Vince's relentless line of questioning, angrily confessing to having used physical force to restrain Amy against her will, thus admitting culpability in her rape.

Vince is immensely satisfied at having punctured Jon's sense of moral rectitude, and reveals that he has recorded the confession onto tape via a concealed recording device. Jon is shocked at Vince's betrayal, but has little time to come to terms with its full ramifications; Vince reveals that he has invited Amy, now an Assistant District Attorney living in the Lansing area, out to dinner for the evening, and that she will soon be arriving at the motel. It is strongly suggested that Vince still holds a candle for Amy even after all this time, and Jon tries desperately to persuade Vince to hand over the tape before she arrives. However, Vince steadfastly refuses: he intends to hand it over to Amy unless Jon apologises to her for his brutal actions of ten years ago.

Amy arrives, and proves to be more than a match for both men. She is highly professional and icily detached; although she is mildly surprised to see Jon at the motel, there is a strong suggestion that she has little real interest in the lives of either man, having only turned up as a matter of polite civility due to her close relationship with Vince in the distant past. Amy is not in the least bit intimidated by the macho posturing of Vince, nor is she moved by the anxious sincerity of Jon. After some substantial urging by Vince, she reveals that she did not consider her sexual relationship with Jon to have been non-consensual, though this only compels both men to conclude that she is in denial over the brutality of the event. Vince offers Amy the tape of Jon's confession, while Jon offers her a heartfelt apology. Amy, however, refuses both, proving that she neither needs nor desires Vince's support or Jon's remorse. Although her composure never cracks, she eventually grows quietly outraged, unsure of what it is that either man believes they truly require from her to reach their respective catharses. Ultimately frustrated at the emotional impasse that they have reached, she pulls out her cellphone and calls the police, informing them of Vince's possession of illegal substances and Jon's self-confessed sexual abuse. She tells the two men that they have only around four minutes until the police arrive, forcing both of them to consider whether they should flee the scene or finally face the consequences of their actions.

With *Tape*, Linklater manages to cram a huge amount of emotional drama and psychological complexity into the film's claustrophobic one-room location. Through Belber's immensely concentrated script and a small but immensely skilled cast, the film explores many issues surrounding the way in which people rely on their awareness and the acuity of their observation, particularly with regard to how far they can rely on the accuracy of their memories over time. It is an interesting counterpoint to *Waking Life*, where there was absolutely no boundary to the outlandish locales and extreme situations offered up by the narrative. Here, constrained by the most circumscribed of environments, Linklater focuses entirely on the complexities of his characters to extremely striking effect, tackling many difficult issues including whether there can ever be any one inalienable sense of absolute guilt and innocence, responsibility and irreproachability, or blame and virtue. Belber makes particular use of the fact that, with the ambiguously-detailed crime at the heart of the matter having taken place a full decade previously, the audience remains as unsure about the true nature of the offence at the end of the film as they are at the beginning of it. Are Amy's recollections more accurate than those of Vince and Jon, or are the two men correct in their assumption that she is blocking the brutality of the event from her long-term memory? We are also forced to question whether Vince may be almost as guilty as Jon in his attempt to force Amy into a particular mode of behaviour to meet his own selfish ends. That she subverts both of their expectations to such devastating effect proves beyond any doubt that she has firmly put the misfortunes of her past behind her by virtue of her own individual self-determination, requiring the aid of no-one else to do so – most especially Jon and Vince. Critic Roger Ebert sagely observed that the tape of the title is a particularly effective device in linking these three characters, due to the fact that although it physically belongs to Vince (who repeatedly reminds Jon that it remains his own private property to do with as he pleases), it contains Jon's private memories as only he can relate them, and his account of these memories directly and inescapably involves Amy.[75]

Tape's cast is uniformly excellent. Ethan Hawke's belligerent, manipulative Vince is brilliantly rendered, from the fiendishly engineered way that he traps his old schoolmate into a confession of his guilt to his hazy affectation of being high on drugs (as we later discover, the character is never anywhere near as addled as he leads us to believe). Hawke is perfectly complemented by respected stage veteran Robert Sean Leonard. Leonard's portrayal of Jon, a superficially cleancut if mildly hypocritical young man on the brink of potential success in his early directorial career, is exceptionally well performed, with Belber carefully peeling back the layers of Jon's polished exterior to explore the decidedly murky ethical core which lies beneath. Hawke and Leonard had worked together many years beforehand – and to considerable acclaim – in Peter Weir's critically well-received *Dead Poets Society* (1989), and both actors ensure that while they make the increasingly fragile friendship between Vince and Jon convincing and believable, this on-screen reunion will ultimately prove to be as tense and as emotionally shattering as a battle between mortal enemies, much less a rivalry between old friends. The depth and range of these psychological issues are exceptionally well articulated by Uma Thurman, who brings a pitch-perfect approach to the frostily aloof Amy. Thurman lends the character an undeniable strength and glacial calm which contrasts faultlessly with Vince's forceful, swaggering bluster and Jon's hand-wringing indignation, and it is of little surprise that her sophisticated performance was to be nominated for Best Supporting Female at the Independent Spirit Awards in 2002.

Tape proved to be largely successful with most critics, many of whom cited the merits of the film's calculated unpredictability,[76] ultimately indeterminate ramifications,[77] robust performances and Belber's clever, well-employed use of subtly combative dialogue.[78] A number of commentators cited the sharp characterisation and skilful exploration of interpersonal communication to be reminiscent of other low-key, small-scale dramas such as David Mamet's *Oleanna* (1994),[79] whereas many noted Linklater's understated achievement in shooting the entire film in a six day session, with only a two week rehearsal period beforehand.[80] Perhaps inevitably, however, the film's unrelenting intensity and reliance on conversation rather than physical action was to lead a few reviewers to label the film pretentious,[81] overly talky,[82] and even dull.[83] These disapproving comments would prove to be largely in the minority though, with others praising the film's skilfully-handled mounting pressure and Linklater and Belber's ability to derive surprisingly wry humour from even the most rarefied of conflicts.[84]

With *Tape*, Linklater was to receive a Special Mention for the Laterna Magica Prize at the 2001 Venice Film Festival, an award which he received in conjunction with his work on *Waking Life*. The film was considered to be a more refined adaptation than had been the case with *subUrbia* and, with his successful harnessing of new digital film-making tools, *Tape* further underscored Linklater's reputation as a director who was at ease at the very cutting edge of the industry, showcasing uncompromising issues and a challenging narrative with pioneering technology.

9

SCHOOL OF ROCK (2003)

Paramount Pictures / Scott Rudin Productions / MFP Munich Film Partners GmbH & Company I. Produktions KG.

Director: Richard Linklater
Producer: Scott Rudin
Screenwriter: Mike White

Main Cast
Jack Black – Dewey Finn
Joan Cusack – Rosalie Mullins
Mike White – Ned Schneebly
Sarah Silverman – Patty Di Marco
Adam Pascal – Theo
Lucas Papaelias – Neil
Chris Stack – Doug
Lucas Babin – Spider

Following his last two successful and critically-acclaimed films, both of which had showcased distinctively unconventional approaches to their subject matter, Linklater was again to throw a curve-ball to spectators' anticipation by creating *School of Rock*, his most mainstream feature since *The Newton Boys* and one which would become one of his most popular with audiences. With its family-friendly approach, good natured script, brisk rock soundtrack and hugely energetic central performance, *School of Rock* was to firmly propel Linklater's reputation to new heights, elevating his recognition as a highly-skilled independent film-maker into the wider annals of American popular culture.

School of Rock featured a screenplay by Mike White, known both as an experienced screenwriter and actor in independent cinema, but by far the film's most recognisable attraction was the inspired casting of rising star Jack Black. A prolific performer since the early 1990s, Black had appeared in a variety of supporting roles on film including *Dead Man Walking* (1995), *The Cable Guy* (1996), *High Fidelity* (2000) and *Shallow Hal* (2001), as well as a number of television roles including appearances as part of the memorable *Tenacious D* features (1997-2000). In *School of Rock*, Black was very much to take centre-stage, and it is the manic charm of his slovenly rockobsessed anti-hero that lends the film much of its hyperactive appeal and entertainment value.[85]

Things do not augur well for the fortunes of rocker Dewey Finn (Jack Black). Now on the wrong side of thirty, his performance talents are questionable and his band's big break looks as unlikely as ever. He is appalled when, following yet another lacklustre gig, his disillusioned fellow band members vote to unceremoniously evict him from the very group that he himself had founded. This news does not impress his friend and landlord Ned Schneebly (Mike White), to whom Dewey owes hundreds of dollars in unpaid rent. Years ago, Ned had also once played in a band with Dewey, but has long since thrown in the towel and trained as a substitute teacher after coming to the conclusion that, quite aside from never having impressed the record companies, his musical talents might simply not have been good enough to deserve a breakthrough. Egged on by his nagging killjoy girlfriend Patty Di Marco (Sarah Silverman), Mike insists that Dewey face up to the fact that his musical career is a permanent non-starter and that he must attempt to find alternative employment in order to pay him back.

Dewey is somewhat dumbfounded at this turnaround in events, particularly as he believes that his rock talents are contribution enough to society. However, after a few abortive attempts to devise an effortless money-making scheme, he receives a phone call intended for Mike from the prestigious Horace Green elementary school. The school are offering a temporary teaching placement, and Dewey wastes no time in impersonating his friend, agreeing to assume the responsibilities of one of Horace Green's fifth-grade teachers in order to generate some much-needed cash.

Quickly cobbling together an eclectic teacher-esque wardrobe, complete with tweed jacket and quaint bow-tie, Dewey only just manages to succeed in convincing the school's uptight principal Rosalie Mullins (Joan Cusack) of his scholarly credentials. The truth, however, quickly becomes evident – he hasn't the foggiest clue how to teach his new class of erudite, hot-housed pupils, and hopes to coast along by keeping them in permanent recess. This doesn't play well with the intense set of ten year old overachievers, who are gravely concerned by his deviation from (indeed, complete abandonment of) their cherished curriculum, and they quickly become bored by his obvious desire to make easy money by whiling away the hours in class, shirking his educative responsibilities as he devises new ways of keeping Principal Mullins off the scent of his desperate scam.

Things quickly change when he accidentally happens upon the children's music class and discovers that many of his pupils have quite accomplished musical talents with a variety of different instruments. Considering their aptitude to be wasted on anodyne renderings of classical music pieces, Dewey hatches a plan to form his class into a rock band before the conclusion of his temporary placement at the school. If he can turn his strait-laced charges into seasoned rockers within the few weeks available to him, he schemes, it might just be possible to enter them into the local Battle of the Bands event and scupper his former band-mates' chances of winning the grand prize.

Dewey's plan is considerably more difficult to pull off than he imagines, however, and requires his every effort to organise the class into wannabe rock gods while diverting the school authorities' attention from his risky machinations. Convincing the pupils that the incessant band practice is actually part of an inter-school assignment, he swears them to secrecy in order to keep their parents from discovering the truth. But in time, he finds that the pupils have many talents beyond just music, and he slowly begins to consider them on individual terms rather than as simply a means to an end. Coaching them in the history and background of rock as well as its many interpretations and techniques, he begins to grow fond of their infectious enthusiasm for the project, and ultimately their joint desires for success begin to converge – although for very different reasons.

However, just as the big date beckons for their stage performance, disaster strikes. Ned and Patty discover Dewey's duplicity at the same time that he is struggling to convince a packed parents' evening that he has been doing more during term-time than just teaching their children that rock and roll is less a simple musical genre, more a state of mind. With his true identity now rumbled and Principal Mullins leading an angry mob at his tail, can Dewey still manage to get his young performers onto the line-up of the Battle of the Bands before the consequences of his actions catch up with him?

School of Rock presents a simple premise which is executed brilliantly from start to finish. Once again, Linklater confounded all critical expectation by presenting a film which contained his trademark themes of anti-authoritarianism and freedom of personal responsibility within a resolutely family-friendly framework (as critic J. Hoberman noted in his review of the film, there may be plenty of rock 'n' roll in *School of Rock*, but no sex and drugs to go with it).[86] Mike White's perceptive screenplay is careful to develop all of the characters with both respect and a fine-eyed attention to detail, irrespective of their age. First and foremost, Dewey Finn is presented to us a complicated character – much more complex than the protagonists of most generic family features – whom we discover to be both likeable and unfathomable in roughly equal measure. Jack Black delivers a performance of a lifetime, infusing Dewey with more than just an deeply ingrained love of rock; Black indisputably makes the role his own with his nonstop frenzied dynamism and energetic contortions, and it is little wonder that *School of Rock* has become one of the best-known (and best regarded) roles of his career, even after later successes in films such as Peter Jackson's high-profile remake of *King Kong* (2005). Yet in the hands of Black and Linklater, Dewey is much more than just a musically-charged clown; a deeper aspect of his character is suggested that makes the audience want to explore his steadfast desire to cling to the comforts of his past, to the hopes of unrealised fame that are not quite yet extinguished. Yet if Dewey's ambitions are little more than a relic of the pre-MTV rock era, he doesn't consider the anachronism of his desires to be a particularly troublesome stumbling-block, for we know beyond doubt that he truly believes that it isn't he who is out of step, but today's world. Hammering out his unorthodox curriculum to the sound of some of rock's greatest classics, it is Dewey's infectious enthusiasm to regain an elusive golden age that affects those around him so potently, whether they actively want it to or not. By the film's conclusion, he has not only changed the outlook of his students, but also the expectations of their parents, Ned, and even Rosalie Mullins.

The other adult characters are likewise well sketched out, from White's neurotically disillusioned Ned to Joan Cusack's inspired turn as the magnificently apprehensive Principal Mullins. She too becomes much more than a straightforward comedy stooge, thanks to Cusack's skilled and expressive rendering of the character's many foibles. (As we discover in the bar scene and subsequent discussion in Dewey's van, Mullins herself fears the possibility that she may have turned into the anxious caricature that she has always hoped to avoid.) The only largely unsympathetic character appears to be Patty, though given her function as an all-purpose spoilsport this was perhaps inevitable. However, as many commentators noted, some of the best characterisation is saved for the many impressive child actors who make up Dewey's class at Horace Green.[87] From the socially-uneasy Lawrence (Robert Tsai) to the image-conscious Tomika (Maryam Hassan), and from the eloquently self-confident Summer (Miranda Cosgrove) to the edgy, paternally-hectored Zack (Joey Gaydos Jr.), there is no weak link in the roll-call of striking young acting talent on display throughout the film, and Linklater and White do not shirk from presenting the pupils as fully-formed characters at all times, never as lazy ciphers. Just as pleasingly, all of these young characters each have very distinctive and engaging personalities, and even those who are most sceptical of Dewey's madcap scheme are never portrayed as obnoxious or mean-spirited.

The skilful promotion of the popular Jack Black and the inspired selection of rock and roll anthems which made up the soundtrack were key to the film's major commercial success, as was the clever subversion of school rebellion clichés (rather than the traditional pattern of pupil revolt against repressive teachers, Linklater seems to take gleeful satisfaction in presenting a pseudo-teacher who tries everything in his power to persuade his students to abandon educational selfrepression in favour of questioning the nature of authority).[88] School of Rock was also to be received positively by critics, who praised the film for presenting rounded characters in spite of its madcap comic premise,[89] the energy of Jack Black's bravura performance,[90] the obvious care taken in keeping the film's anarchy tightly controlled,[91] and the skill evident in making the narrative consistently entertaining in spite of a few of the less plausible (but always necessary) twists in the plot.[92] Roger Ebert seemed to speak for much of the critical community when he commented that perhaps the film's most laudable quality was its ability to present a thoughtful and enjoyable comedy for all of the family whilst never once insulting the intelligence of the viewer (regardless of their age).[93]

School of Rock's critical and commercial success was to be mirrored in its performance at awards ceremonies, where it was to be very warmly received. Among the many plaudits gained by the film was a MTV Movie Award in 2004 for Jack Black (Best Comedic Performance) as well as a nomination at the same ceremony for Best On-Screen Team for the young ensemble of actors who had made up Dewey Finn's class of pupils. Black's performance was also to be nominated for a Golden Globe (2004), a Golden Satellite Award (2004), and a Teen Choice Award (2004). Ilene Starger won the Artios Award for Best Casting for a Comedy Feature Film at the 2004 Casting Society of America Awards, and the film's rock soundtrack album was nominated for a Grammy, also in 2004. The film was also nominated for a number of technical awards, mostly with regard to its music editing, as well as Craig Wedren's original soundtrack which was to win a BMI Film Music Award in 2004.

School of Rock had proven to be a major commercial hit for Linklater, and had also entered him into the awareness of many casual moviegoers who may otherwise have been more or less oblivious to his significant stature in the world of independent film.[94] Whilst many were impressed at the ease with which he had again made a successful transition from distinctive freewheeling features to a narratively conventional and highly commercial feature, more still were to voice their admiration for the way in which he refused to tone down his enlightened, freethinking views for the purposes of mainstream film-making, instead couching his potent objectives of examining the authenticity and justification of authority within a deceptively straightforward comedic storyline. The fact that he could achieve this objective with such panache whilst still producing an entertaining and popular film was to further enhance his reputation as a major directorial talent, as well as bringing his talents to the attention of a wider audience than ever before.

10

BEFORE SUNSET (2004)

Detour Filmproduction / Castle Rock Entertainment

Director: Richard Linklater
Producers: Anne Walker-McBay and Richard Linklater
Screenwriters: Richard Linklater, Julie Delpy and Ethan Hawke, from a story by Richard Linklater and Kim Krizan

Main Cast
Ethan Hawke – Jesse
Julie Delpy – Celine
Vernon Dobtcheff – Bookstore Manager
Louise Lemoine Torres – Journalist #1
Rodolphe Pauly – Journalist #2
Mariane Plasteig – Waitress
Diabolo – Philippe
Denis Evrard – Boat Attendant

The announcement of *Before Sunset*'s release was to provoke considerable surprise amongst the film-going community. The fact that Linklater was to direct a sequel of any kind was in itself unprecedented in his career thus far (though some may argue that *Waking Life* was at the very least a thematic continuation of *Slacker*). However, the fact that he had chosen to produce a follow-up to one of his best-known works – and one which already seemed to be something of a closed circle in terms of both premise and narrative – was to raise the eyebrows of many critics. *Before Sunrise* had appeared to encapsulate an entire relationship (a providential genesis, meaningful rapport, fleeting but significant bonding and eventual parting) of its two star-crossed lovers so perfectly that it was difficult to imagine what kind of direction a sequel was likely to take. Given that *Before Sunrise* remained one of Linklater's most popular films, a degree of scepticism was voiced with regard to whether he could possibly come close to matching the original film's unique style and charm. Characteristically, of course, Linklater was to be undeterred by the challenges that these expectations posed, and set out to create a sequel which was every bit as distinctive and engaging as the original, though in very different ways.

The careers of both Ethan Hawke and Julie Delpy had developed very impressively since their appearance in *Before Sunrise*. Hawke had starred in films as diverse as Andrew Niccol's *Gattaca* (1997), Alfonso Cuaron's *Great Expectations* (1998) and Michael Almereyda's *Hamlet* (2000) before being nominated for an Academy Award for Best Supporting Actor in Antoine Fuqua's *Training Day* (2001). Delpy had likewise continued to develop a strikingly varied range of film roles, including Billy Wirth's *MacArthur Park* (2001), Ravi Kumar's *Notting Hill Anxiety Festival* (2003) and perhaps most notably *Looking for Jimmy* (2002), which she had also written and directed. Her other work had included an appearance in Jerry Ree's acclaimed short film *CinéMagique* (2002), a prominent television role in Joseph Sargent's adaptation of Fyodor Dostoyevsky's *Crime and*

Punishment (1998), and a high-profile seven episode recurring appearance on TV's *E.R.* during 2001. Both Hawke and Delpy were to bring not only their distinguished acting talents to *Before Sunset*, but also their considerable combined writing prowess due to the fact that they were to collaborate with Linklater in the creation of the film's script.[95]

It has been nine years since the events of *Before Sunrise*. Jesse (Ethan Hawke) is now a successful writer in his mid-thirties, and is rounding off a European book tour with a reading from his new novel at a prestigious Parisian bookshop. As he is concluding a questions and answers session with an eager group of journalists, he is stunned to notice Celine (Julie Delpy) watching him from the periphery of the audience. As they have never been in contact with each other since their intense day together in Vienna back in the mid-nineties, their reunion is both euphoric and awkward in equal measure.

Jesse has an hour or so to kill before he is due to check in at the embarkation lounge of the airport for his flight home. Keen to catch up with Celine after their many years apart, he arranges with the bookshop's manager (Vernon Dobtcheff) and the chauffeur who has been assigned to him (Diabolo) to pick him up by car a while later, so that he can join Celine for a short tour of her native Paris before he leaves the country.

At first the reunited couple's discussion has a slightly self-conscious, formal edge to it. Celine reveals that she is now a committed environmental campaigner in a *laissez faire* relationship with a war photographer, whereas Jesse reveals that he is married to an elementary school teacher with whom he has a young son. They recall their decade-old promise to each other that they would meet again in Vienna six months after their previous meeting, and Celine notes that she was never able to make that date due to the fact that her grandmother's funeral (the same relative that she had been visiting in Budapest during her encounter with Jesse on the train where they first met) was being held on the same day. Jesse, however, had readily travelled to Vienna from the United

States only to meet with disappointment, and had always wondered why Celine had not been there to meet him. As they had never exchanged addresses or phone numbers, given their belief that a long-distance relationship would be doomed to fade and die, they were to have no other way to get back in touch with each other.

As their unexpected meeting continues, Jesse and Celine discover much more about the direction that the other's life has taken since their parting. It quickly becomes clear that Jesse's book is semi-autobiographical in nature, detailing his fond memories of that one perfect night with Celine. Celine reveals that it was only through reading about the novel that she was able to put two and two together and catch up with Jesse at the Paris bookshop venue. Jesse is clearly amazed and delighted by her announcement, as this had in fact been his exact aim in writing the book in the first place (its eventual bestseller status being clearly little more than a secondary consideration to him).

As their impromptu tour of Paris takes them to a pleasantly inviting café, a verdant public garden and even a short ride on the Seine in a tourist sightseeing boat, further revelations about their lives are gradually teased out. In spite of his success in the publishing world, Jesse is deeply dissatisfied with his life. His marriage has become stagnant, and the only thing keeping him from instigating a divorce from his wife is his love for his son Hank, upon whom he clearly dotes. Celine on the other hand seems never to have got over the intense passion and affection that she had shared with Jesse during their past meeting, and has found that none of her subsequent relationships have come close to matching the fire of the bond that they had shared in Vienna. Both voice their disappointment that things hadn't turned out differently; Jesse is particularly gutted when he discovers that Celine had been living in New York City in the late nineties, as he himself had been, and that he may have narrowly missed meeting her there while she was studying for a Masters degree at a university near to him.

The pair grow ever more wistful as their time begins to run out. The chauffeur arrives to pick up Jesse and deliver him to the airport, but Jesse insists that they take Celine along for the ride, in order to drop her off at home on the way back. They grow upset at the prospect of parting once again, and share increasingly powerful expressions of their feelings at fate having reunited them both – now older and very different people than before – only for professional, familial and parental obligations to get in their way. But Jesse has one last request of Celine before they must go their separate ways – one which surprises her, and leads to an equally unanticipated conclusion.

Both Hawke and Delpy reconnect instantly with their respective roles, making the improbable but serendipitous reunion between Jesse and Celine a joy to behold. Delpy brings to Celine a staggeringly wide range of compelling characteristics; she is witty and wise, hopeful but also a little disillusioned.[96] Hawke too is always completely believable as the successful novelist who, in spite of his obvious professional accomplishments, is jaded and unsettled. (It is interesting to note that Hawke himself is, like the character of Jesse, a published author, having written two highly successful novels to date[97] – *The Hottest State,* later adapted by Hawke into a film which he was also to direct (2006),[98] and *Ash Wednesday.*[99]) Both actors excel in bringing their characters to life once again, reminding the audience of the matchless passion of *Before Sunrise* while emphasising the broadening of their life experiences and the deepening of their shared disenchantment with their respective fates. Celine's enthusiasm for her globetrotting environmental work, for instance, is overshadowed by her deep dissatisfaction at the geopolitical state of the world, leading her to question whether her efforts have any lasting meaning beyond their immediate short-term benefits (her idealistic worldview remains in sharp contrast to Jesse's pragmatic, market-oriented viewpoint).[100] Jesse, on the other hand, is clearly balancing the immense satisfaction of his publishing success against the crippling disappointment he feels at his moribund, loveless marriage. These emotional anxieties are never overplayed, however, and it is never less than a joy to behold the profound re-ignition of the two characters' youthful attraction as the deeply shared bond slowly burns away at the psychological burdens that age has bestowed upon them. Rarely had either actor performed more memorably than in *Before Sunset*, even taking into account the critical success of its illustrious predecessor.

The incredible performances of Delpy and Hawke are further emphasised by the subtle stylistic distinctions that Linklater had drawn between *Before Sunrise* and *Before Sunset*. Whereas the original film had delicately compressed the events of almost 24 hours into a running time of less than two hours, *Before Sunset* takes place in real time, injecting an even greater sense of naturalism into the discourse between Celine and Jesse.[101] Likewise, *Before Sunrise* had featured a small but memorable selection of brief appearances by supporting characters, such as the Palm Reader and Street Poet, but *Before Sunset* features no quirky incidental cameos at all, focusing solely on the way in which the increasing power of Jesse and Celine's shared feelings is developed and expressed. The audience is never less than fully aware of the slowly building intensity of the couple's attraction, their regret over what might have been, and their unspoken hope for the future. Even the dialogue – the jewel in the crown of both films – is subtly different this time around; the dry wit and teasing flirtatiousness are both still there in abundance, of course, but the interplay demonstrates a general air of wistful melancholy in place of the playful, light-hearted whimsy of *Before Sunrise*. At all times we are aware of the fact that these are the same two people with whom we had become so familiarly acquainted in their youth, but now they each bear different and equally profound hallmarks of age and experience.

It is important to note that while both films were exceptionally well served by their respective screenplays, *Before Sunset* is significant not only in what is said but also in what remains left unsaid. Jesse and Celine's body language, though explored very effectively in *Before Sunrise*, is refined to an entirely new degree here, with the gesture and physicality of both characters expressing almost as much as their verbal exchange. This is evident in instances such as Jesse's spontaneous grabbing of Celine's hand as he guides her to the bench in the public garden (unexpected given the slightly reserved distance between them which precedes it), and even more so during the car ride to the airport when Celine touchingly extends her hand to reach out to an oblivious Jesse and, entirely unseen by him, then silently withdraws it.

Another interesting question raised by *Before Sunset* is, of course, how the film affects the cameo appearance of Celine and Jesse which takes place in *Waking Life*. As it is plain that the couple have never encountered each other in the nine years between their Viennese and Parisian meetings, it appears to be largely up to the viewer to decide whether the ambiguous *Waking Life* sequence is itself a brief, low-key sequel to the events of *Before Sunset*, or whether it instead takes place in one of the alternative realities described so vividly by Linklater's character at the beginning of *Slacker*.

Before Sunset performed exceptionally well with critics, even including some who had openly disapproved of *Before Sunrise*.[102] Like *Before Sunrise*, the film's style was compared with the works of Eric Rohmer and Louis Malle, but it also invited critics to contrast its approach with a variety of other prominent features from the past including David Lean's *Brief Encounter* (1945)[103] and Woody Allen's *Annie Hall* (1977),[104] whereas the startling effectiveness of the film's ending was compared to the conclusion of George A. Romero's *Martin* (1978).[105] Commentators praised a number of different aspects of the film including Hawke and Delpy's graceful resumption of their roles,[106] Linklater's masterful handling of the tangible, inexorable passing of time throughout the course of the narrative,[107] and the fact that although the dialogue was delivered so naturally that it appeared indistinguishable from spontaneous conversation, it had actually been very meticulously planned out at every stage rather than having been improvised on location.[108] Also, in spite of the fact that Linklater had shot *Before Sunset* in a single fifteen day session,[109] the film was commended for its lack of any apparent technical impediment or over-engineering of any of its situations.[110] (Indeed, the location filming highlights Linklater's particular skill in delicately employing Parisian landmarks like Notre Dame Cathedral and the River Seine as subjects to be actively engaged with through the characters' conversational interplay, rather than as merely a superficial backdrop to the action.) Some critics even voiced the opinion that another sequel would be desirable, to discover the manner in which Jesse and Celine's destiny had played out after the film's ambiguous conclusion,[111] although others suggested that for maximum impact, a further nine years should elapse from the time of the film's release before audiences discover the characters' fate.[112]

Before Sunset's multifaceted script was nominated for the Best Adapted Screenplay Oscar at the 2005 Academy Awards, and the film's script was also to receive nominations for an Independent Spirit Award, Writers Guild of America Award and Online Film Critics Society Award. *Before Sunset* was also nominated for the Best Film Award at the Gotham Awards, and gained Linklater a nomination for the Golden Berlin Bear at the Berlin International Film Festival in 2004. Julie Delpy's performance was to win her the Best Actress awards at the Empire Awards and the San Francisco Film Critics Circle Awards. Delpy was also nominated for Best Actress at the Online Film Critics Society Awards in 2005, where the film itself was nominated for Best Picture. *Before Sunset* was additionally nominated for a number of other international awards.

With *Before Sunset*, Linklater had delivered a film which had surprised moviegoers as much as it had delighted them. Whereas many had initially voiced dismay at the prospect of a sequel which would inevitably be forced to clarify the enchanting ambiguities of *Before Sunrise* (not least being a definitive answer as to whether the couple ever did succeed in reuniting in Vienna), the film not only managed to match the original's warmth and charm, but also deepened the dimensions of the protagonists' relationship still further, conjuring up a uniquely magnetic allure as the audience are drawn – ever so briefly – into the lives of these two passionate strangers, fanning the embers of a long-dormant romance as they come to terms with the paths that their lives have taken, their regrets at being forced to grow apart, and the hope that is rekindled in them during this unlikely chance meeting. There is little doubt that Linklater, Hawke and Delpy were all at the top of their game when filming *Before Sunset*, and the result is truly something special to behold.

11

BAD NEWS BEARS (2005)

Detour Filmproduction / Geyer Kosinski / Media Talent Group

Director: Richard Linklater
Producers: J. Geyer Kosinski and Richard Linklater
Screenwriters: Bill Lancaster, Glenn Ficarra and John Requa

Main Cast
Billy Bob Thornton – Morris Buttermaker
Greg Kinnear – Roy Bullock
Marcia Gay Harden – Liz Whitewood
Sammi Kane Kraft – Amanda Whurlitzer
Ridge Canipe – Toby Whitewood
Brandon Craggs – Mike Engelberg
Jeffrey Davies – Kelly Leak
Timmy Deters – Tanner Boyle

After the release of *Before Sunset*, his first sequel, it seemed oddly logical that Linklater would choose as his next project the first remake of his career.[113] His selection was an interesting one, for Michael Ritchie's *The Bad News Bears* (1976) had long been a gleefully subversive family favourite in America, especially amongst baseball fans (and indeed sporting fans in general). Featuring an exquisitely ill-tempered performance by Walter Matthau as the harddrinking coach of a Little League baseball team, the film was successful enough to spawn two sequels (Michael Pressman's *The Bad News Bears in Breaking Training* (1977) and John Berry's *The Bad News Bears Go to Japan* (1978)), along with a short-lived television series of the same name (1979-80). It seemed fitting that Linklater, having so effectively explored the unorthodox educational aspects of childhood in *School of Rock*, should now switch his attention to an equally unconventional exploration of youth leisure-time activities. Indeed, the project seemed almost tailor-made for him given that the spirit of *School of Rock* had, on its release two years previously, been compared to the original *Bad News Bears* feature.[114]

Replacing Walter Matthau in the central role of coach Morris Buttermaker was Academy Award winner Billy Bob Thornton, who had been awarded an Oscar for his screenplay for *Sling Blade* (1996), which he had also directed. He was additionally nominated for the Best Actor in a Leading Role Award for his performance in *Sling Blade* (also at the 1997 Academy Awards ceremony), as well as a later nomination in 1999 for Best Actor in a Supporting Role for his appearance in *A Simple Plan* (1998). Thornton delivers a perfectly honed performance as the cynical, borderline-alcoholic Buttermaker, replacing Matthau's crusty, curmudgeonly pessimism with a darkly sarcastic world-weariness that seemed ideally suited to this modern update of the *Bad News Bears* story. However, while Linklater ensures that the film's setting is brought into the immediacy of the here and now, he also takes care to preserve the anarchic charm of the original.

Morris Buttermaker has fallen on hard times. Once a

professional baseball player with a brief tenure in the Major League, he has now been reduced to eking out an existence as a pest exterminator as he slowly pickles himself in cheap booze. His only focus beyond drinking lies in his varyingly successful attempts at seducing any woman unlucky enough to cross his path. His aimless way of life takes an unexpected turn when he finds himself hired by Liz Whitewood (Marcia Gay Harden), a hotshot attorney and local councilwoman, as coach of a Little League baseball team named The Bears. Whitewood is determined to fight what she perceives as alleged discrimination in the Little League selection process, insisting that all children should be allowed to participate in baseball regardless of their sporting ability.

Unfortunately for Buttermaker, ability is something that the Bears are lacking in the extreme. Their number is made up of a ragtag collection of children who, while generally well-meaning, have little conception of even the most basic fundamentals of the game. Some are unfit, some can't speak English, some have major attitude problems, and one of them finds his catching capability hampered by the fact that he is unable to get around without the use of a motorised wheelchair. Buttermaker is further exasperated by persistent appearances from Roy Bullock (Greg Kinnear), coach of rival team The Yankees. Bullock is a smarmy and sanctimonious car salesman, totally single-minded in his determination for his team to succeed, who has obvious disdain for both the Bears and their new coach.

The Bears' first game of the season is a total disaster, largely due to the fact that Buttermaker has already written off the team as a lost cause and neglected their tuition. As the Yankees trounce them in competition, he concedes the match in order to spare the Bears further humiliation. However, the children's obvious disappointment at the outcome – coupled with his anger at Bullock's patronising condescension – makes Buttermaker resolve to improve the team's performance. From now on, he decides, the Bears will be 'bad news' for their rivals. After much cajoling,

Buttermaker manages to persuade Amanda Whurlitzer (Sammi Kane Kraft), the young daughter of one of his ex-girlfriends, to join the team. Buttermaker had trained Amanda into a highly skilled pitcher some years back, and is mightily relieved to discover that far from having lost the knack, her throw is still nigh-on faultless. He also eventually manages to recruit Kelly Leak (Jeffrey Davies), a local miscreant with hitherto-undiscovered throwing and catching skills. The other team members are a little wary of Kelly's enrolment, as his felonious exploits have become legend around their school, but in spite of his delinquent mindset he soon proves that the scope of his sporting potential is every bit as impressive as Buttermaker had suspected.

After following a long and difficult learning curve, the Bears eventually shake their losing streak and begin to score victories over their rivals. Although the team spirit is shaky at times, Buttermaker manages to hold everyone together until they eventually reach the championship final... and discover that they will once more be facing off against their arch-rivals, the Yankees. Undeterred, the Bears throw themselves into the game, employing every skill that Buttermaker has taught them (and even discovering a few more along the way). But with Bullock absolutely determined to win, parental expectation at fever pitch on the spectator stands and antipathy between the teams in constant danger of boiling over, will the Bears' performance finally see off their opponents once and for all?

Bad News Bears remains at all times a faithful adaptation of the Michael Ritchie original, with only a few minor cosmetic alterations applied – mostly for the purpose of situating the narrative within the context of a present day which is replete with laptop computers and the Atkins Diet.[115] Matthau's original Buttermaker cleaned out swimming pools for a living, for instance, in contrast to the nonconformist extermination business which seems better suited to Thornton's rendering of the character. While some critics noted that Buttermaker's alcoholism and promiscuity were made more explicit in the remake, others observed that references to casual drug abuse had been toned down from those in the original.[116] Yet there are many more similarities than there are differences, such as Linklater choosing to retain the original film's stirring excerpts from Bizet's *Carmen* which were used to accompany the team's performance on the field.

Ultimately, the film's screenplay by Glenn Ficarra and John Requa (who had also worked with Thornton in Terry Zwigoff's comedy *Bad Santa* (2003)) was such a truthful rendering of the style and content of the original film (even including some character names and situations) that the screenwriting billing includes a posthumous credit to the late Bill Lancaster, who had written the script for *The Bad News Bears* back in the mid-seventies. Yet for all its fidelity to Michael Ritchie's film, the new screenplay does firmly establish its own identity, as is perhaps most notable from the freshly developed direction of Thornton's Buttermaker in comparison to Matthau's, and the acidic bite of his dialogue. Thornton wrings sardonic mirth out of his every moment of screen time, and it is difficult to dislike the hopeless, womanising loser that he portrays – especially as Buttermaker ultimately confirms that he is every bit as conscious of his drink-addled shortcomings as everyone else is (something that the audience has likely suspected all along).[117]

Although Thornton is very much the driving force of the film, he was not the only major acting talent on display in *Bad News Bears*. Marcia Gay Harden had won a Best Supporting Actress Oscar for her performance in *Pollock* (2000) at the Academy Awards in 2001, and was also nominated for Best Supporting Actress for her role in *Mystic River* (2003) at the 2004 Oscars ceremony. She manages to bring an interesting and unexpected dimension to the character of Liz Whitewood, elevating her from a stereotypical workaholic legal expert and neurotic parent into a rather more rounded individual – a single parent with genuine concern for her son's wellbeing, rather than someone who is living their life vicariously through the achievements of her child.

Her co-star Greg Kinnear was likewise no stranger to critical acclaim, having been nominated for Best Supporting Actor for his role in *As Good As It Gets* (1997) at the Academy Awards ceremony of 1998. If anything, his character of Roy Bullock is even more incongruously complex than that of Whitehead, for although Bullock is introduced in the first act as a mealy-mouthed and slyly antagonistic character, by the end of the film (and especially in the climactic championship final) we have received a vague glimpse of other depths to this competitive adversary. This is especially true of his interactions with his son, proving that not only is he a caring parent at heart, but that he is not so obsessed with winning that he will encourage his offspring to succeed at any cost. It is thus thanks to Kinnear's performance that we are left wondering whether Bullock is really the hypocritical bullying rival (and figure of fun) that we were led to believe, or whether a basically decent individual lurks beneath the surface – a strength of characterisation not always to be found in a knockabout family comedy.

The film's impressive young cast make even the most unsympathetic characters among their number ultimately likeable. Notable among them are the pugilistic Tanner Boyle (Timmy Deters), diminutive in frame but on a short fuse at all times; the generally affable but massively hot-housed Toby Whitewood (Ridge Canipe), harried son of Liz Whitewood; the overweight and short-tempered Mike Engelberg (Brandon Craggs), a target of many jokes who never fails to give as good as he gets; the pessimistically defeatist Matthew Hooper (Troy Gentile), who is confined to a wheelchair (and often to the dugout too), and the nerdish Prem Lahiri (Aman Johal), the team's most intelligent member who seems more interested in performance statistics than in actually playing the game. The film is replete with entertaining banter between these mismatched team-mates, both on and off the field – not only with their various opponents, but most usually amongst themselves. Special mention is due for Sammi Kane Kraft's performance as ace pitcher Amanda

Whurlitzer. She and Thornton strike up a touching on-screen rapport that underscores the fact that Amanda is clearly the daughter that Buttermaker never had, and their shared affection is made all the more poignant by the way that both characters work so hard conceal their true feelings, neither wishing to appear 'soft' in the eyes of the other. Jeffrey Davies also impresses as all-purpose ne'er-do-well Kelly Leak, whose sullen intransigence masks a deep-seated desire to belong and be accepted.

Linklater again demonstrates his lightness of touch with comedy situations, and indeed Buttermaker's path to redemption (of sorts) in turning his hotchpotch of a team into championship finalists is laced with all manner of amusing vignettes. Most notable among them are Buttermaker's long, thankless trawl to find his team a sponsor (he eventually persuades a dubious 'gentleman's club' to fit the bill, with the added bonus of bringing some rather unconventional cheerleaders into the mix), and the beautifully-rendered awkwardness of the interaction between Toby Whitewood and Buttermaker when the older man is unexpectedly discovered having spent the night with Toby's mother. The way that Thornton articulates Buttermaker's entertainingly tongue-tied discomfort, and his ingeniously quick-thinking solution to the situation, are brilliantly handled. Critical reception of *Bad News Bears* was significantly polarised. Given the considerable audience affection surrounding the original film, it seemed reasonable to predict that the views of commentators would be divided, and whilst some critics praised Linklater's film for its sense of fun,[118] gifted cast of young actors,[119] and Thornton's acerbic central performance[120] and deadpan delivery,[121] others questioned the need for a remake of a film that seemed to have made its point so succinctly thirty years earlier,[122] and even ventured the opinion that the driving force in producing a remake of such a successful film may have been motivated as much by commercial marketing than it was by creative choice.[123] Some of the negative criticism may have been exacerbated by the fact that *Bad News Bears* had been released at around the same time as a number of similarly-themed sporting comedies including Steve Carr's *Rebound* (2005) and Peter Segal's *The Longest Yard* (2005), effectively flooding the market and taxing the tolerance threshold of reviewers.[124] Following the film's release, the non-adult cast of *Bad News Bears* would go on to win the award for Best Young Ensemble Cast Performance in a Feature Film at the Young Artist Awards in 2006, and the film itself was nominated for a Teen Choice Award and Golden Trailer Award, both in 2005.

By presenting a perennial tale of triumph over adversity in an appealing and completely unsentimental way, Linklater had reinforced *School of Rock*'s theme of against-the-odds success, playing out against the backdrop of moderate mayhem to good effect (albeit in a slightly more low-key fashion than *School of Rock*'s overtly anti-authoritarian agenda). In many eyes, the film ably recaptured the mischievously defiant charm of Michael Ritchie's original, remoulding it for modern audiences whilst still managing to keep the formula fresh for the many fans of the classic seventies' film.

12

A SCANNER DARKLY (2006)

Detour Filmproduction / Warner Independent Pictures / Thousand Words / 3 Arts Entertainment / Section Eight Ltd.

Director: Richard Linklater
Producers: Tommy Pallotta, Jonah Smith, Erwin Stoff, Anne Walker-McBay and Palmer West
Screenwriter: Richard Linklater, from the novel by Philip K. Dick

Main Cast
Keanu Reeves – Bob Arctor
Robert Downey Jr – James Barris
Woody Harrelson – Ernie Luckman
Rory Cochrane – Charles Freck
Winona Ryder – Donna Hawthorne
Mitch Baker – Brown Bear Lodge Host
Melody Chase – Arctor's Wife
Alex Jones – Arrested Protester

A *Scanner Darkly* was a significant film for Linklater in a number of ways. Noteworthy was his return to the pioneering new digitally interpolated rotoscoping technique, Rotoshop, which had been developed by Bob Sabiston and employed to such striking effect in *Waking Life*. Here, however, it was to be used less obtrusively, with even greater refinement, and for very different reasons.[125] But Linklater's choice to adapt a novel by the late Philip K. Dick was also a significant one. His interest in the writer's work had been apparent from *Waking Life*, where Linklater's 'Pinball Playing Man' discusses of one of Dick's many essays at the film's conclusion, and indeed Dick's persistent exploration of the themes of human perceptions of reality and his deep suspicion of the role and motivation of central government in the modern age seemed tailor-made for Linklater's leading edge film-making.[126]

Philip Kindred Dick (1928-1982) is one of the most important figures in twentieth-century science fiction, and arguably one of the most significant American authors of the post-War period.[127] He has become best-known for his challenging and psychologically probing novels which include *The Man in the High Castle* (1962), *The Three Stigmata of Palmer Eldritch* (1965), *Ubik* (1969) and *Flow My Tears, The Policeman Said* (1974), as well as a great many short stories. A multiple literary award-winner in his lifetime, it is difficult to overstate Dick's intricate skill and momentous impact on both literary science fiction and indeed American fiction in general, and this influence has been seen to continue even since the time of his death. An extremely prolific writer, adaptations of many of his novels and works of short prose fiction have been popular in film, television, radio and on stage. There have been a number of significant cinematic adaptations of his work, most notable among them being Ridley Scott's *Blade Runner* (1982) (based on the novel *Do Androids Dream of Electric Sheep?* (1968)), Paul Verhoeven's *Total Recall* (1990) (from the short story *We Can Remember It For You Wholesale* (1966)), Christian Duguay's *Screamers* (1995), Steven Spielberg's *Minority Report* (2002) and

John Woo's *Paycheck* (2003). It is no small testament to Dick's skill as a writer that with each passing year, his damning indictments of modern society, authoritarianism and human nature seem ever more prescient, and indeed his intensely keen foresight and the uncomfortable potency of his finely-drawn psychological awareness would be of special relevance to Linklater's adaptation of one of Dick's best-known novels, *A Scanner Darkly* (1977).

Some years in the future, the world is awash with a highly addictive (and gravely damaging) narcotic drug known as Substance D, covertly developed from a small blue flower and smuggled to all points of the globe. Trafficking of the narcotic has become endemic, and the American government is struggling to track the supply and demand of the illegal substance within their country, gradually establishing a highly sophisticated monitoring system to trace the communication and movement of citizens in order to pin down the source of the drugs.

In Anaheim, California, Bob Arctor (Keanu Reeves) is an anti-narcotics agent in the employ of the government who is responsible for stymieing the flow of Substance D in the immediate area. For some time he has been working undercover in a ramshackle house in the locality which he shares with a number of drug addicts including the addled Ernie Luckman (Woody Harrelson) and the conceited, thoroughly inscrutable James Barris (Robert Downey Jr). Other regular visitors to this curious hideout are Charles Freck (Rory Cochrane), who is heavily addicted to Substance D and now suffers disturbing symptoms of long-term exposure to the drug, and Donna Hawthorne (Winona Ryder), a cocaine addict who is also the group's supplier of Substance D. However, it soon becomes clear that Arctor himself has become addicted to the drug during the course of his covert operations, which greatly complicates matters. His initial plan had been to manipulate Donna into revealing her source of Substance D, thus allowing the police to shut down the operation at its foundation. Instead, he finds himself romantically attracted to her, and becomes drawn ever deeper into the murky, drug-soaked world that he has been assigned to infiltrate.

Back at police headquarters, Arctor is known only as Agent Fred, his visual identity masked by a scramble suit – a full-body technological gadget which constantly obscures an individual's features, voice and gender in order to ensure that no two operatives are ever able to identify each other (thus avoiding the potential for corruption within the department). Fred regularly reports to his immediate superior, Agent Hank (voice of Mark Turner), who has been monitoring the situation within Arctor's house via a comprehensive system of concealed video cameras. By a process of elimination, Hank has now determined that Fred is in fact one of the house's occupants, but is unable to establish which one he might specifically be. He thus orders Fred to intensify his scrutiny of the situation, specifically with regard to heightening observation of Arctor himself, whom Hank believes may be the key to the whole investigation.

Now faced with the intricate task of supervising a surveillance operation of his own undercover identity, Fred/Arctor finds that his addiction is further encumbering his ability to perceive the difference between his two discrete selves. As the inhabitants of Arctor's house become ever more paranoid, suspecting that their movements are being monitored by the state, Arctor himself becomes increasingly immersed in his clandestine role, slowly losing his ability to recall his other identity as Agent Fred and suffering acute hallucinations. Meanwhile, Barris quietly becomes distrustful of Arctor, suspecting that his romantic relationship with Donna is merely a front for a covert professional association between the pair. Barris thus deduces that Arctor and Donna are both members of a terrorist cell, which fuels his already-rampant anxieties.

Barris approaches the police about his suspicions, and ironically ends up airing his wild notions to Agents Fred and Hank. However, Fred is unmoved by Barris's detailed betrayal of Arctor, as he now has no way of differentiating between his 'real' and undercover identities. Hank has Barris remanded in custody 'for his own protection', but his testimony is of little benefit as Hank has already deduced Fred's true identity and thus already knows that he has no connection to either terror organisations or the source of the drugs supply. Police psychologists have also become conscious of Fred's impaired mental functionality due to his heavy abuse of Substance D, deducing that conflict has been agitated between the right and left hemispheres of his brain. Hank informs Fred that he will be reprimanded on account of breaking the law.

Hank then reveals that he is fully aware that Arctor is also Fred (and vice-versa), which comes as a total shock to him. This heightens Fred/Arctor's state of confusion still further, and – exhausted and crushed by the ramifications of his drug use – he has no choice but to comply with Hank's insistence that he attend a facility operated by New Path, a mysterious corporation which manages rehabilitation clinics throughout the country.

What Fred/Arctor remains entirely unaware of is that Hank's alter-ego is none other than Donna. Far from being the drug runner that Arctor had originally suspected, Donna is actually working to enforce a government agenda – to plant an operative within New Path in order to ascertain the corporation's true motives. Therefore both of Fred/ Arctor's separate identities have been manipulated by Donna and her superiors to achieve this end, with the consent of neither of his two selves.

At New Path, Fred/Arctor reacts badly to his sudden withdrawal from Substance D, and suffers extensive neurological damage. After a long period of mental and physical rehabilit-ation, he is given a new name – Bruce – and shipped out to one of the corporation's secluded farming facilities. Now suffering profound mental defects, he is put to work tending the vast cornfields. Eventually, he discovers that beneath the rows of corn, thousands of tiny blue flowers are being cultivated – the organic source of Substance D. Although mentally incapable of deter-mining the true nature of the flowers, he is subconsciously compelled to pick one from the ground and conceal it in his boot, determining to pass it on to his friends the next time that he returns to the New Path clinic. (It is left to the audience's judgment as to who these 'friends' may be.)

A Scanner Darkly is an extremely faithful adaptation of the Philip K. Dick novel, accurately translating not only its content but also its oppressively claustrophobic, paranoid approach to its subject matter. Apart from updating the film for an indistinct near-future setting (Dick's novel having been set in 1994), only a small number of variations are in evidence between the book and Linklater's screenplay, such as the explicit revelation that Hank is in fact Donna (Hank's identity is only suggested in the novel, but never fully revealed), and the elimination of novel character Jerry Fabin from the events of the film. Linklater utilises Sabiston's rotoscoping effect very successfully in heightening the edgy disorientation of the narrative, and this is particularly effective in the realisation of the constantly shifting scramble suits, with their dizzying visual characteristics. Highly efficient too is the skilful contrast between Fred's continuously changing exterior aspect and the unnervingly confined Arctor speaking from within the suit's interior, growing ever more psychologically disturbed as the film continues. Bob Sabiston's software is applied in a very different way to its previous employment in *Waking Life*; although Fred/Arctor's drug-influenced perceptions could conceivably suggest that the same kind of dream-state environment is evident in *A Scanner Darkly*, the effect is much more restrained throughout the film. Even the cockroach transformation sequence, where Arctor's observational acuity grows ever more unreliable, appears much more low-key than the vibrant conceptual buoyancy and shifting visual styles of *Waking Life*, and the moody, oppressive effect suggested here seems much more inclined to unnerve and disorientate the audience than to suggest the wild and exciting subconscious possibilities suggested by Linklater's earlier film.

The casting of star Keanu Reeves was also an inspired choice. Well known to audiences from a high-profile career reaching back to the mid-eighties, Reeves was at the time enjoying considerable acclaim for his role as Thomas 'Neo' Anderson in Larry and Andy Wachowski's *The Matrix* trilogy (comprising *The Matrix* (1999), *The Matrix Reloaded* (2003) and *The Matrix Revolutions* (2003)). Although *The Matrix* series had featured a similarly Descartes-inspired exploration of a fractured reality, its apocalyptic far-future backdrop seemed a world away from the foreboding imminence of Dick's grim, despondent realism, and Reeves brilliantly subverts the kind of cool heroism displayed by Neo to create the perplexed dejection and idiosyncratic mumbling mode of speech of Agent Fred/Bob Arctor. The shuffling, confused Arctor has a perfect foil in the rangy physicality of Robert Downey Jr, whose surreal verbal articulacy in the role of James Barris contrasts sharply with his eccentric, spasmodic mode of speech. Downey Jr excels in expressing Barris's quick (if oddly oblique) wit, along with his devious, paranoid scheming, and his uniquely mannered portrayal reminds the audience of the reason why his acting skills had gained him a nomination for an Academy Award in 1993 for his leading role in *Chaplin* (1992). He gives a particularly well-observed performance following a malfunction with the accelerator pedal of Arctor's car, an unfortunate accident which Barris uses to gradually manoeuvre the other men (and possibly even himself) into believing is part of an intricately planned state-controlled plot to have them all murdered.

Past Oscar nominations could also claimed by two of Downey Jr's co-stars, Woody Harrelson (for Best Leading Actor in *The People Versus Larry Flynt* (1996)) in 1997, and also Winona Ryder, who was nominated for Best Supporting Actress in 1994 (for *The Age of Innocence* (1993)) and Best Actress in a Leading Role in 1995 (for *Little Women* (1994)). This tightly-knit quartet of actors creates a fascinating collective character study, the qualities of each contrasting effectively with the other as the film progresses. Ernie Luckman, for instance, has all the traits of a spaced-out surfer dude who has strayed into dark and uncertain territory, yet when the thin surface of his easygoing disposition is scratched he can be seen to match Arctor and Barris step for step when it comes to agitated paranoia. Donna Hawthorne, on the other hand, is a much more evenly collected character, encouraging Arctor's affections whilst steadfastly refusing his physical advances. Her intractable and continuous rebuff of Arctor on a physical level raises Barris's suspicions as much as it inspires a vague, unrealised infatuation towards her from Luckman. Ryder impeccably carries off Donna's duality of purpose, demonstrating her character's deft ability to flawlessly manipulate the proceedings around her, and even managing to outscheme the arch-conspirator Barris. Completing the central ensemble is Rory Cochrane, whose frenetic, twitchy performance as Charles Freck – constantly in motion and haunted by vivid hallucinations which have tangibly aggravating physical symptoms – seems to form a kind of extreme flip-side of the affably stupefied Ron Slater from *Dazed and Confused*. Cochrane brings great pathos to the slow-motion disintegration of Freck, heavily addicted to Substance D and even more thoroughly disorientated than the inhabitants of Arctor's house, yet he still manages to bring just enough dark humour to the role to take the edge from Freck's hopelessly bleak situation.[128]

The critics were generally supportive of *A Scanner Darkly* following its release, though there were a few dissenting voices nonetheless. While some reviewers praised the film for the great care taken to respect Dick's original text,[129] others considered it to be too faithful to the deliberate, idea-driven novel, divesting the film of momentum.[130] Some commended the thoughtful use of Bob Sabiston's digital rotoscoping technique,[131] while others questioned why Linklater had felt the need to employ the process at all.[132] However, a majority of commentators found aspects of the film worthy of approval, including its relentless sense of disquieting claustrophobia,[133] willingness to engage with potent political issues,[134] speculative and theoretical vigour,[135] and the fact that it never shies away from engaging with the difficult range of concepts evident in Dick's novel.[136]

A Scanner Darkly was awarded the Austin Film Award at the

2007 Austin Film Critics Association Awards, and also won the Best Animation Award at the Online Film Critics Society Awards in the same year. It was additionally nominated for Best Animation at the Golden Trailer Awards in 2006, and was also nominated for two of the most prestigious prizes in science fiction, the Saturn Award for Best Animated Film from the Academy of Science Fiction, Fantasy and Horror Films (2007), and the Hugo Award for Best Dramatic Presentation (2007).

With *A Scanner Darkly*, Linklater had created quite possibly the most faithful cinematic evocation of Philip K. Dick's style and thematic concerns since Ridley Scott's atmospheric *Blade Runner* almost a quarter of a century earlier. Praised by many admirers of science fiction for its fidelity to the source text, while still augmenting the dialogue and technology evident in the film to reflect cultural and scientific advances made since the time of Dick's novel, Linklater's film offers further exploration of the nature of existence in the modern world – namely the importance of self-expression in the face of growing surveillance of public life. In terms of free speech, it is interesting to compare the treatment of Alex Jones's outspoken protester character – unceremoniously silenced and bundled off by the oppressive authorities – with Jones's unfettered cameo appearance in *Waking Life*, where he has the ability to freely broadcast his views just as the audience are at liberty to draw their own conclusions about the statements that he makes. Thus, like Dick's novel before it, Linklater's defence of freedom of expression within the film is of paramount importance to the core of its narrative, and *A Scanner Darkly*'s preoccupation with Orwellian scrutiny of the masses, the culture of suspicion, and corporate interference with the direction of society is, in the grand tradition of the very best of the science fiction genre, a cautionary tale with bold allegorical resonance.[137]

13

FAST FOOD NATION (2006)

BBC Films / HanWay Films / Recorded Picture Company /
Participant Productions

Director: Richard Linklater
Producers: Malcolm McLaren and Jeremy Thomas
Screenwriters: Richard Linklater and Eric Schlosser, from the
book by Eric Schlosser

Main Cast
Greg Kinnear – Don Henderson
Ana Claudia Talancón – Coco
Bobby Cannavale – Mike
Catalina Sandino Moreno – Sylvia
Wilmer Valderrama – Raul
Ashley Johnson – Amber
Patricia Arquette – Cindy
Ethan Hawke – Pete

Fast Food Nation was released in the same year as *A Scanner Darkly*, and although the two projects are wildly divergent in style, Linklater's core theme of concern for the direction of the society in which he lives remains the same. However, in place of *A Scanner Darkly*'s censorious assessment of the surveillance society and state oppression, *Fast Food Nation* was instead to set its sights firmly on the motivations of big business in a similarly sharp but equally thoughtful examination. Even more apparent than had been the case with most of Linklater's other directorial output, *Fast Food Nation* is unquestionably a film which has serious and unambiguous political motivation, and the issues that the film raises are much less oblique than the dense social critique of *subUrbia* or the muted, low-key geopolitical observations of Jesse and Celine in *Before Sunset*.[138]

Fast Food Nation was based upon the best-selling book of the same name which had been authored in 2001 by Eric Schlosser, who was also to co-write the screenplay with Linklater. The original work had been a forensically-researched, comprehensive non-fictional account of the fast food industry and its global influence which was quickly to find a huge audience across the world.[139] For the film, however, Schlosser and Linklater were to forgo a docu-dramatic style of storytelling in favour of creating a range of fictional locales and organisations, with a large cast of characters who would articulate the book's key themes with a bitingly satirical and hardhitting narrative drive.[140]

Business prospects couldn't be better for Mickey's, a multinational fast food corporation celebrating one of their biggest successes, The Big One: a burger meal which is outstripping even their most optimistic expectations. Much of The Big One's success lies in the publicity talents of Mickey's vice-president of marketing, Don Henderson (Greg Kinnear), who is tipped for great things by his employers.

However, the path to market domination is not entirely smooth for Mickey's; activists have been successful in gaining access to samples of frozen burger meat and have subjected them to analysis, discovering that they contain a high concentration of bovine faecal matter. Sensing the potential for public relations disaster, Mickey's chief executive dispatches Henderson to the town of Cody in Colorado – home of their principal suppliers, Uniglobe Meat Packing – in an attempt to uncover the reason behind this risk to public health.

Henderson arrives in Cody and takes the official visit of Uniglobe Meat Packing's premises, which he finds to be spotlessly clean and run with a high degree of professionalism. Finding this to be at odds with the dire concerns of Mickey's board of directors, Henderson then calls in on Cody's local branch of Mickey's, where he meets hard-working customer assistant Amber (Ashley Johnson) and store manager Tony (Esai Morales). Tony furtively explains to Henderson that the approved tour of the UMP plant gives only a very restrictive view of working conditions there, and that the real story is rather less idyllic than UMP's officially-sanctioned version of events would suggest.

Tony puts Henderson in contact with Rudy Martin (Kris Kristofferson), a local ranch owner, who gives him a very different kind of tour around Cody. Martin is deeply concerned about incursions onto his land by illegal mobile narcotics labs and new housing estates springing up all around the boundary of his ranch. However, he also describes UMP's ruthless business practices to Henderson, emphasising their use of a workforce of overburdened, exhausted Mexican immigrants and breaches in hygiene and safety procedures due to their single-minded concentration on running their production line at the fastest possible speed.

Martin's sobering account of UMP's mercilessness towards its employees and callous disregard for the law leads Henderson to seek out Harry Rydell (Bruce Willis), an independent inspector who has acted as a long-time contact associate between UMP and Mickey's. The cynical Rydell is proud to have negotiated a good deal for Mickey's, and is affronted by Henderson's enquiries about UMP's probity. Although Rydell does not deny the major breaches in conduct that Henderson outlines, he sees no ethical conflict in the company's business practices, citing the considerable wage benefits for the average Mexican worker in comparison to their average salary back over the border, which he feels should offset any potential risk to their health. With regard to the faecal content of UMP's meat, Rydell is adamant that the cooking process is more than sufficient to offset any potential threat to the public, and feels satisfied that no further investigative action is required.

Henderson is left to balance his concerns about the UMP plant with the prospect of damaging his career. As he has a family to support, and some of Rydell's comments had suggested sinister power-play taking place at the highest levels of Mickey's board of directors, Henderson comes to the inescapable conclusion that he can take no suitable action to bring UMP to book without risking impairment to his long-term prospects at Mickey's. Reluctantly, he withdraws from Cody empty-handed.

Meanwhile, a group of Mexicans are making a desperate border-crossing in order to gain entry into the United States. Among them are Raul (Wilmer Valderrama), his partner Sylvia (Catalina Sandino Moreno) and her sister Coco (Ana Claudia Talancón). After a harrowing journey with a number of others, they are successful in being smuggled into the country by Benny (Luis Guzmán), only to wind up in Cody. Subsequently, many are to find themselves employed by UMP, and are quickly disillusioned by the company's cavalier disregard of the wellbeing of its workforce. Coco in particular finds herself the focus of brutal foreman Mike (Bobby Cannavale), whose lecherous advances and the offer of hard drugs further accentuate the unprincipled quagmire affecting every level of the UMP organisation.

After a while, the group of Mexicans find themselves thoroughly disenchanted by the rigours of life under the yoke of the oppressive UMP. Sylvia gets a lower-paid but marginally more satisfying job at a local hotel while helplessly watching Coco fall under the malevolent influence of Mike. However, everything quickly changes when Raul is badly injured during a catastrophic workplace incident. Keen to avoid taking any responsibility for Raul's industrial accident, UMP quickly concoct test results indicating that they had discovered traces of illegal narcotics in his blood stream, absolving them of culpability for his fate. Faced with expensive bills for medical care, Sylvia is forced to give up her job at the hotel and plead with the repellent Mike to find her a better-paid position within UMP. As it transpires, Mike can only find her a job on the kill floor, a blood-smeared abattoir which brings her face-to-face with the relentless killing machine that drives UMP's fortunes.

In the meantime, Amber is growing tired of her humdrum existence behind the cash register at Mickey's and desperately hopes for more out of life. She is conscientious and intelligent, doing well at school but quietly terrified at the prospect of following in the footsteps of her single mother Cindy (Patricia Arquette), who is cheerful and sociable but also appears directionless and resigned to a life of compliant banality.

Amber is eventually shaken out of her stupor by the unexpected arrival of her uncle Pete (Ethan Hawke). Pete can sympathise with Amber's plight, as his complacent drift into adulthood has left him profoundly disappointed with what might have been. He implores her to follow her dreams rather than accept defeat too easily, advising her that it is much better to at least try to reach her highest aspiration than merely to be left with regrets in later life as he has been.

Moved by Pete's earnestness, Amber eventually finds herself gravitating towards a group of student activists nominally led by the feisty Alice (Avril Lavigne), who have heard local stories of UMP's casual brutality and are keen to raise awareness of the company's wrongdoing. Seemingly oblivious to the plight of the virtually indentured Mexican workforce, the group focus instead on the poor living conditions of the hundreds of cattle being herded wholesale into UMP's slaughterhouse. However, in spite of the best intentions, the activists' attempts at encouraging a large-scale bovine jail-break are sadly doomed to failure.

The film ends on a downbeat but interestingly ambiguous note, with the activist group appearing even less able to throw a spanner into the works of UMP's production line than Don Henderson had been. Henderson, on the other hand, is seen back in the plush Californian head office of Mickey's at the end of the film, spearheading another major marketing campaign for the company as though his investigation at Cody had never taken place. This seems in stark contrast to the hopeless future faced by Raul and Sylvia; just as working at UMP has ruined Raul's livelihood, we are left to decide for ourselves how long it will take to do the same to Sylvia.

Fast Food Nation is a film which is angry and despairing in equal measure, suggesting both outrage at the cruel, dehumanising effects of unbridled acquisitiveness at any cost and despondency at its corrosive consequences for the operation of society. The film forms an interesting counterpoint to *A Scanner Darkly*, subtly suggesting that the insidious tyranny of unfettered corporate self-interest forms a kind of shadowy parallel to the oppressive, all-seeing authorities depicted in the previous film.[141] This said, Linklater is careful to avoid any correlation between the fictional Mickey's burger franchise and any real-life fast food chains, even specifically mentioning a number of well-known corporations throughout the narrative in an attempt to distance the film's social commentary from any specific commercial target and thus keeping the film's withering satire firmly aimed at the cumulative consequences deriving from the industry in general.

Linklater and Schlosser develop a very large ensemble cast of characters to demonstrate Uniglobe Meat Packing's all-encompassing influence on the town of Cody, and to this end the film is aided greatly by many excellent performances. Although many of the biggest star names in *Fast Food Nation* are only on-screen for short periods, such as Kris Kristofferson, Bruce Willis and popular singer Avril Lavigne, they are able to impress the characters' individual traits upon the audience due to memorable performances that stand out amongst the mundane world of corporate uniformity that surrounds them. The characters' lives overlap and intersect in a variety of interesting and rewarding ways, and this process brings many other standout appearances to the forefront throughout the course of the film. Ashley Johnson impresses as the socially conscious Amber, assiduous but not yet beaten into conformity by the slow-motion corporate takeover of Cody. Patricia Arquette and Ethan Hawke also satisfy as the touchingly mismatched brother-and-sister team, both superficially jovial but ultimately disheartened by missed opportunities and coping with their dissatisfaction in very different ways. Ana Claudia Talancón, Wilmer Valderrama and Academy Award nominee Catalina Sandino Moreno (for her leading role in Joshua Marston's *Maria Full of Grace* (2004)) all give extraordinary performances as the maltreated immigrant workers, each forced to come to terms with their new life in a hostile environment but constantly struggling with the odds that are stacked against them. Their nemesis, the odious Mike, is perfectly played with sneering malevolence by Bobby Cannavale, who wrings every ounce of malice out of an essentially rotten and depraved character.

Greg Kinnear's complicated portrayal of Don Henderson is central to the first half of the film, and his investigations provide a springboard for many of the incidents which take place later. Henderson does not seem to be a typical white-collar clone, and when confronted by his superiors' apprehension about the conduct of UMP he is keen to investigate fully on their behalf. However, as he digs deeper and uncovers some less than savoury truths along the way, Kinnear faultlessly underplays Henderson's dawning realisation of UMP's ruthlessness and the resulting ethical dilemma that ensnares him with regard to how he should deal with the fallout from the unfolding revelations. This is realised impeccably in his departure from the hotel in Cody, where he is faced with a dead-eyed reception assistant whose droning intonation and automaton-like procedures draw parallels between the hotel's coldly impersonal service and the bland corporate gloss that affects much of the rest of the town – including its branch of Mickey's.

Henderson's departure from the narrative halfway through the film is significant, for it denotes the end of his investigation before it had even remotely threatened UMP's practices. His abrupt exit accentuates Linklater's point that this is no simple morality tale, and that no one individual – regardless of how well-meaning they may be – can possibly impede the UMP juggernaut. This ultimately leads into the disillusioning build-up towards the film's gruesome closing sequences on UMP's kill floor, which unflinchingly depicts the brutally efficient production-line slaughter of live cattle. These scenes have become among the film's most chillingly iconic, and are a powerful metaphor for the coldly uncompromising ruthlessness of the corporation which is responsible for this grisly but disturbingly proficient bloodletting.[142] Yet in spite of his sustained condemnation of corporate excess throughout the film, Linklater does not provide any comfortable solutions to the problems that he highlights, and even subtly suggests that no obvious way out exists for either the characters or the society that they live in.[143]

By eschewing a documentary format in favour of a fictionalised approach to their subject matter, Linklater and Schlosser were to avoid critical comparison to other prominent and controversial features which had engaged with similar themes, such as Morgan Spurlock's *Super Size Me* (2004) and Mark Achbar and Jennifer Abbott's *The Corporation* (2003). Indeed, most commentators considered that the main thrust of the film was in fact more similar to Upton Sinclair's hard-hitting book *The Jungle* (1906), which had discussed exploitation of an immigrant workforce exactly a century beforehand.[144] The film did, however, benefit from the pre-existing high profile of Schlosser's book, which was noted by some reviewers.[145] Perhaps because of its profoundly issue-based nature, *Fast Food Nation* sharply divided the critics on its release. Some commentators seemed impressed by Linklater's large interlocking array of characters, which brought to mind the acclaimed ensemble social examinations of Robert Altman,[146] others considered the characters to be too generic in nature,[147] and that their appearances were too brief to engender a satisfactory level of audience interest.[148] While a number of critics praised the film's performances,[149] and in particular were to note that Linklater's sympathetic handling of members of Generation Z (through the treatment of Amber and her activist friends) matched his equally careful rendering of his more familiar Generation X characters (in particular, Pete and Cindy),[150] others were contrastingly to find the cast lifeless and curiously inert given the film's provocative socio-political content.[151] Linklater and Schlosser's treatment of the film's themes were also to prove contentious: just as some reviewers noted *Fast Food Nation*'s detailed proposal for societal improvement[152] and the unwavering depiction of impersonal corporate environments full of oppressed workers,[153] there were others who lambasted the film for presenting what they regarded to be a largely onesided argument,[154] or claimed that the fictionalisation of Schlosser's factual source text had not been effective.[155] Although Linklater had split critical opinion many times before, *Fast Food Nation* has arguably been the most divisive of all his features among commentators, having received both high praise and concerted criticism since the time of its release.

Fast Food Nation was nominated for the Golden Palm Award at the Cannes Film Festival in 2006, and also gained Wilmer Valderrama a nomination for the Best Actor award at the 2007 Imagen Foundation Awards. The film had once again emphasised Linklater's commitment to examining major social issues, particularly in concert with the themes dealt with in *A Scanner Darkly*, but had also underlined his ability to skilfully manage a very large ensemble cast (and all of the complex interactions between them) as well as bringing a humanistic appeal to the drearily austere and uninvitingly impersonal world that he creates in the town of Cody.[156]

14

INNING BY INNING: A PORTRAIT OF A COACH (2008)

Detour Filmproduction

Director: Richard Linklater
Producer: Brian Franklin

Main Cast
Augie Garrido
Pete Donovan
Cliff Hatter
Bill Kernan
Seth Johnston
Dave Weatherman
Rick Vanderhook
Cathy Clark

Richard Linklater's next film was to be a sporting documentary entitled *Inning By Inning*. Once again pulling the rug from beneath the feet of critical expectation with considerable panache, Linklater's first full-length documentary film saw a shift in format from the judiciously fictionalised adaptation of *Fast Food Nation* to this entirely factual account of a prominent sporting figure, all the while never losing any of Linklater's characteristic directorial flair in the transition.

Inning By Inning focuses on the career of the much-admired American sportsman August (Augie) Edmun Garrido Jr. (1939-), who has followed his vocation in coaching college baseball teams since 1969 to enormous professional acclaim. Garrido is currently coach of the University of Texas baseball team, and over the years the teams that he has coached have won national titles on five occasions. Garrido himself has earned many accolades, including National Coach of the Year awards, on five separate years to date during his career. While Linklater's interest in baseball had been well established throughout the course of his earlier films, most obviously in his remake of *Bad News Bears*, the tongue-in-cheek anarchy of the earlier film's comedic Little Leaguers is firmly supplanted here by an enlightening and deeply respectful account of Garrido's long and successful time working in the world of college baseball. Linklater's high regard for the sport, and the people who are involved in it at every level, is every bit as palpable as his infectious enthusiasm for the game itself.

Employing a skilful mosaic of archive footage and specially filmed material of Coach Garrido at work, Linklater pieces together a detailed picture of a man who is not only vastly successful in his chosen discipline, but also a passionate and sophisticated person who is concerned with the character development of individual players as much as he is with their sporting prowess. The footage of Garrido and his players is intercut with a considerable amount of interview material from a wide range of contributors, including sports commentators, prominent personalities who are acquainted with Garrido, and a range of players and professionals with whom he has worked throughout the course of his long career.

Immediately obvious from his philosophical comments to camera and his rousing pre-game speeches to his players is the fact that Garrido not only cares deeply about the tactics and technicalities of baseball, but also about the feelings and judgements of his various members of his team. Whether watching from the dugout or talking one-on-one with individual players, Garrido always appears to be profoundly concerned about the relationship that exists between the game and those who play it – and, in turn, the people who are influenced by it in a broader manner, such as players' families and the team's supporters. He sees his remit as extending further than simply managing his team's approach to the methodological dynamics of baseball, that most quintessential of American sports, and pinpoints the fact that beyond the immediacies of playing and winning the game, there is significant scope for personal growth and character enhancement.

Even more extraordinary, given the length of his career in the sport, is the strong suggestion throughout the film that Garrido himself is still discerning new aspects of individual improvement which are inherent in the game even after all these years. There is a sense that although times change, with fashions and cultural mores in a state of constant flux, the appeal of baseball remains essentially invariable – and yet, precisely because of this consistency, its perennial prominence in American sporting life means that just as social trends keep changing, the potential ways that the game can influence lives also keep on shifting and evolving. For all his truth-seeking contemplation, there is no doubt that Garrido remains thoroughly committed to getting the very best out of his team in terms of performance – a fact that his outstanding record of wins bears ample testimony. Linklater makes good use of footage showing Garrido passionately arguing over points with umpires and vocally articulating his concerns in the dugout to prove that, like any coach, he detests losing a game

– even as he acknowledges that losing is sometimes an inevitable part of life, irrespective of how hard anyone may try to avoid it. Yet Linklater clearly delineates Garrido's philosophy that defeat can also be forged into a developmental tool: an important catalyst in learning how to win.

Drawing in a number of interviews from Garrido's childhood friends as well as his sister, Linklater paints a compelling picture of the man's life-long relationship with baseball, from his first taste of competitiveness in the sport during his youth through to his early realisation that he had an intense calling to become a coach. From these formative years, he would rise to the very pinnacle of college baseball, and his unswerving dedication to achieving this goal can be seen to inform his later commitment to encouraging his team to give of their best – a responsibility which, as Linklater deftly articulates, Garrido has always tackled with the utmost seriousness. The film emphasises the impressive scope of Garrido's career, encompassing not only the sheer length of its duration but also the scale of his sporting achievements. Analysing Garrido's early successes as a player in Fresno State, Linklater constructs a detailed representation of the way that he came to use his own experiences as a baseball player to create a firm foundation that would ultimately inform his multifaceted approach to coaching later in life – an approach which balances the significance of each individual player's distinct strengths in tune with the overall importance of the combined team. As he explains passionately, a team is more than simply the sum of its parts, and good team spirit is absolutely crucial in securing long-term sporting achievement.

Instead of chasing the dream of professional Major League baseball in his youth, Garrido was determined to become a coach. His coaching career began in 1969, at San Francisco State, and following a stint with Cal Poly (1970-72), he began a very successful period of coaching at Cal State Fullerton from 1973 through to 1987. Linklater explores Garrido's immensely positive influence on the team, building it up from relative obscurity to huge success through the use of his principled discipline and unparalleled talent for establishing a unity of purpose amongst players. Progressing through his different teams' College World Series wins over the years, Garrido's gradual rise to national renown is charted with considerable panache, including his time coaching at the University of Illinois (1988-90), his return to Cal State Fullerton (1991-96), and his tenure at the University of Texas, which began in 1997.

Because of its non-fictional nature, *Inning By Inning* is something of an atypical feature for Linklater, and yet his obvious admiration and enthusiasm for the subject matter means that the film is never less than compelling. He develops an intimately detailed portrait of a hugely articulate and complex figure, whose professional distinction and highly individual personality makes for an absorbing documentary experience. Linklater constructs a comprehensive study of not only Coach Garrido's professional career, but by extension a persuasive depiction of what makes baseball the unique sport that it continues to be. By drawing together a remarkable number of contributors from the whole spectrum of Garrido's life, from his early childhood right through to the present day, Linklater ensures that every element of the coach's sporting philosophy is brought to light: the battle of confidence over fear, the need to respect the team as well as the individual, and the fundamental enjoyment of the game are all stressed continuously throughout the duration of the film.

What seems particularly telling is Garrido's supposition that baseball doesn't develop character so much as it actively exposes character. While we are shown that baseball is important to many lives, what really counts is the individual team player – not just in terms of what they put into the game, but in what they personally take out of it. As well as being depicted as an impeccable model of sportsmanship, Garrido is portrayed as a man of considerable intricacy, being both charming and deeply contemplative. Seeming as comfortable talking directly to individual players as he is addressing them collectively, his winning combination of technical prowess and team psychology – coupled with an intrinsic understanding of the spiritual and emotional elements of the game – mark him out as an exceptional character. He appears concerned more with holistic wellbeing than he is with simply winning a game at any cost, for he realises that without the former there can never be any success with the latter.

Linklater's proficiently-blended melange of specially-shot sequences and effectively selected archive footage are particularly successful in conveying the full span – and developmental path – of Garrido's career. Always combining to delineate the achievements of a passionate man who has never been less than willing to push himself to the very limit for his game and his team, Garrido has continually adapted over the course of his four-decade-long career to allow his coaching techniques to subtly adjust for the changing needs of new generations. And yet, for all that, Linklater carefully underscores the fact that Garrido's approach also remains constant in many ways, not least in its dedication to the support and personal growth of the individual player. The capacity of Garrido's sporting career to span several decades of American history is very efficiently articulated through Linklater's inspired choice of still photography throughout the film, and this is particularly true of the closing credits sequence, which – like the rest of the film – is greatly enhanced and supported by Michael McLeod's evocative score.

Inning By Inning marks an interesting side-step in Linklater's career, and one which clearly shows that the scope of his creative film-making talents is not constrained by fictional narratives. All of his characteristic directorial verve and enthusiasm are unmistakably on display throughout the film, and he takes obvious care in his depiction of Augie Garrido as an inspirational figure who has enhanced countless lives through his aptitude for sports teaching and the furtherance of his vocation. And yet this is not solely a sporting film, either; although it centres upon baseball, with Garrido as its narrative focus, it is at heart no less philosophical than *Waking Life*, nor in its way is the film any less concerned with the crucial role of the individual than *Slacker* had been. Critical appreciation for *Inning By Inning* was generally warm, with commentators praising the film for its willingness to challenge preconceived notions about baseball, skilfully toppling many truisms about sportsmanship along the way.[157] Other reviewers voiced admiration for Linklater's sheer exuberance in his depiction of both the game and those who are involved in it at every level,[158] while the precise accuracy of his psychological insight was also singled out for commendation.[159]

Once again, Linklater had challenged his audience to think carefully about the nature of the world around them, and through Garrido's motivating life story he emphasises the fact that in America – just as in baseball – anything is possible for someone who is willing to try their hardest and work relentlessly towards the achievement of their dreams. It is a sentiment which is particularly well-suited to Linklater's upbeat, optimistic awareness of individual aspiration, and owes more to the vibrant, youthful hopefulness of *Dazed and Confused* than it does to the apprehensive moral concerns of the more recent *A Scanner Darkly* and *Fast Food Nation*. With its irrepressible sense of warmth and buoyancy, *Inning By Inning* provided an appealing yet unanticipated development for Linklater, and its preoccupation with individual personal development would be an issue of further consideration during the course of his next motion picture.

15

ME AND ORSON WELLES (2008)

Detour Filmproduction / CinemaNX / Cinetic Media / Framestore / Fuzzy Bunny Films

Director: Richard Linklater
Producers: Richard Linklater, Mark Samuelson and Ann Carli
Screenplay: Holly Gent Palmo and Vincent Palmo Jr, adapted from the novel by Robert Kaplow

Main Cast
Zac Efron – Richard Samuels
Claire Danes – Sonja Jones
Christian McKay – Orson Welles
Ben Chaplin – George Coulouris
James Tupper – Joseph Cotten
Zoe Kazan – Gretta Alder
Eddie Marsan – John Houseman
Kelly Reilly – Muriel Brassler

With his most recent film, Richard Linklater was to make a return to the kind of richly-detailed historical locale that he had visited in *The Newton Boys*. Yet the early twentieth-century Americana presented in *Me and Orson Welles* is a far cry from the safe-cracking action of his earlier film; by exchanging the wide open spaces of the Midwest for the urban bustle of New York City in the period immediately preceding World War II, Linklater was to present his audience with a unique and fondly-remembered time in American theatrical lore: a tale of the Mercury Theatre under the auspices of the legendary Orson Welles.

The name Orson Welles (1915-85) is one which needs little introduction to anyone with even a passing interest in stage, screen or radio drama. His ground-breaking *Citizen Kane* (1941) is regularly cited as one of the finest motion pictures ever committed to film, whereas his radio adaptation of H.G. Wells's *War of the Worlds* (1938) achieved international renown due to the mass panic that it caused at time of broadcast (the news report format of its narrative causing some listeners of the period to believe that a Martian invasion really was underway). But at the time of *Me and Orson Welles*, an adaptation of Robert Kaplow's well-regarded 2005 novel of the same name, we are given a glimpse into the period immediately preceding Welles's meteoric rise to show-business renown, when he was simply a respected young actor in New York City and the Mercury Theatre was little more than a derelict building, a mere husk of past glories. But as Welles prepared to bring Shakespeare to the New York stage, a legend was about to be born.

In the New York State of 1937, Richard Samuels – nearing the end of high school – is growing tired with academic pursuits. A creative spirit, seventeen-year-old Richard (Zac Efron) has a passion for theatre and a desire to take to the stage. Wandering through New York City, he meets an aspiring young writer named Gretta Alder (Zoe Kazan) in a music shop and strikes up an impromptu conversation with her. Richard finds Gretta's enthusiasm for her craft to be compelling, and encourages her to follow her ambitions. She finds the support of this well-meaning stranger to be oddly endearing, and as they part she tells him that she hopes that they will meet each other again.

Later that day, Richard stumbles across a near-derelict building and discovers it to be the Mercury Theatre, recently brought under the control of the great Orson Welles (Christian McKay). Knowing Welles from his considerable repute as an actor on both stage and radio, Richard quickly moves to catch his attention with a demonstration of musical skills and a gift for improvisation. Impressed by Richard's display of chutzpah, Welles recruits him into the role of Lucius in his forthcoming production of Shakespeare's *Julius Caesar*, casually dispensing with the previous incumbent of the part.

Somewhat awestruck by his apparent good fortune, Richard is swept along by events as Welles introduces him to production assistant Sonja Jones (Claire Danes). Immediately infatuated with the beautiful and intelligent Sonja, Richard seems both surprised and thrilled when she appears to return his affections. He is also attracted to the fact that, like himself, Sonja is incredibly ambitious and determined to get ahead in her career. It is obvious why Welles values Sonja so highly; her administrative talents are unparalleled, and her capacity for keeping the cogs of the production in motion – through a mixture of cool efficiency and flattery towards backers as required – make her indispensable to the management. She is also, quite incidentally, the unattainable object of desire for most of the Mercury's male cast and crew.

Richard soon discovers that the world of theatre is much less glamorous than he had imagined. Welles is a challenging individual to work with, tyrannous and snootily condescending towards his perceived underlings. Few of the cast are brave enough to make a stand against the imperious Welles, though there are occasional exceptions. Theatre manager John Houseman (Eddie Marsan) is close to being driven to distraction by Welles's constantly shifting date for an opening night, while respected English actor George Coulouris (Ben Chaplin) is frustrated by

Welles's direction; he feels that contemporary military uniforms chosen for Caesar and the other characters, for instance, is more a testament to Welles's inability to afford the costumes appropriate to ancient Rome than an attempt to make Shakespeare's play more relevant to the present day with an allegory of the rise of European fascism.

Welles's difficult behaviour causes Richard as much puzzlement as it does disillusionment. Although his socialite wife Virginia Nicholson (who is rarely present at the theatre) is heavily pregnant, Welles is having a brazen affair with the play's lead actress Muriel Brassler (Kelly Reilly). However, it is clear that his romantic conquests don't end there – it doesn't take Richard long to realise that Welles is staggeringly promiscuous and has no compunction in satisfying his prodigious sexual appetites with any attractive woman who is willing to consent to his advances. On a whim, Welles invites Richard to join him for the afternoon as he heads off to deliver a pre-arranged dramatic performance on CBS Radio. During the car journey to the studio, Welles gives some brief background detail about himself, explaining that both of his parents had died during his youth and speaking warmly of his affection for Booth Tarkington's Pulitzer Prize-winning novel *The Magnificent Ambersons* (1918). Later, during the recording of the radio play, Richard is impressed when Welles begins to improvise near the drama's conclusion, speaking powerfully as he draws in some of the influences that he had earlier mentioned from Tarkington's novel. He later leaves in a cab with beautiful studio assistant Lorelei Lathrop (Imogen Poots), leaving a confused Richard in his wake.

A chance encounter with Gretta at a nearby New York museum gives Richard the opportunity to discover how her writing efforts have been faring since they last met. Rather self-consciously, she explains that she has composed a short piece about a girl who regularly likes to visit a museum (based largely on her own life experiences), and although rather confused at the story's apparent lack of incident Richard encourages her to seek publication. He offers to pass the story on to Sonja, who has a contact who works on the staff of *The New Yorker*. While he can't guarantee success, he feels that it would be worth a try. Thrilled, Gretta willingly agrees to go along with his plan.

Back on stage, Richard is confused and self-conscious about his lack of acting experience, but in truth this is among the least of the problems facing the production. Welles's impatience at the rough edges of his cast's performances causes friction, leading to some discord amongst the other players. Then Richard has an untimely accident with a match in the dressing room, causing the theatre's ramshackle sprinkler system to burst into action and drench the auditorium, the costumes and the stage. There is also conflict when Welles openly usurps the credit for the production's design from the affable hard-working designer who he has employed, even in spite of the young man's tireless effort. This culminates in the designer threatening to tear his work apart rather than allowing Welles to steal his credit, while Welles seems on the cusp of throttling him. Only the diplomatic Houseman is able to defuse the fracas.

Meanwhile, Richard's efforts to court Sonja's affections meet with mixed results. He becomes confused at how driven she seems in the effort of advancing her ambitious career plans, rather than concentrating on the romance that he feels that they are fated to share. As the play's opening approaches, Welles draws tickets from a hat to pair up members of the cast and crew, who must then go for a drink together (which Welles is personally funding). Richard unabashedly cheats in order to ensure that he and Sonja are teamed together, and they enjoy a cordial date which eventually leads to them spending the night together at Welles's secret love nest in the city. Elated, Richard is moved to declare the true depth of his feelings for her the next day, but to his hurt confusion she appears coolly unresponsive to his declaration of love.

The play's preview matinee is a rather rough affair, which leads Welles to become exasperated at everything from the efficiency of the stage lighting to the timing of the musicians. It does, however, lead him to discover any structural weaknesses in the production prior to the all-important opening night which is now only a day away. But everyone involved is painfully aware that the play remains perilously under-rehearsed. As they leave the theatre in the evening, Richard hangs around to meet Sonja on her way home, only to discover that Welles has told her that he wants her to spend the night with him. Staggered by this news, to say nothing of being deeply aggrieved, Richard has no choice but to watch as she wanders back into the theatre in pursuit of Welles.

Richard's anger builds, however, and knowing the location of Welles's clandestine apartment he lies in wait for their emergence the following morning. Welles seems both surprised and slightly sheepish to find Richard there, but brushes off the encounter and orders the younger man to hail him a cab. As he does so, an anxious Sonja demands to know what Richard is doing there, and reveals that she had willingly agreed to sleep with Welles because he had offered to introduce her to film producer David O. Selznick (who would later produce 1939's famous *Gone With the Wind*) in return. Richard rebukes her for her lack of fidelity, but Sonja seems stunned by his naivety. Incensed by the under-handed scheming behind Welles and Sonja's tryst, Richard angrily rounds on Welles, who in turn is furious at the younger man's insolence: he fires Richard from the Mercury staff on the spot. Becoming even more irate, Richard rebukes him for his moral licentiousness, questioning how he can sleep around so wantonly when he has a pregnant wife at home. Enraged at the very mention of Virginia, Welles pours out his wrath on Richard, attacking him for his lack of both talent and consequence. But his ranting is meaningless; Richard has already decided that he wants nothing further to do with Welles or his work.

As the day progresses Welles seeks out Richard, eventually finding him in a nearby park sitting contemplatively on a bench. Seemingly contrite, Welles apologises for his earlier angry words and ensures Richard that rather than being bereft of talent as he had originally implied, he actually believes the young man to be a naturally gifted actor. Richard is surprised to hear this, and after securing a number of concessions – including the return of the stage designer to his rightful place on the play's production credits – Richard agrees to resume the role of Lucius for the opening night later that day. He remains sceptical of Welles's apparent repentance, however. As the cast and crew scramble to get things in place for the fast-approaching production, Richard becomes ever more suspicious of Welles's sincerity when the director sharply disregards him, avoiding interaction or eye contact. His mistrust deepens when Coulouris suffers severe stage fright and Welles reassures him by using more or less the same warm words that he had spoken to Richard in the morning.

The actual production, when it arrives, is a triumphant success, enthralling the audience and cementing Welles's reputation amongst the New York critics. However, during the euphoria of the post-performance party, stage veteran Joseph Cotton (James Tupper) takes Richard aside and contritely explains that Welles's original dismissal still stands. Welles had never actually forgiven Richard for having the audacity to stand up to him, but had nonetheless required Richard's presence on opening night to help ensure that every element of the production was a success. With the play's future now secure, Welles no longer has any use for Richard, and has already cast another actor in the role. Incensed, Richard prepares for a showdown with Welles, but Cotton manages to talk him down. Although clearly derisive of Welles's cowardice in refusing to confront Richard directly in the first place, Cotton explains that Welles will never back down and risk losing face – especially in front of his cast and crew. Bearing in mind the fate of Richard's predecessor as Lucius, it seems that history has repeated itself. Thoroughly disgusted, Richard leaves the theatre only to stumble across Sonja, waiting near the sidewalk for the arrival of David O. Selznick's car. The famous producer, it seems, is her date for a lavish party being held by

Welles elsewhere in the city. It soon becomes apparent that Sonja was fully aware of Welles's plans for Richard from the outset, but by now he is too disillusioned to care. Wishing each other well, they part on good terms, but Richard's distaste at his treatment is tangible.

Choosing to draw a line under his experiences, Richard throws himself back into academic life, determined to graduate from high school with decent grades. He particularly impresses his English teacher with his familiarity with the text of Shakespeare's *Julius Caesar*. Returning to the museum, he meets up with Gretta, who excitedly shows him a letter of acceptance from *The New Yorker* – they have agreed to publish her short story. She also explains that she had attended the opening night of *Julius Caesar* at the Mercury, though Richard breezily informs her that he has turned his back on a career in acting now, claiming that it didn't pay as well as he had hoped. And after all, his entire experience at the Mercury had lasted only a single turbulent week. Both clearly relishing the opportunity of romance and an exciting shared future, they head out of the museum together, looking ahead to a destiny that will be of their own making rather than a career privy to the manipulations of the arrogant Welles and those like him.

What is immediately obvious from *Me and Orson Welles* is the incredible care that Linklater takes to present a very particular time and place from history. Pre-War New York is painstakingly recreated, from the details of the artists in the music store where Richard first meets Gretta all the way through to fine points such as posters encouraging voters to re-elect Mayor Fiorello Henry La Guardia, who served three terms in office between 1934 to 1945. Yet what truly impresses is the transformation of the Mercury Theatre from a near-dilapidated state into a crisply professional venue within the course of a week – an important aspect of the film, which reminds us both of the crew's efficient professionalism combined with Welles's reputation as a hard taskmaster. The tiniest of minutiae is faithfully reproduced, from the complex system of period stage-lighting all the way through to the Mercury's claustrophobic backstage areas. For a film so intimately concerned with the workings of a theatrical production, the film's milieu remains effortlessly convincing with no anachronistic lapses ever in evidence throughout. This is especially true of Nic Ede's brilliant costume design, replicating everything from Welles's expensive tastes in fashion to the contemporary gear of the stage hands. Michael J. McEvoy's score also displays an exceptional lightness of touch, conjuring up the febrile energy of the city at that time.

Zac Efron impresses as the wide-eyed teenager experiencing the highs and lows of theatre life for the first time. Having made appearances in many popular television shows such as *ER*, *CSI: Miami* and *Navy NCIS*, as well as having a part in Adam Shankman's *Hairspray* (2007), his early career has been best-known for his high profile performances in Kenny Ortega's *High School Musical* (2006) and its sequels. Playing against his heartthrob persona, Efron handles well the demands of a challenging role, one which calls upon everything from elation and euphoria to disillusionment and disgust. Through his performance, Richard achieves a touching rapport with the sweet Gretta (a nicely-pitched performance by Zoe Kazan), but it is the complicated chemistry that he shares with Claire Danes's Sonja which stays in the memory. Danes had previously appeared in a comprehensive array of well-received films including Gillian Armstrong's *Little Women* (1994), Baz Luhrmann's *Romeo + Juliet* (1996), Jonathan Kaplan's *Brokedown Palace* (1999) and Stephen Daldry's *The Hours* (2002), as well as appearing alongside *Me and Orson Welles* cast-mate Ben Chaplin in Richard Eyre's *Stage Beauty* (2004). She invests Sonja with both drive and considerable pathos, creating a character who is utterly determined to reach the top by any means necessary, but who ultimately appears to be a better rounded individual than the shallow superficiality of her ruthlessly ambitious intentions may initially suggest. The conflict between Richard's inexperienced romantic expectations and

Sonja's calculating, single-minded aspiration create a compelling tension between both themselves and Welles, and also makes Richard's attraction to the quietly artistic Gretta (who desires success on merit rather than by sleeping her way to the top) all the more believable. That their optimistic faith in a bright future directly precedes the horrors of the fast-approaching Second World War makes the film's conclusion all the more poignant.

However, there is no doubt that in terms of performance the film belongs to Christian McKay, who delivers an outstanding portrayal of the deeply multifaceted Welles. Aided by the perceptive characterisation which is offered by Holly Gent Palmo and Vincent Palmo Jr's screenplay, McKay evokes an uncannily accurate depiction of Welles's appearance and mannerisms, to say nothing of his highly individual performance style. Yet it is in his depiction of Welles's complicated personality that McKay's interpretation proves to be most remarkable. Moving with regularity from the high-energy professionalism of a talented performer at the very top of his game through to the monstrously domineering and darkly egotistical nature that is never far from the surface, McKay delicately grafts together a complex portrayal of a figure whose charisma and occasional generosity of spirit is outbalanced by a vastly high opinion of both himself and his skills. Together, these many aspects form a truly compelling tapestry of a troubled genius, whose immense artistic gifts and aloof distance ultimately isolate him from the prospect of meaningful interaction with those around him (even as these same people flock to the light of his success like moths circling a light-bulb). As a result, there is a sense that his company need him, are in awe of him, and possibly even respect him (at least, to some degree), but stop short of actually liking him.

McKay deftly manages to sidestep the possibility of the young Welles ever becoming caricatured as an essentially shallow figure in terms of his personality; for all of the casual promiscuity and infidelity, and the sneering contempt which underlies his jocular façade, his obvious capability and towering intelligence – as well as a rare flicker of munificence (such as his impromptu invitation for Richard to join him at the recording of the CBS radio drama, or an infrequent vague glimmer of awkward guilt) – suggests greater depths to his character than the rampant self-centredness and nonchalant amorality may otherwise suggest. McKay had previously appeared in a number of stage productions, as well as in Wyndham Price's film *Abraham's Point* (2008), but his performance as Welles seems almost certain to be his break-through role. At time of writing, he has already been nominated for the Most Promising Newcomer Award at the British Independent Film Awards in 2009, and given the strength of his performance in *Me and Orson Welles* there is a firm possibility of further nominations in awards ceremonies throughout 2010.

Linklater and the Palmos work hard to examine the deep complications of Welles's character, never trivialising or oversimplifying them. While the depiction is certainly no rose-tinted view of either the man or his talents, neither is it wholly critical. With the revelation of his parents' untimely death, which has obviously had significant ramifications for the still-young Welles, there is a strong suggestion that his constant demand to be in control of all situations at all times – along with his apparent need for never-ending sexual gratification – are the result of an immense but ultimately fragile ego, desperately seeking the affirmation stolen away from him with the early passing of his mother and father. This constant dichotomy between bullying and neediness, chipper buoyancy and violent tantrums, comes to characterise a difficult and rather obnoxious man, but one who is indisputably brilliant at his craft. Ignoble and disingenuous, his mocking insincerity underpins the fact that his cast and crew (including those with whom he is having affairs) are all little more than dispensable instruments to the might of his creative will... and yet, given his manifest character flaws, it is difficult not to pity the objectionable figure that Welles is revealed to be by the end of the film.

There are many inspired nods to Welles's later career

peppered throughout the film, not least the presence of Ben Chaplin's gifted but loftily affected George Coulouris and James Tupper's laconic, world-weary Joseph Cotton. Both Coulouris and Cotton would of course collaborate with Welles again in the years ahead to great acclaim. Welles's high regard for Booth Tarkington's novel *The Magnificent Ambersons* naturally presages his later film adaptation in 1942, and there is also a very subtle allusion to Welles's later, ambitious production *Chimes at Midnight* (1966), adapted from his play *Five Kings* which had originally been produced for the New York stage in 1939.

Me and Orson Welles has been regarded warmly by critics on both sides of the Atlantic, with some commentators singling out Linklater's scrupulous recreation of thirties theatre (comparing it favourably with other attempts to do so in film, such as Tim Robbins's *The Cradle Will Rock*, 1999)[160], while many others chose to focus on Christian McKay's astonishingly faithful portrayal of Welles's mannerisms and speech patterns.[161] A number of reviewers centred on the way that the film has proven ample testimony to Linklater's continuing artistic versatility as a director[162], while still others decided to stress the film's impeccably accurate employment of historical detail and the ambience of both the Mercury Theatre and the New York City of the pre-War period.[163]

With *Me and Orson Welles*, Linklater presents a remarkably mature and far-reaching adaptation of a perceptive and thought-provoking novel. As much a declaration of affection and respect for a golden age in American theatre as it is a profound and touching coming-of-age drama, the film is first and foremost a challengingly provocative portrait of the corrosive effects of excess and egotism, a cautionary tale of the damaging consequences which result from climbing the slippery pole of fame at any cost to oneself. This warning seems all the more immediate due to the fact that it is epitomised by a certain legendary figure of dramatic performance coming to symbolise the true cost of seeking pre-eminence and renown at the cost of all else: a faintly monstrous but avowedly charming genius, immensely talented but full of essentially empty gestures, building an empire on shifting sands whilst simultaneously – and unwittingly – sowing the early seeds of his own eventual downfall. This over-riding message, that the venal trappings of fame should never be allowed to distract the artist from presenting the very best work of which they are capable, is one which resonates down the decades, and proves once again that Linklater is never inclined to shirk from infusing a breezy, entertaining film with a weighty subtext: as Richard and Gretta discover, the only truly meaningful recognition that is worth having can ultimately be earned only through unerring artistic integrity and sheer hard graft, qualities which the true historical Welles possessed in abundance. But by the film's conclusion, we are left in no doubt that everything else about fame is essentially transitory: like the sleight of hand shown in this fictionalised Welles's parlour tricks, celebrity has always been little more than the stuff of smoke and mirrors, and Linklater seems keen to emphasise that it is who we are and what we do – rather than how others perceive us – that truly defines the nature of an individual.

ILLUSTRATIONS

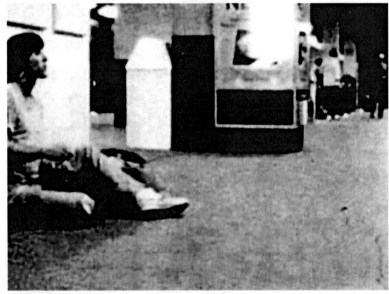

(Detour)

(Universal)

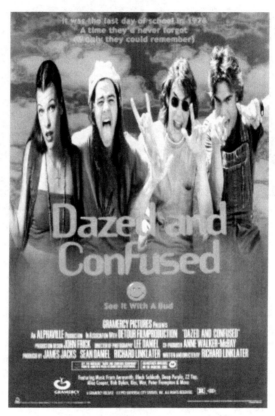

(Universal)

(Sony/ Castle Rock)

(Castle Rock)

(20th Century Fox)

(Fox Searchlight)

(Lion's Gate)

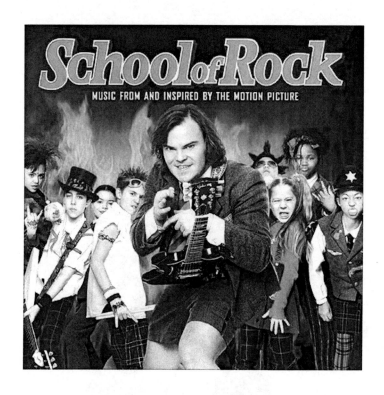

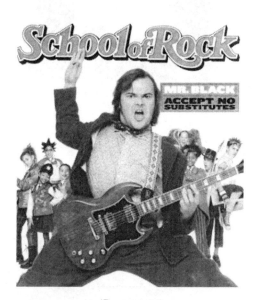

(Paramount)

(Paramount)

(Paramount)

(Warner Independent)

(Warner Independent)

(Warner Independent)

(Warner Independent)

(Fox Searchlight/ Tartan)

(Detour)

(Freestyle Releasing/ Warner Bros.)

(Freestyle Releasing/ Warner Bros.)

CONCLUSION

NOTHING REEL EXISTS?

As we have seen over the course of his diverse and influential career, Richard Linklater is a highly distinctive directorial talent; comfortable in the creation of the most niche of independent features and the most commercial of mainstream films, the only predictable thing about him is his consistent unpredictability. We have witnessed the fact that he is a film-maker who always finds something extraordinary in the ordinary, and who is never blind to the beauty of the smallest details of everyday life, no matter how mundane or commonplace they may seem at face value.

Both a highly talented director and a superb screenwriter, the acuity of his observation of human behaviour and communication is always handled frankly and usually with considerable warmth and optimism – refreshing sanguinity given the jaded attitudes of the post-modern world into which he has released his films. However, rather than allowing his constantly shifting choice of subject matter and sometimes surrealistic approach to separate him from his intended audience, quite the opposite is true: Linklater is an artist who always likes to keep people guessing, and in an industry which seems at times to be firmly wedded to the rigid format of the three-act structure and the inflexibility of perceived audience expectation, he gleefully continues to rewrite all the rules with considerable panache.

As the title of this conclusion suggests, it can be argued that the central theme in Linklater's work is the search for the authentic, be it social or cultural. He often posits the question of what makes a cultural experience genuine, or whether it is the very nature of sincere and unaffected interaction between individual people that is, at a fundamental level, the most important tithe that binds society together (even as he questions, in the tradition of Alexis de Tocqueville, whether the long established economic and democratic freedoms of American civilisation – though eminently desirable – have essentially and inadvertently isolated the lives of individual citizens from each other). In this sense, it is important to note that the terms 'authentic' and 'realistic' need not be mutually exclusive, for even

Waking Life's most bizarre dreamscapes and *Slacker*'s peculiarly eccentric characters and situations are never completely divorced from the erratic yet invariable nature of the human condition, nor is his keen observation of personal interaction ever obscured by a backdrop of the fantastic and outlandish. Indeed, more than most directors Linklater appears to be the perfect cultural commentator for our times, fully embracing the stylistic challenges presented by the post-modern world and always allowing his sensitive eye for character development and multifarious social phenomena to harness the thought-provoking irrationalism of our deconstructed age. In short, he has proven himself at all times to be a thoroughly contemporary *auteur*, and has been much praised for his brave recognition of the fact that straightforward rational solutions do not always sit comfortably in an irrational world of labyrinthine moral complexity.

It is significant to note that, given how many of Linklater's features have been set or filmed in and around Texas (and specifically in Austin), he is most definitely an artist with extensive international concerns, and these are reflected in his interest in the universality of the human condition as well as his clever examination of intercontinental differences and similarities. The latter is especially true of *Before Sunrise* and *Before Sunset*, particularly noteworthy being his continual suggestion that the socio-political issues which appear to divide different nations, and even sections of societies within these countries, obscure far deeper commonalities which are all too often ignored. His credentials as an observer not just of America but of the world at large are even further reinforced by his strong influences from international cinema, particularly the masters of classical European film,[164] and this has been echoed by the critics' identification of his sophisticated and wholly distinctive directorial style, earning comparisons between his filmic style and the likes of Max Ophuls, Eric Rohmer and Luis Buñuel, while the philosophical underpinnings of his directorial methodology have often been considered to be very much in the tradition of the pioneering theories of the *Cahiers du Cinéma* movement.[165]

Linklater's fascination with society and social mores is also mirrored in the way that he has been so inexorably linked with the cultural phenomena surrounding Generation X. Although Linklater himself is older than the majority of what has come to be categorised as mainstream Generation X, the subjects of his films tend to closely follow the development curve of that generation, moving beyond the memorable observations of teenage Gen-X made in the eighties films of John Hughes and Allan Moyle and evolving into Linklater's examination of an uncertain and often directionless Gen-X adulthood throughout the nineties. There is an undeniable sense of progression from the gleefully purposeless twenty-something denizens of *Slacker* and the affably world-weary duo Celine and Jesse of *Before Sunrise*, to the nihilistic cast of *subUrbia* and the angst-ridden Jon and Vince of *Tape* – slowly leaving the youth of their twenties behind them – finally edging towards the nostalgic, offbeat optimism of *School of Rock*'s Dewey Finn, who seems almost scandalised to find himself having wound up on the wrong side of thirty. In short, as Generation X grew up, so too were the themes and subjects of Linklater's films seen to constantly advance, mature and develop.

This evolution of the Generation X themes common to the eighties has an added importance to Linklater's work in another respect. The tongue-in-cheek assertion of *Dazed and Confused*'s students of the mid-seventies that the 1980s were likely to be an exciting, vibrant and above all 'radical' time clearly struck a chord with Linklater, whose own late-eighties feature, *It's Impossible to Learn to Plow by Reading Books*, is undoubtedly his most visually grim. If the eighties presented a time of arch-materialism and a definitive turning point in the young adulthood of Generation X, it also presented a range of political issues (including the ramifications of the end of the Cold War and the emerging New World Order) that Linklater sought to examine and comment upon – particularly with regard to their legacy to the following decade.

Although Linklater often injects a note of anti-authoritarianism into his work, often strongly so, his characters tend to be erudite and well-informed, rarely acting predictably and never protesting vacuously against a nebulous establishment that they do not understand. Only rarely do characters in Linklater's films discover that they cannot influence the world around them in some way, even if that influence is only subtle in nature. Indeed, quite the contrary is true; when Linklater presents characters in opposition to conventional authority, it is precisely because they have a deliberately argued and premeditated antipathy towards the establishment that the audience are encouraged to sympathise with them. This is evident from Dewey Finn's quasicomic insistence that 'stickin' it to the Man' is absolutely central to the makeup of rock 'n' roll in *School of Rock* all the way through to the dizzying paranoia of *A Scanner Darkly*, where Agent Fred/Bob Arctor finds himself hopelessly submerged by the inconstant nature of the role of the individual in a state which is slowly coming under the control of an insidiously creeping totalitarianism. Linklater always takes the issue of individual freedom very seriously (even when his treatment of the subject may superficially appear light-hearted), and he has sought to underscore its importance in a number of different ways over the course of his career.

Just as *A Scanner Darkly* had vividly re-emphasised Philip K. Dick's literary concerns about pervasive state control for the modern age, Linklater appeared to be every bit as concerned about the potentially dehumanising aspects of modern society – specifically, with regard to how to recognise and actively combat them. This is certainly obvious from the vibrant urban collage of *Slacker* and social kaleidoscope of *Waking Life*, where discussion and contemplation are at the forefront of proceedings, but the theme is also interestingly handled in his more mainstream features such as *Bad News Bears*, an underdog story with a theme of meeting goals through inclusive attitudes,[166] and *The Newton Boys*, where the protagonists' unabashedly criminal activities are counterbalanced by their quirkily civil qualities of politeness and gentlemanly conduct at all times. *The Newton Boys* also furthered Linklater's examination of the behaviour of the establishment, contrasting the Newtons' amiable and largely guileless approach to their criminality with the internecine plotting of the shadowy organisations seeking to bring the brothers to book, not so much out of concern for their customers or the general public as for the sake of their own commercial interests. This theme of the burgeoning consumer culture and the isolating effect upon the individual that may be argued to have developed alongside it was also explored in the unambiguously political *Fast Food Nation*, and – to similarly striking effect – in *subUrbia*, where it is suggested that much of the lethargic characters' nihilism is being driven by their place in an overly commoditised society, and that they are reacting against the questions of individual self-worth that this has generated. In bringing Eric Bogosian's vitriolic stage play to the big screen, Linklater manages to infuse the unsympathetic band of characters depicted throughout the narrative with a kind of sparing but intricate humanity and a darkly laconic wit, but even so the film remains almost certainly his starkest – a harsh warning against the ineffectual direction that some aspects of society and youth culture were seen to be taking at the time.[167]

Linklater never puts forward any glib answers to solve the multifarious ethical issues of *subUrbia*, and he was to engage with the complexities of moral relativism even more deeply in *Tape*. A masterpiece of moral ambiguity, *Tape* delicately (and at times deviously) explores the intricacies of psychological perception and remembrance of specific events, yet it also manages to force the audience to think carefully about the responsibility and culpability of the individual. As the film progresses, we are unsure which character we are supposed to be sympathising with; by the conclusion, we are uncertain about whether we should in fact be sympathising with any of them. Linklater carefully manages Stephen Belber's elaborate manipulations of the audience's perception of guilt and what it means to be a victim, and ultimately suggests that veracity and impartiality are factors that are much less certain in life than they may initially appear.

More often than not, Linklater's characters find themselves on a journey, both philosophically and geographically, and his films frequently feature a recurring motif of different nodes of public transport, such as bus terminals, train stations and airports. This is most obvious in *Slacker*'s laid-back travelogue around Austin, where the notions of Baudrillard, Descartes and Joyce become landmarks just as familiar as the city's physical attractions. Wiley Wiggins' bemused central character in *Waking Life* is even more explicitly on an expedition, though it is through much less familiar terrain – namely, through dreams (not necessarily his own) and ultimately an examination of the nature of existence: what it truly means to be 'real'. By exchanging the actors and performers of *Slacker* for an even wider interdisciplinary range of thinkers and artists, *Waking Life* explores the way that the personal voice is rendered authentic,[168] and joins its predecessor in both passively and explicitly opposing the dangers of unchecked and unjustified power. This creates a common link between *Waking Life* and *A Scanner Darkly*, not only in terms of the importance of freedom of expression, but also in the vital consequence of maintaining the certainty of one's own authentic identity, lest an inauthentic one be imposed upon us by external forces.

The theme of journeying inevitably takes us to what may be Linklater's greatest achievement – *Before Sunrise* and *Before Sunset*. Although *Before Sunrise* had delighted audiences and almost universally impressed the critics at the time of its release, Linklater managed to surprise everyone by seamlessly recapturing its unique charm with a perfectly-pitched sequel which succeeded on every level and even managed, in the main, to win over those few who had been unconvinced by the original. Both films shared common characteristics, from the staggeringly multifaceted performances of Ethan Hawke and Julie Delpy to the oddly fluid quality taken on by time during their respective meetings; the passing of the hours, though inevitable, appears to be a malleable and indistinct process, only indirectly affecting the course of the two protagonists' fated encounter (even in spite of the fact that this temporal pliability persists only for their meeting's abruptly-curtailed duration). Interestingly, this rarefied and teasingly temporary isolation from time, and from the concerns of the wider populace surrounding the pair, led some critics to question whether Jesse and Celine could, in fact, be considered to be both existing and functioning outside of the confines of Generation X as well, including all of the baggage that the term suggests.[169] Indeed, Celine and Jesse's highly intense relationship is initially free from most other baggage too – when they first meet, they are full of youthful exuberance, temporarily separated from their families and responsibilities and able to fully enjoy the experience of their brief meeting with only the prospect of their inevitable separation threatening to inhibit proceedings. By the time of their second encounter, however, their life experiences have grown dramatically, as has the collective burden of their responsibilities. Through the magnificently understated articulation of Delpy and Hawke, Linklater was to use *Before Sunset* to explore a whole range of issues including fading youth and the prospect of the ageing process, commitments that are desired and others which are less so (but to which the characters are tied nonetheless), and the acute frustration of a single missed opportunity which has had life-changing ramifications for both of them.

Although *Before Sunset* was to answer some questions that *Before Sunrise* had left enigmatically ambiguous – including, obviously, whether the pair ever had been reunited in Vienna six months after their fateful first meeting – Linklater ensured that rather than destroying the mystique, as many critics had feared, the subsequent revelations which were to unfold would instead deepen audience understanding of the characters even further, due to the adroit way in which these questions were answered. The film constantly engages with the contrasting themes of passion and frustration, hope and despair, and elation and regret; by the time Linklater reaches the conclusion, we feel as though we have lived through the powerful emotion of the couple's unpretentiously passionate reunion alongside them, and have come to truly know them in a way that few other narratives could hope to match. The films express the importance of robust but unrealised devotion with matchless eloquence, yet in both features it is just as significant to note that what is left unsaid is almost as important as what is explicitly uttered; Linklater proves the point many times throughout the two films that communication is much more than a merely verbal exercise, and this adds a distinctively human aspect to Jesse and Celine's multilayered interaction. The remarkable effect of Linklater's skilful character depiction has been refined to such a striking extent, especially in later films, that it has led some critics to hail him as one of the most psychologically observant and inventive directors currently working in America, never allowing the pursuit of a philosophical or socio-political agenda to obscure the meaningful and sympathetic development of his characters.[170] Indeed, Linklater's treatment of Celine and Jesse typifies his general approach to characterisation; that is, to always render characters with care and respect, providing them with realistic and plausible motivations, believable psychologies and convincing behavioural qualities, regardless of their function within the individual film in question.

Even more recently, audiences have seen Linklater extend this methodology to engage with the depiction of real figures from recent American history, both in fictional and non-fictional frameworks. With *Inning by Inning*, the life's work of Augie Garrido is delineated with historical accuracy and deep respect even while Linklater's keen eye for conveying the broadest possible range of psychological complexity is being fully engaged throughout. Although the film succeeds in exploring the many significant achievements of Garrido's career, this function is ultimately subsumed by Linklater's enthusiastic determination to examine the intricate character which lies behind this remarkable and enigmatic sporting figure. Linklater's contemplative scrutiny of Garrido's desire to emphasise team spirit and personal growth in the sportsmen with whom he works is successful in sketching out a deeply thoughtful approach to the coach's discipline, blurring the lines between sport, philosophy and art. As such, the film has again underscored Linklater's dexterous balance between percept-iveness and respectful appreciation of character and personality. This has been demonstrated further in *Me and Orson Welles*, where he shows no apprehension in presenting a bold and uncompromising depiction of the eponymous thespian. The sheer renown of this legendary actor/director's celebrated status in film history leaves Linklater entirely undaunted, and he acutely draws out Welles's multifaceted character traits with all of the wit and verve that he had lavished upon the Newton brothers a decade beforehand.

Regardless of whether he is depicting the touching romance of two strangers or the deep-seated love that human beings have for new ideas and fresh concepts, Linklater is one of the most optimistic and upbeat directors currently working in independent film. His focus on the need for constant interaction between people and groups is constantly expressed through his emphasis on the importance of ongoing dialogic interplay and the exchange of theories, knowledge and understanding. To be human, Linklater stresses, is to be a social animal; to take an interest in the world around oneself and, what's more, actively participate in it. He does not deny that the modern world is a dangerous and at times deceptive place, but always throughout his work there is a prominent notion that – in spite of the perils of a jaded, cynical society with an electorate which appears increasingly apathetic and drained of hope for the future – we still live in a vibrant and exciting world that remains full of exhilarating possibilities. As films like *Waking Life* strongly signal (particularly during its Eamonn Healy and Robert C. Solomon sequences), there will always remain room for new ways of thinking, for coherent challenges to hitherto-accepted socio-political norms. Such contestation, Linklater suggests, can encourage civilised, consensual and positive developments in the manner by which people interact and coexist, particularly with the advent of new communications technology (though as *A Scanner Darkly* suggests with the bugging of Arctor's mobile phone and the multitude of hidden cameras in his home, this development is also not without its own darker, more sinister side). With current prevailing attitudes of reductive world-weariness, concern over perceived social atomisation and fears of the formation of an all-encompassing surveillance society, Linklater's hopeful attitudes seem like a breath of fresh air in the most uncertain of times, stressing constructive possibilities and optimistic aspirations for the future whilst simultaneously never oblivious to the perils that, if not adequately addressed, may potentially lie just around the corner.

The influence of Linklater's film-making has been far-reaching, being noted most conspicuously in the work of Kevin Smith[171] and the Mumblecore movement.[172] The impact of his filmography has undoubtedly been highly significant in the world of independent film, particularly (but certainly not exclusively) in his native United States, yet perhaps even more exciting is the prospect of his production of ever more innovative work in the future. Details have recently emerged about a new and highly ambitious project, provisionally entitled *Boyhood*, which Linklater commenced filming at the beginning of the century. A speculative release date has been cited for midway through the next decade, though Linklater himself has not given official confirmation of this.[173] Although the fine detail of the project is not yet known, it is believed that the film will centre upon a young boy's development through adolescence and into early adulthood. By filming sections of this feature on a year-on-year basis, Linklater will be ensuring that the depiction of his protagonist's advancement through life is treated with the utmost accuracy and realism: a typically bold and pioneering experiment on his behalf. However, his work on *Boyhood* is not the only future project that has caught the imagination of film commentators. Unconfirmed speculation continues to persist among many pundits about the potential production of a highly anticipated third (and possibly final) instalment in the *Before Sunrise* cycle at some undisclosed point in the future, particularly following the widespread critical success of *Before Sunset* in 2004, and Linklater has also tentatively spoken of other potential projects in recent interviews. [174] By planning so far ahead, Linklater continues to emphasise his dedication to presenting a wide-ranging and varied corpus of work, never failing to keep his audience guessing as to the next move in his ever-changing career.

Linklater is a director wholly unafraid of the critics, and he has proven on innumerable occasions that he is never one to pander to critical expectation. Virtually impossible to fit into any readily-available political pigeonhole, he is one of the most literate of film-makers, with an extensive knowledge not only of classic cinema, but also fine art, music, literature and many social, political and philosophical issues. Indeed, even Linklater's production company, Detour Filmproduction, reflects his high regard for film history, as it is said to be named after Edgar G. Ulmer's cult B-movie *Detour* (1945), considered by some to be one of the most notably philosophical commercial American films of the forties. [175] His deep respect for film-making also has a permanent living monument in the Austin Film Society, which he founded in 1985 with cinematographer Lee Daniel, and the two have been much praised in subsequent years for promoting Austin as a vibrant nucleus for making independent films.

Richard Linklater is many things – boundlessly creative, intensely autonomous, powerfully literate and penetratingly perceptive. In possession of one of modern independent film's most intriguing and accomplished careers, it is clear that he is still seeking new goals to achieve, new expectations to exceed, and brave new approaches to pioneer. Yet perhaps the most impressive of all Linklater's accomplishments is the simple fact that, after fifteen films released over the past two decades, there is still no such thing as 'a typical Richard Linklater film'. And given his unique directorial skill, it seems certain that there never will be.

SCENE BY SCENE:

BEFORE SUNRISE

In the eyes of many commentators, **Before Sunrise** *has become one of the most critically acclaimed of all Richard Linklater's films. With its contemplative pacing, an inspired premise and dialogue which is simultaneously insightful, philosophical and playful, the feature has become one of the most immediately identifiable landmarks in Linklater's entire filmography. This section will take a closer look at the manner in which Linklater's directorial skill, together with the carefully constructed screenplay he created with Kim Krizan and the emotionally-charged performances of Ethan Hawke and Julie Delpy, combined to bring about a film which has proven to be among the most enduring of his career thus far.*

Before Sunrise opens with a shot of train-track rolling by at speed, followed by a tracking shot of scenic European countryside. These rural scenes are interspersed by a shot of a railway bridge receding into the distance, and a busy river scene complete with a large moored vessel. As we now move into the interior of the train, a young woman with a shoulder-bag can be seen walking along one of the carriages, entering a passenger compartment via a sliding door.

Interestingly for a film which is so intimately concerned with the nature of romance, Linklater chooses to open *Before Sunrise* with a vocal argument between a disaffected middle-aged couple. The man is intent on reading a newspaper; his female partner's attention appears to be drifting. They look to be in their mid-forties, speak German, and although their dispute begins in a low-key, darkly sardonic manner, it soon turns increasingly loud and unpleasant. While they squabble, we are introduced to Celine. She is very attractive, in her mid-twenties and casually dressed. Currently trying to read from a paperback book, it is obvious that she is finding it difficult to concentrate due to the altercation that is taking place on the other side of the compartment. Her expression shows a mixture of mild irritation and discomfort at being forced to endure the couple's progressively more vocal argument. We then cut to a few other passengers – a young man sleeping, and then an elderly couple sitting together – before we are eventually introduced to Jesse. Like Celine, he is in his mid-twenties, attired informally, and possesses understated good looks. He is also trying to read a book, albeit a hardback as opposed to Celine's softcover, and is gazing distractedly out of the train window at the world passing by.

Moving to a wide-angle shot of the carriage, we can now see that Celine is seated directly across the aisle from the warring couple. They continue to argue, and the female partner eventually slams her hand down onto the man's newspaper, grabbing it from him and moving it away. Their quarrel persists. By now, Celine has had enough. She picks up her travelling bag from the seat next to her, gets up, and moves further down the carriage away from the incessant sound of altercation. Finding a vacant seat, she stuffs her bag into an overhead storage compartment and sits down, resuming her book. Jesse is on the opposite side of the aisle from her, and – though also still reading his own book – spots Celine's movements nearby. They both impart a subtle glance, each aware of the other's presence. Juxtaposed with Celine and Jesse's apparent shared attraction at first sight, the arguing couple can still be heard in the near-distance further along the carriage.

Even at this very early stage, we are aware of a mutual sense of desire between Celine and Jesse – though very delicately restrained at this point – which quickly establishes the film's central theme. From the tiny momentary looks that they both take at each other, and also in Celine's particular choice of seat next to Jesse, there is a definite suggestion that their fateful meeting is not only attributable to good fortune, but also an instant emotional empathy with one another. Jesse and Celine continue to eye each other up, though both are very circumspect about their motions. Moving back to a wide angle shot, the female member of the warring relationship decides that she has had enough of the spat that she and her partner have become embroiled in. Heatedly, she gets up from her seat, storming along the aisle of the carriage and heading out of the compartment. Her partner follows closely behind her. Jesse watches their departure with wry amusement. He smiles across to Celine, who politely returns the gesture.

Jesse asks Celine if she was aware of the cause of the argument, checking that she speaks English upon hearing her French accent. His own accent is distinctively American, with a faint ring of the East Coast. In English, Celine replies that she doesn't speak much German, and thus is as much in the dark as he is about the source of the couple's falling out. She jokes about the ability of couples to tune each other out as they grow older together, and Jesse appreciates her sense of humour. Jesse asks her what she's reading, and Celine holds up her paperback to reveal that it is a compilation edition of work by Georges Bataille, including *Madame Edwarda* and *The Dead Man*. She then asks the same question of Jesse, who likewise reveals his own reading matter – his hardback is a copy of Klaus Kinski's autobiography, *All I Need is Love*. Neither appears to have much to say about the other's choice of reading material.

Here we see the mutual rapport more clearly established between Celine and Jesse; not only from the thought-provoking works that they are choosing to read, written by two highly distinctive if entirely diverse artists, but also from the appreciation they strike up with regard to each other's dry wit and philosophical insight. They already seem intrigued by each other, even although they haven't yet formally introduced themselves.

The battling Germanic couple re-enter the carriage, encroaching upon the relative calm that had settled in their wake. Still quarrelling, though now less vociferously than before, their voices trail off as they head back to their seats. Seeming less than enthralled by the couple's return, Jesse suggests a move to the lounge carriage, and asks Celine if she would like to join him. She agrees, and packs her book away into her bag. Together, they head along the aisle into a connecting compartment, and then move into the adjacent carriage. The atmosphere is much more convivial than had been the case with the awkwardness of their previous location, and they soon find a vacant table, taking seats opposing each other. Picturesque rural terrain continues to roll past outside the nearby window of the carriage.

Jesse asks Celine how she came to have such a good command of the English language. She replies that she had spent some time being educated in Los Angeles, and had also lived in London for a while. Celine then turns the question on its head, asking Jesse how he came to speak English so well, and he replies that he is an American. Sensing sarcasm in the presumption that he is monolingual, he is quick to tell her that he studied French for four years in high school, but – quite in spite of his best efforts – his attempts to converse with native Francophone speakers fell flat on its face when the time came for him to actually visit France. Celine is amused by his self-effacing honesty about his perceived shortcomings.

This sequence establishes one of the recurrent themes in the film: that of cultural difference. Not only are Celine and Jesse naturally inclined towards dissimilar perspectives – a fact which is emphasised by the fact that they are both very individualistic people – but to some degree their divergence in worldview is caused by not only their distinctive personalities but also the effect of their nationalities on their attitudes and opinions. Linklater draws this distinction very subtly, and the issue continues to manifest itself in a restrained and sensitive way as the film progresses.

Jesse asks where Celine is heading, and she replies that she is travelling back to Paris, where she is studying at La Sorbonne. When he enquires about what had brought her on this particular train journey, she replies that she had been in Budapest visiting her grandmother. Celine is visibly charmed when Jesse, in an automatic gesture of courtesy, asks after her grandmother's health even although he knows absolutely nothing about her. She asks him where his own destination is and he replies that he is heading for Vienna, where he intends to fly back to the United

States. Celine, curious, asks if he is currently on holiday, but Jesse seems reluctant to talk about the situation, answering only that he himself is unsure of the exact purpose of his stay in Europe. Enigmatically, he adds that he has been travelling around on various different trains for the past two or three weeks. Now even more inquisitive because of his apparent evasiveness, Celine asks if he had been travelling with friends, but Jesse remains tight-lipped, saying only that he had met an acquaintance in Barcelona recently.

Jesse's disinclination to discuss the function of his visit to Spain becomes significant later. Not only does it offer an early clue to his presence on the train, but the ramifications of his earlier experiences in Europe inform much of his viewpoint at this point in his life and, as a result, throughout much of the film. Likewise, Celine's playful curiosity is revisited several times throughout the film, and always seems much more understated than Jesse's generally more direct mode of questioning.

Celine senses that Jesse hasn't really enjoyed much of his visit to the continent, which he mutedly confirms, though he does add that the forced monotony of long-distance travel has given him plenty of time to think about things in his life. Somewhat out of left field, he then regales her with an elaborate idea that he has concocted for a cable access television show, which would feature rolling twenty-four hour coverage of individuals living ordinary lives – three hundred and sixty-five different people from all over the world, studied in depth for a single day each. Celine is confused at why anyone would want to watch uninterrupted coverage of all the boring, unremarkable minutiae that makes up an ordinary life, but Jesse's view differs – in his opinion, there can be great beauty in the tiny mundane details that comprise everyone's subtly different approach to living.

This sequence offers another insight into Celine and Jesse's respective psychologies, as well as highlighting Jesse's occasional propensity for fanciful notions as opposed to Celine's more tangible stories of her life experience, which denote her deep sense of emotional awareness. Yet as his acute observations about the appeal of the everyday signify, Jesse too is in possession of profound reserves of emotional sensitivity, although he does generally tend to demonstrate it in less perceptible ways.

As they continue to talk, a uniformed waiter heads up the carriage aisle towards them and hands out two menus. They both look over the contents of the menu as the camera slowly pulls back, revealing the rest of the carriage. Jesse wryly observes that in his opinion, European culture is generally not service-oriented. While they keep on perusing, the shot changes to the still-rolling scenery outside the window. When we move back to the carriage, we can see that a finished meal lies in front of Jesse and Celine, their respective plates now empty.

Obviously now midway through a further thread of conversation, Celine is ruminating on her father's uncanny ability in the past to convert her childhood idealism – all of her passionate dreams and aspirations – into practical ambitions with solid targets and achievable objectives. Jesse replies that by the time he had got into the education system, he had become well-versed in screening out other peoples' attempts to impose their will on his goals in life, and was resolved to fulfil his own notions of self-determination instead. He remembers his family's attempts to educate him about the nature of death in his infancy, and how he had come to realise that there was more uncertainty and imperceptibility to human existence than they had ever suggested to him. Celine envies his *laissez-faire* view of death, as for her it is a shadow which follows her doggedly through life. She lives in constant fear of not only death, but the manner in which it may take place. For this reason, she always avoids flying where possible because of the overwhelming sense of danger that it brings her. Jesse is intrigued by her candidness.

Celine's revelations about her fear of death are significant, for they conversely inform much of her attitude towards life – her spontaneous inclination to live in the moment, for instance, and her deep appreciation of her own existence. Just as Jesse has anxieties about the *direction* of his life, as we see demonstrated more clearly later, Celine's apprehension tends to be geared more towards the finite *duration* of life itself (most particularly with regard to being morally satisfied with her actions prior to any unanticipated termination of her existence).

The train has now almost arrived at Vienna, and Celine mentions that Jesse will need to disembark soon. Jesse seems disappointed; he has enjoyed talking to Celine so much that he wishes that they had met earlier, so that their conversation would have lasted longer and that they would thus have got to know each other better as a result. Cutting to a Viennese railway platform, the train can now be seen coming to a rest at the station. Once its doors have opened, passengers begin to leave with their luggage.

Back in the carriage, Jesse – now holding his jacket and bag – is heading back to where Celine is sitting. She smiles curiously at his return. Jesse tells her that he has a crazy idea, but one which he nonetheless wants to ask her about. He says that not only has he taken great pleasure in chatting with Celine, but that he feels a certain kind of emotional connection with her. Celine agrees with his assertion, feeling the same way. As he has a day to kill before his plane is due to leave for America, Jesse suggests that she disembark with him, spend the time before his plane leaves getting to know each other, and then catch the next train to Paris after he has flown back home to the States. Going further, he explains that in ten or twenty years time, if she is married and finds that her relationship with her then-husband is running out of steam, she will inevitably begin to question what life would have been like with other men that she had met earlier in her life. This way, Jesse tells her, she can discover that he is in fact just as tedious and apathetic as her future husband will be, thus doing herself a huge favour in years to come – there will be no need to agonise over what might have been. Laughing at his unconventional way of convincing her, she agrees to join him for the day in Vienna. She grabs her bag, and together they head out of the carriage.

Here we see Celine taking the leap of faith that ultimately drives the rest of the film's narrative. Although neither of the two have yet asked each other their name, and in spite of the many potential dangers that Jesse outlines about trusting a stranger, Celine still feels sufficiently drawn to Jesse to risk spending more time with him in a city that neither of them are well acquainted with. Her decision, as we will see, has far-reaching effects for both of them.

Stepping out onto the train platform, Celine looks around uncertainly. She seems unfamiliar with Vienna, and this venue in particular. Jesse takes her bag for her, and suggests that they find a locker to store it in. She agrees. The camera follows their feet as they head further into the station. Celine is wearing flat casual shoes in black, while Jesse favours black Converse trainers. The camera moves to cover the upper section of their bodies as they move on. Celine asks Jesse's name, and he replies that although his name is actually James, everyone calls him Jesse. She also tells him her own name for the first time.

We watch as a train departs the station as the camera pans up and around an exterior location, finally settling on Jesse and Celine as they emerge onto a flyover bridge. Clearly now feeling slightly self-conscious at making small-talk, Jesse comments on the pleasant condition of the bridge. Celine laughs, commenting that she too feels slightly embarrassed by the unconventional situation that they find themselves in. She suggests that they look at Jesse's guide-book to the city in order to find something to do. Jesse, however, decides to ask a couple of nearby Austrians instead, as they are currently standing in close proximity looking over the bridge onto a river.

He asks if they speak English and they confirm that they do, though they joke that as a tourist maybe he should consider speaking German for a change. When he asks about museums and galleries, one of the men replies that in his opinion these places are rarely much fun to explore and will, at any rate, be closing soon for the day. He asks what they're doing in Vienna, and what they expected to find there. Celine jokes that they're on honeymoon, while Jesse elaborates that he'd got her pregnant, suggesting that a shotgun wedding had taken place. The Austrian laughs, telling him that he is an unconvincing liar. His friend suggests that Jesse and Celine come to a play that they will be appearing in that night, as they are both amateur actors. They give a rambling account of the play, *Bring Me the Horns of Wilmington's Cow*, which has complex socio-political overtones and appears to be rather postmodern in nature (it features a cow with an inclination towards canine behaviour which has the ability to smoke). Celine and Jesse appear nonplussed by the sprawling explanation. The men point out the address of the play's venue, which is near the Wiener Prater, and tell them that it will be starting at 9:30pm. The two actors are both keen that Jesse and Celine should attend, but neither of the couple seems entirely convinced of the play's dramatic merits. Jesse does offer his assurance that they'll try to make it along if they can, however. Thanking the Austrians for their friendly advice, Celine and Jesse head off the bridge as the two men move away in the opposite direction.

This sequence demonstrates not only a little subtly-employed cultural satire in the two actors' enquiry about whether Jesse can speak German (thus deftly turning on its head Jesse's usual opening question of whether any stranger he is talking to is fluent in English), but also the growing rapport that is building up between Celine and Jesse. They very rapidly overcome their feelings of awkwardness at their unusual situation, such that they are soon comfortable enough to form a spontaneous double-act when Jesse jokes about being on honeymoon. There is also irony in the actor's question about what the pair expected to find in Vienna – because neither of them know the city well, there is little indication that they have any expectations at all, with the exception of getting to know each other better.

A tram is heading along a track atop a bridge, passing an

historic cathedral. Scaffolding can be seen constructed around one of its spires. In the distance, church bells can be heard ringing. Moving inside the tram, Celine and Jesse are heading towards a seat at the rear of the vehicle. Viennese traffic moves along, visible from the window as it flows around the tram in the background. Jesse suggests that as they're going to be spending some time together, it's time that they asked each other some direct questions – with the proviso that both must answer with complete honesty. Jesse goes first, and asks Celine about the first time she had felt sexual desire towards someone. She tells him about a talented swimmer she had met in youth while at a summer camp, who she had developed a serious crush on. They had both felt attracted to each other over the course of the summer, though she had played hard to get and had rebuffed his offer of a date. When the camp was over, they had exchanged a promise that they would always keep in touch with each other, though it had never come to pass. Jesse eagerly assures her that he is also an exceptionally good swimmer, which makes her laugh. Then it is her turn to ask a question; she enquires whether Jesse has ever been in love. Jesse replies that yes, he has, and then quickly tries to move on to another question. Celine feels cheated that she should have given such a long, detailed answer to his question about sexual desire when Jesse had only used a one-word response to her own query. He responds that sexual attraction and love are two very different things; in the past, he had told someone that he loved them and had at the time been sincere in his assurance of that fact, but love has ultimately become such a complex notion to him that he now feels unsure whether he could really call it a selfless or full-blooded devotion in retrospect. Celine seems slightly disappointed at his frankness about the issue, appearing distant as he relates his viewpoint to her, but reluctantly admits that she knows what he means. When he asks her how she would have responded to the same question, she acknowledges that she would probably have lied rather than provide a straight answer, though it would at least have been a longer and more entertaining account than Jesse's one-word response.

Jesse's frankness about love is interesting, for his faint tone of cynicism is – we later discover – heavily influenced by his earlier experiences in Spain, and disguise much stronger romantic notions that are cloaked by his apparent scepticism. Celine's account of her summer romance is also significant; her acceptance that long-distance relationships are almost impossible to maintain indefinitely comes to inform the dilemma that she and Jesse must face at the end of their shared time together, and foreshadows the film's conclusion.

Jesse asks Celine what kinds of things really annoy her. Celine responds that she could give him a very long list – she hates strangers asking her to smile, or the thought that brutal wars are being waged around the world while people remain apathetic about the suffering of others. She also detests the manipulative effects of the mass-media on the public, and more than anything else despises the fact that when she's visiting a foreign country, people find her 'Frenchness' endearing and subsequently treat her in a patronising way. Jesse appears quietly impressed by the passion with which she delivers her answers. Celine then asks Jesse the same question; what kind of things does he consider a problem? Jesse jokes that Celine is probably enough of a problem on her own, which they both laugh at, but he then goes on to describe a quandary that had occurred to him while travelling through Europe. Taking off his jacket, he describes his worry to her – if human souls are reincarnated, how can it be that not even a million people lived on the Earth fifty thousand years ago, and yet the planet is now sustaining a population of almost six billion. How, he asks, are the souls divided up? He postulates the notion that perhaps modern humans are possessed of only a tiny proportion of what constituted a soul in the past, for otherwise there is no indication of where new souls would originate from. Celine laughs at this concept, baffled at his diffuse line of reasoning. Jesse joins in her amusement, suggesting that his idea is so outlandish that it actually makes its own kind of sense. As the tram grinds to a halt, Jesse grabs his coat as he and Celine head through the door and out onto the pavement beyond. Jesse's evocation of this almost surreal issue of philosophical uncertainty, which stands in stark contrast to Celine's more concrete response, is representative of his character not only in its wryly abstruse nature, but also in its inscrutability. Because the question relies on supernatural proof that cannot be discerned in empirical terms, it seems bound to be forever unanswerable in the world of human experience. (Indeed, the issue is raised again in Celine and Jesse's sequence within Linklater's later film, *Waking Life*.)

An establishment shot of a record shop can be seen; its exterior signage reads *Schallplattenhandlung*. Moving inside, we are treated to a variety of vinyl singles dangling from the ceiling, suspended by lengths of string. Jesse is idly flicking through a selection of album sleeves showing artists as various as Ella Fitzgerald, Gordon Lightfoot, The Searchers and Frank Zappa. As the camera pulls back, we can see that the shop is a true independent music store, full of old-fashioned touches like hand-written category signs, framed photographs and sketches on the walls, and a vintage gramophone system on display. Jesse walks across to Celine, who is browsing records on the other side of the shop. He expresses his general approval of the store to Celine. She agrees, noting that it even still has a listening booth. Celine holds up a vinyl LP, an album by Kath Bloom, and asks Jesse if he has heard of her. He replies that he hasn't. Celine seems slightly surprised at this, believing her to be an American artist. Jesse suggests that they try the record out in the listening booth, and Celine agrees. They head to the back of the shop and enter the booth, Jesse drawing a sliding glass door closed behind them.

We see a close-up of Celine's hand as she touches the record player's stylus down onto the surface of the album. Guitar music starts to play, and the pair look slightly self-conscious at being in such close proximity to each other due to the cramped interior dimensions of the booth. When the vocals begin, Bloom can be heard singing *Come Here*, a moving love song with undeniably romantic lyrics. This makes the pair look even more embarrassed, if not altogether uncomfortable. At one point, Jesse looks as though he's about to reach for Celine, perhaps weighing up the notion of putting his arm around her, though he ultimately decides against it. They smile at each other occasionally, sneaking the odd glimpse into their companion's eyes, but look away as often as they actually make visual contact.

The scene in the listening booth is one of the most touching early scenes in the film, as Jesse and Celine appear to feel simultaneously comfortable and awkward at being in such close proximity to each other. There is a definite suggestion, especially from Jesse's stance and gesture, that there is consideration given to moving beyond this self-consciousness and making physical contact in a more tangible way, though the decision to avoid doing so raises the question of what later opportunity will present itself for them to do so.

We cut to a park. Celine and Jesse are strolling along a path at an unhurried rate. An expansive stately home can be seen behind them. As Jesse expresses his awe of the scenic vista, we are treated to shots of various fountains, monuments and statuary in the area. Cutting away again, we see Jesse and Celine running to catch a tram, which they manage to reach just in time. Further shots of Viennese street scenes, replete with other passing trams, then roll by from the viewpoint of the tram window. Inside, the pair continue to talk excitedly, their dialogue inaudible. The tram comes to a halt, and Celine – not expecting the sudden change in speed – seems to have difficulty keeping her balance. The door slides open, and they disembark.

We are now in an area of lush, green grass. A rabbit, apparently disturbed by something, hops away into the distance. Celine spots it as she and Jesse descend a flight of stone stairs. As they wander along the small grassy region, Celine recognises the nearby Friedhof der Namenlosen graveyard (the 'Cemetery of the

Nameless in Simmering'), which she had once visited while still a teenager. She tells Jesse that on her last trip there, the groundskeeper had explained that the cemetery was largely populated by bodies of unknown people that had washed up from the River Danube – hence the graveyard's name. Celine ruminates on the fate of these unknown people and the fact that if they were alone in the world, nobody would be aware of their passing and thus their respective histories would inevitably have to be invented by others. She feels particularly sentimental as they stop by the grave of a thirteen year old girl, for that had been her own age when she had first encountered the burial place. Her expression is contemplative as they move away from the graveside.

Here we see the theme of Celine's preoccupation with death rising to the surface again. Her remembrance of the young girl's grave, dead before her time, and indeed her observation of the unknown corpses which have to acquire a conferred identity rather than retaining their own authentic distinctiveness, are obviously issues which haunt her. Coupled with her earlier ruminations, there is a sense that much of Celine's uneasiness with her life derives from this fundamental anxiety that if she dies alone and unremembered, all of her thoughts and achievements disregarded, that she would feel as though all of her life experience would have been for nothing. Thus there is a sense that she would ultimately feel at risk of being just as forgotten and overlooked as the nameless people buried in the cemetery.

Next we see a dramatic establishment shot of the famous Ferris wheel at the Wiener Prater. The sky shows that the afternoon has now turned to twilight. Moving inside one of the wheel's spacious passenger compartments, Jesse and Celine are surveying the glorious view outside. Celine points out the Danube, though Jesse seems unfamiliar with this famous European river. Alone together in the carriage, the pair draw closer as they continue to admire the view. Next to the open window, Jesse obliquely expresses his desire to kiss Celine, though he ultimately leaves the thought unsaid. Celine, however, immediately picks up on his unspoken attraction – she gently puts her arms around him, kissing him tenderly on the lips. Jesse reciprocates with equal sensitivity. The embrace lasts only a moment before they mutedly break apart, but seconds later Celine decides to engage Jesse in a warm hug. They hold each other in silence.

In this crucial scene, the shared physical attraction which was immediately established between Celine and Jesse on the train, and made more obvious in the listening booth, reaches its natural conclusion with their first kiss together. As they both wholly consent to the embrace – Jesse in suggesting the notion, and Celine in initiating it – there is an immediate poignancy that emphasises Celine's emotional spontaneity while, at the same time, the encounter neatly explodes Jesse's earlier muted disparagement of romantic love while conversing in the tram.

A raucous party track strikes up as we see a group of teenagers spinning around on a fairground ride. Cutting to a scene nearby, sightseers are wandering around the Prater grounds. Next, we see Celine putting a coin into a 'test your strength' amusement machine. Impromptu music can be heard striking up from the contraption – Boots Randolph's *Yackety Sax* – and Celine laughs as she and Jesse dance along to it. In a smooth manoeuvre, Jesse elbows the machine as he passes, and it registers his strength as 70 out of 100. He seems quietly impressed.

As they meander through the Prater, Celine discusses her parents. She explains that they had been full of revolutionary fervour in the sixties, and though her father had become a successful architect later on, she felt grateful to be able to enjoy the freedoms growing up that her mother and father had fought so hard to achieve. Yet, she opines, she herself must now engage in different conflicts from those that her parents had to consider. Jesse is unsure of the existence of such nebulous adversarial forces in culture and society, however; in his opinion, no matter what way parents attempt to raise their children, they inevitably always fail. He uses his own mother and father, now divorced, as an illustration. Remembering a fierce argument that had taken place in front of him in youth, where his mother had accused his father of never wanting her to have given birth to Jesse, he has come to consider this experience as a major formative influence in his life. Celine is saddened by his account, though Jesse assures her that it had actually come to imbue him with greater self-determination as an individual. Celine says that although her own parents had stayed together over the years, she still feels that it is important and beneficial for youth to have iconoclastic urges. Thoughtfully, she asks if Jesse knows anyone who is actually in a happy relationship. Thinking about it, he replies that although he knows some couples who appear to be happy, it may only be a superficial assessment as he has no way of gauging how honest they really are with each other. Celine agrees with this summation; she has recently discovered that her grandmother, who was together with her husband for decades, had spent years pining for another man. Jesse suggests that this was probably for the best – had she actually got to know this alternative partner better, he would almost certainly have proven a disappointment due to her having invested so much expectation in his romantic allure. Celine is unconvinced by his apparent cynicism, however. Not only does Jesse have no actual knowledge of her grandmother or the man that she yearned for, but his own actions on the Ferris wheel spoke of a more romantic character than that which he is now projecting. Trying to change the subject, he jumps up to grab hold of a roundabout as he passes.

In this sequence, we see Jesse's anxieties about parenthood and adult responsibility being presaged – he will deal with these issues more thoroughly later. For Celine, however, it again demonstrates her uneasiness with the development of her life – she discusses social and moral struggles that she feels must be engaged with, just as Jesse appears sceptical about this need. Yet their respective concerns about marriage and long-term partnerships clearly transcend cultural barriers, as their thoughtful responses prove. Jesse's apparent scepticism about romantic love, filtered through the lens of the account of Celine's grandmother, is now undermined by his actions on the Ferris wheel – a fact which Celine wastes no time in emphasising to him.

Near a town square, a horse-drawn carriage bearing a man and woman is passing on the road as a pair of robed monks walk by. As the camera pans across, we can see an elaborate fountain, and a café with a variety of outdoor tables. It's evening now. The camera follows the monks as we hear Jesse joking about their sense of fashion style, and then eventually pans across to reveal both he and Celine as they sit at one of the nearby restaurant tables. They kiss again. As they break apart, Celine spots a palm-reader in the vicinity. The middle-aged fortune teller notices them, and moves across to their table – a prospect which does not thrill Jesse. After ascertaining that she can speak English, Celine agrees to pay in order to have her palm read. The fortune teller explains that Celine is searching; she is an adventurer who is creative and imaginative. She also warns that Celine must achieve inner peace before she can connect effectively with other people. Asking if Jesse is a stranger to Celine, the fortune teller also briefly examines his palm and deduces that the two will be quite safe together – apparently Jesse is still in the process of acquiring knowledge (though it is left to our own interpretation whether by this she means that he is still learning about himself, about life and the world around him, or indeed all of these things). After Celine provides the payment for her consultation, the fortune teller explains to them both that as everything on Earth came to be formed from the universe's original Big Bang, they should both consider themselves to be stars, as they are ultimately composed of the same material as stellar matter.

As the palm reader departs, Jesse seems amused by the whole encounter. He scoffs at her vague predictions, which he asserts were so general that they could have been deduced by more or less anyone, and puts forward the theory that if fortune tellers ever actually told the truth, they would all go out of business. In his opinion, people only ever consult them to hear what they want to hear, rather than receive an accurate prediction of the future. Celine laughs at Jesse's unabashed scepticism, particularly as she had enjoyed the reading's strangely quixotic intensity.

This sequence again emphasises the key difference between Celine and Jesse; whereas Celine seems enchanted by the fortune teller's optimistic predictions of a constructive and positive future, Jesse is quick to challenge the ambiguity of her equivocal account. Yet even this variance may not be quite so neatly discerned as it appears at face value; as we have already seen in Jesse's approach to issues of romantic love, what he says can often contrast with how he feels.

Fooling around as they wander down a well-lit Viennese street, Celine notices a poster for a Georges-Pierre Seurat exhibition and seems regretful that they won't have the chance to see it – it won't go on show until the following week. She points out one of the paintings that will be on display – *La voie ferrée* – and explains that she had seen it in exhibition once before and had felt oddly mesmerised by it at the time. Celine points out other aspects of Seurat's style that she finds admirable, particularly the way in which he makes his human figures appear curiously ephemeral in relation to their backgrounds.

Celine and Jesse head up a flight of steps towards a cathedral. They decide to see if it's open, only narrowly managing to avoid the path of a passing car as they do so. Inside, Celine gazes in wonder at the beautiful scenes painted on the ceiling as she roams amongst the lit candles and religious iconography. As she takes a seat next to Jesse on a pew, she explains that she had visited a similar church with her grandmother only a few days ago. Celine discusses the fact that although religion has little place in her life, she still feels for the people who seek and gain comfort from it – in particular the ability of faith to span and profoundly affect different generations. Jesse accurately deduces that she is close to her grandmother, and Celine talks about the strong connection that she feels to her. Building upon the topic of age, Jesse says that he has always felt like a young teenager at heart, practicing at being an adult but not quite reconciled to the fact that he is now a mature human being. Celine laughs, likening their romantic embrace on the Ferris wheel to an old woman kissing a young boy. Jesse discusses his experience of attending a Quaker wedding, where the bride and groom knelt down and stared directly at each other for an hour before being pronounced husband and wife. Celine is moved by his account, considering the ceremony he describes to be charming. They sit in silence for a while, and then Jesse relates a story of an atheist friend who had offered a $100 bill to a homeless man only to drive away with it when the man had professed a belief in God. Celine is reproachful towards his friend's cruelty; Jesse agrees, though he can still manage to laugh at (rather than with) the illnatured humour of his one-time acquaintance.

Here we see the way that Celine and Jesse's differences strengthen rather than threaten the bond that is growing between them. Celine's rejection of mainstream organised religion is offset by her own personal sense of spirituality; Jesse's slightly taciturn approach to the matter of faith at this point is telling, suggesting less clarity in his own beliefs. This corresponds with earlier indications of Jesse's restlessness, and the lack of evident direction in his life. Yet for all their apparently dissimilar approaches to faith and spirituality, their candidness about their own respective stance on a highly personal matter continues to augment their unswerving honesty with each other.

Jesse and Celine are now wandering along a riverside path, still fooling around playfully. Jesse asks her if she would now have been safely home in Paris, had she not agreed to spend time with him in Vienna instead. She says that she wouldn't yet have arrived, and in turn asks him what he would be doing at this point in time. When he replies that he'd likely have been killing time at the airport, mourning the fact that she hadn't joined him from the train, she jokes that she might have disembarked at Salzburg with someone else instead. When he feigns outrage at this, she smiles and tells him how much she has enjoyed his company thus far. Jesse readily agrees with this summation, telling her that he has also taken great pleasure in getting to know her better. Celine abstractedly discusses the tactics and stratagems that go into conventional dating, and they talk about the irritations that eventually surface in the behaviour of partners during a long-term relationship. When Jesse asks her if there's anything about him that irritates her, she replies that she'd found his behaviour after the fortune teller's palm reading to be mildly distasteful – his cynicism almost made it seem like he was unhappy at the focus of the discussion being taken away from him. However, her criticism is well-intentioned, and Jesse takes it in good part.

Jesse is preparing a rebuff to Celine's defence of the fortune teller when they are interrupted by a man sitting at the water's edge. His clothing appears slightly the worse for wear, the implication being that he may be living on the streets. He speaks to them in German initially, though Celine tells him that she only understands a little of his language, and Jesse none at all. The man then begins to talk in English, slightly hesitantly, and gives them a proposal; he is not asking them to part with money, but instead requesting that they give him a word instead. He will then embed that word within a poem and, if they appreciate it, he invites them to pay him as much as they feel his work is worth. They agree, and Celine decides to offer the word 'milkshake' to the poet. As the poet begins to jot a composition into a pocketbook, Celine and Jesse quietly walk a little distance from him in order not to disturb his concentration. Jesse wryly asks Celine if, prior to encountering the street poet, they were in the process of having their first argument. Celine doesn't think so, but Jesse is unconvinced by her denial. She ventures the opinion that conflict isn't necessarily always a negative thing, as sometimes positive effects can derive from it. She also suggests that this may be one reason why she's still studying – sometimes it can feel comforting to have something to struggle against, like the establishment. Jesse speculates that competitiveness, which he feels is deeply entrenched in the makeup of their generation, may play a role in the predilection of individuals towards such conflict.

As Celine asks Jesse if the competitiveness that he's speaking about may possibly have been a driving factor in him asking her to leave her train and join him in Vienna, the poet interrupts them – he has completed his composition. He hands it, written on a torn-out page of his pocketbook, to Jesse. However, before Jesse has a chance to unfold it Celine plucks it out of his hand and returns it to the poet with a request that the artist read his own work out aloud. The poet gladly does so. His poem (*Daydream Delusion*) is a haunting work which suggests the deep need for the unity that love can bring, the importance of affection, and the necessity of mutual appreciation between romantic companions in an ever-changing and unpredictable society. Jesse and Celine appear both moved and impressed by the poem, and they each give him some money in exchange for it. Smiling, the street poet accepts their payment graciously, returning to his original position near the water's edge as the pair resume their journey.

As they continue their wanderings, Celine still appears touched by the poet's words, the piece of paper remaining in her hands. Jesse, however, is less influenced by the man's elegiac charm, instead speculating that he had probably put together a generic poem and simply included whatever word that a passer-by would happen to give him. Celine is again bemused by his apparent cynicism. They carry on walking, and for a while they discuss the relative nature of time. Jesse is perplexed by the fact that modern society relies on time-saving devices which, through their application, free up time for their users that is immediately squandered on doing other mundane tasks. Celine replies that the concept of time is qualified in any respect, regardless of how one looks at it.

Jesse's scepticism towards the poem's spontaneous creation,

with his suspicion that the poet is simply working a shrewd scam to entice sentimental tourists into shelling out their small change, is counterbalanced by his ready admission that the lyrical text of the poem – no matter how many times it may or may not have been reused – is undeniably the man's own work, and the fact that he does not directly contradict Celine's feeling of captivation at its words. The following dialogue about time heralds the first major examination of this significant issue in the film, and foreshadows the theme of time having taken on strangely variable attributes during the course of Jesse and Celine's night together, which is discussed in greater detail as the film continues.

By now Celine and Jesse have reached the exterior of a slightly run-down, heavily graffiti-scrawled building. Many colourfully-dressed youths are hanging around outside the door. On deciding that it must be a club, Jesse and Celine decide to go inside for a while. Jesse pays the doorman a hundred schillings – fifty for each of them – in order to gain entry. Once inside, they discover the club to be an intimate and inventively decorated venue, and reasonably well-populated. They stop for a moment to appreciate the vocal work of a musician as he sings and plays his guitar on stage. On finishing the song, he meets with an appreciative round of applause from his audience. Jesse asks Celine if she'll buy him a beer, and they head further into the club towards the bar.

As we cut to the bar area, a reasonably slow pan reveals a group of people playing a table soccer game and others seated around tables as we eventually reach Celine, who is playing pinball. Jesse is watching her performance from the sidelines with interest, a bottle of beer in his hand. Celine also has a beer bottle of her own nearby. After a few moments, she loses the pinball that is in play through the machine's flippers, and exclaims in irritation. Jesse, amused at her exasperation, moves over to take his turn at the controls. As he does so, he takes the opportunity to ask her if she's currently seeing anyone in Paris. She replies that she isn't in a relationship at the present time, having split with her previous boyfriend six months beforehand. As they alternate at the controls of the pinball machine, Jesse politely asks for further details, and she replies that although her partner had many failings she had been traumatised by the break-up and had subsequently become fixated on the relationship that had existed between them. She explains that she had sought the advice of a psychiatrist but, upon finding her counsel unhelpful, eventually got over the ordeal of her own volition. Celine then asks Jesse if he's in a relationship. He is initially evasive, but following some persuasion from Celine he eventually confesses that he had saved money over a long period in order to travel to Barcelona, so that he could spend time with his girlfriend. She had been staying there as part of an art history program, which had separated them for some time. However, on being reunited it soon became apparent that things weren't working out, and they subsequently broke up. Jesse appears bitter at the way that events had unfolded, and is still smarting from the graceless way that his ex-girlfriend had chosen to end their relationship. We then follow the pinball through a few close-up shots of the machine's internal gameplay apparatus.

Jesse chooses this sequence to reveal the story behind his journey to Spain for the first time, and the bitterness that he feels at the scenario which had played out between his ex-girlfriend and himself. Although he pays lip-service to the inevitability of a long-distance relationship running out of steam, his pain is still palpable, and there is a definite feeling that he has been hurt even more significantly than he wants to admit to Celine. Yet Celine's own tale of her recently-dissolved relationship is also very informative of her character; though she previously expresses an understated anxiety of appearing distant and reserved, her account here shows the dramatic effect that heartbreak has had on her and the emotional turmoil that she has gone through. (Her inability to deal with the separation from her former partner also provides a subtle foretelling of her personal situation several years later in *Before Sunset*.) Although both Jesse and Celine use humour to play down the rawness of their feelings, we are now in absolutely no doubt of their respective potential for romantic engagement or depth of emotion.

The camera is following Celine and Jesse's legs and feet from behind as they progress up a flight of stairs. We then cut to their upper bodies as they continue to move, now heading towards the camera. Jesse is discussing a breed of monkeys who, inclined to a behaviour that favours sexual procreation, are always docile and happy – proof, he believes, that promiscuity is really no bad thing. Celine deems this to be an old argument that men tend to use whenever they want to justify licentiousness. Jesse then goes on to talk about the perceived willingness of women to put men in precarious or dangerous situations, thus risking their destruction either voluntarily or involuntarily. Celine points out that the same can be said of the role of men in ruining women, but suggests that they move onto another topic of conversation – it is an age-old trusim that they agree there is no point in revisiting. As they stroll along a cobbled road, she ventures that such gender-related discussions have been going on for time immemorial, and never meet with any firm conclusions.

The mild distrust that Jesse expresses towards women never reaches the level of generalised misogyny, borne out of his resentment towards his ex-girlfriend and other past relationships, but appears instead to be a deep wariness of misandry. Celine does not accept this, and is quick to inform Jesse that for every woman wishing to entice a man into a hazardous situation, the same conditions can also be observed if the genders are reversed. Jesse has little appetite to argue the point further, appearing to see her point, and his ready agreement with Celine's decision to curtail this thread of the conversation confirms that both of them acknowledge that the debate is not one which is winnable by either gender.

A belly-dancer is performing on a richly-woven carpet near the main thoroughfare. We cut back to see Jesse and Celine walking nearby. Noticing the dancer's movements, Celine recognises that her performance is actually a birth dance. A passer-by puts some money into a bowl which lies adjacent to the carpet to collect small change from the audience; an oil lamp and the dancer's discarded shoes can also be seen close by. The dance comes to an end, and the crowd applaud warmly. Jesse asks Celine if she thinks that he should leave a donation, and she responds in the affirmative. After he has parted with some of his coinage, he and Celine move off into a commercial area. Brightly-lit shop windows, tastefully decorated, can be seen in the near distance. Celine explains the ritual nature of the birthing dance to Jesse. Once he has heard her account, Jesse openly doubts that his own mother would have approved of this ceremony taking place at his own birth.

As they make their way along a series of narrow streets, Jesse asks – largely rhetorically – what the men do while women partake in such ritual dances. Celine wryly responds that human males should be grateful that their partners don't kill them after mating, as happens in some parts of the insect world. Jesse notes that the destruction of men is a topic that is being raised with increasing frequency in their conversation, a revelation which seems to surprise Celine. She replies that although her independence as a woman is very important to her, loving and being loved is a deeply significant thing in her life. Celine reflects that much of what people do in life is often geared towards attracting and retaining love, and asks Jesse's opinion on the matter.

He takes a seat on a pile of wooden loading pallets nearby, and Celine joins him. Seeming melancholic as well as contemplative, Jesse says that while there are times that he relishes taking on the mantle of husband and father in the future, there are other occasions where he is unsure of how comfortably he would fit into such a function. He adds that this doesn't come from a fear of responsibility, but rather that it derives from an anxiety that he couldn't succeed at it quite as well as he would want to – better to depart the earth knowing that you had excelled at one thing rather than being simply mediocre in the pursuit of another. Celine relates the story of an older employer she had worked for who had, in his early fifties, realised that he had devoted himself single-mindedly to his professional duties at the expense of all else, and was deeply saddened by his awareness of this fact when it was too late to act upon it; his youth was already spent. Happiness and fulfilment, Celine concludes, can only come out of the attempt at forging a meaningful bond between oneself and others, even when such an endeavour may sometimes seem ostensibly fruitless. Thoughtfully, the pair regard each other in silence.

Celine uses this juncture to finally put to rest Jesse's concerns about gender conflict, emphasising the deep need for most people – regardless of their sexual characteristics – to give and receive love. This may not necessarily be limited to romantic love, however – Jesse's evocation of the family unit, and Celine's story of her regretful past employer, enlarge the scope of the issue to examine the many applications of affection and the vital bonds which can establish themselves between human beings. Once again, there is a sense that both Jesse and Celine have discovered a significant shared understanding that they both recognise to be true.

We cut to a wide-angle shot of a classically-furnished restaurant. Dark wooden panelling and elegant wall lights surround the room's perimeter, and the tables are well-populated for late evening. Jesse and Celine are sitting across from one another at a table on the extreme left of the frame. There follows a number of cuts around the room. A waiter arranges two roses in a pint-glass half filled with water; a group of five men and women in their mid-twenties take part in a lively debate in German; a pair of men in their late thirties (one of them smoking a cigarette) chat as they play cards; a pair of bearded intellectuals in their sixties talk energetically (also in the German language) as one brandishes a cigar for conversational effect, and a lonely young woman sits in brooding silence, her spectacles and a packet of cigarettes laid out on the table in front of her. At another table, a disgruntled American couple in their early thirties complain about the service, the man considering that it typifies the decline of European civilisation in microcosm, while by contrast a trio of Austrians in their forties laugh heartily as they enjoy each other's company. Cutting back to Celine and Jesse, smiling at each other over the table, Celine is making a suggestion: she's going to telephone her friend in Paris, who she was supposed to be meeting on her return (though, she suggests, this event will obviously now have to be delayed). Jesse is a little surprised to see that she doesn't intend to literally call her friend; she's suggesting a role-play exercise instead. Pretending to phone her up, with Jesse taking up the role of the Parisian friend, she initially chats to him in French. They each use their hands to mime telephone receivers. Jesse – struggling with the foreign language – quickly suggests that they practice speaking English instead, just for laughs. Celine agrees, and goes on to explain the situation that has unfolded; she relates her meeting with Jesse, her instant attraction to him, and the way that the connection between them had sufficiently bewitched her to the point that she would have been willing to follow him off the train even if he hadn't asked her to. She goes on to speak of his virtues and what interests her so deeply about him, but worries that she may have offered an unappealing depiction of herself as the day has progressed – does he think that she's a scheming, calculating individual, when really she feels that she's a caring and affectionate person? Jesse, still pretending to be her Parisian friend, says that she should trust her instincts; surely her American admirer sees her for the kind, loving person that she really is? When he asks if she and Jesse will be seeing each other again, Celine replies that they haven't discussed the issue, and abruptly changes the subject – now it's Jesse's turn to 'call' one of his own friends. This he does, and Celine replies with an exaggerated 'surfer dude' accent that seems to catch Jesse momentarily off-guard. In character as his friend, Celine enquires about Jesse's encounter with his (now-ex) girlfriend in Spain, and he briefly sketches out the events of his break-up as well as his travels through Europe thus far. He then moves on to discuss meeting Celine, and describes her in such glowing terms that Celine herself appears almost embarrassed to hear his words. He says that he's concerned about what she thinks of him, and she replies that she must have liked him enough to sit beside him on the train in the first place. But then, she adds, what do men ever really understand about women anyway?

This scene, with its spur of the moment role-play session, is one of the film's most touching sequences. By using a play-acting premise to blunt the heightened self-awareness required to directly express their feelings to one another, the pair are able to articulate exactly how much affection they have for the other without the need to suppress the exuberance of their feelings. Yet as is signified with Celine's nimble avoidance of the issue of their potential for being reunited in the future, the fragile issue of their new love being preserved over the miles which divide them is a subject that they still have to address but are clearly afraid to approach.

Jesse and Celine are now sitting on an elevated walkway overlooking a well-lit Viennese street. Jesse casually straddles a low wall, his legs dangling over either side of it, while Celine stands in a relaxed pose nearby. They discuss the strangely rarefied experience that they are living through, almost as though time has stood still and the only thing that matters is their encounter with each other. Celine compares it to a fairytale, and subtly emphasises her sadness at the prospect of their meeting coming to its inevitable conclusion. They briefly kiss again, and then look out into the street together in silence.

We cut to an establishment shot of a ship-bound restaurant moored to the shore. Cutting next to a floating candle on one of the restaurant's tables, Jesse can be heard speaking before the camera eventually moves on to his face. He is talking about the fixed nature of time, which makes our limited tenure on the planet so important. Celine, motivated by the subject of life and experience ultimately being finite, ruminates on the improbable likelihood that they will ever meet again. Jesse is downcast at this prospect, and they consider the possibilities of how they could keep a relationship alive over such a long distance. After they bounce some ideas back and forward, Celine – though unhappy at the conclusion – reflects that it would be irrational and unrealistic to expect the two of them to maintain any kind of true romance under the circumstances, and that such relationships inevitably fade in any respect because of the geographical factors that are at work. Though obviously disappointed, Jesse sees the sense behind her logic and agrees with her; it would be a great pity to allow the memory of their wonderful romantic encounter to become tarnished by allowing it to simply fizzle out. Thus they decide not to exchange phone numbers or addresses, but rather to continue to enjoy the night for what it is – a beautiful but finite experience for the both of them. As they come to this decision, a violinist and accordion player come onto the deck; Jesse is the first to notice them. They shake hands as they pledge to enjoy the rest of their time in each other's company. Celine is upset that the shadow of their parting will now haunt the rest of their time together, but Jesse instead suggests that they say goodbye to each other there and then – that way, they won't have to worry about their actual separation when it eventually comes later on. This they do in a superficially jokey manner, though their respective expressions and significant eye contact clearly show that they are both dreading the prospect of actually leaving one another when the time comes. Celine is the first to break their shared gaze, looking over at the two musicians. Jesse looks newly pensive.

Now that the pair have discussed the inevitability of their parting, there is a sense that the genie has finally escaped the bottle. As Celine surmises, the growing realisation that their time together is running out has the potential to eclipse the remainder of their encounter, as does their shared agreement that they won't make any attempt to keep in touch after they have gone their separate ways. Their growing self-consciousness of these facts, and subsequent attempts to renegotiate them while they still can, does indeed inform their rationale with increasing frequency from this point onwards.

A pair of trams are rolling along a street, one at a higher elevation than the other but both following parallel tracks. The sky has lightened very slightly, signifying that dusk is beginning to approach. A tracking shot of some shop exteriors then follows, suggesting the view from one of the tram windows. We cut to Jesse and Celine descending a flight of stairs, heading towards what appears to be a bar. The corridor is harshly illuminated in red light, and reasonably loud (if slightly muffled) music can be heard from the room at the bottom of the stairs. Jesse is quickly reiterating the details of a plan that they have hatched between them; he plans to procure a bottle of red wine, while she must purloin two glasses. Seemingly in good spirits about this notion, she confirms her understanding of the scheme to him. They emerge into a dimly-lit bar area, complete with a few scattered patrons and an impressive range of bottles on prominent display. Celine and Jesse then go their separate ways, with Jesse making a bee-line for the bartender. Although he doesn't speak much English, the bartender listens attentively as Jesse outlines the unusual story of the romantic night that he and Celine are currently enjoying together. He appears suspicious when Jesse explains that they need a bottle of red wine to put the finishing touches to their experience, but that he no longer has any ready cash left. However, Jesse suggests that he would willingly send payment in full at a later date if the bartender will provide him with the postal address of his bar. Eventually the Austrian man agrees, and they shake hands on the matter. The whole exchange is intercut with Celine surreptitiously removing a couple of wine glasses from a nearby table and secreting them away in her bag. The bartender wanders away momentarily, with Jesse making a silent 'victory' gesture to Celine in his absence, and then returns with the promised bottle of wine. He warmly wishes Jesse a great night, and is thanked sincerely in response. The bartender watches them in silent amusement as they depart.

The camera pans down from some green treetops into an area of lush parkland. An owl can be heard hooting in the near distance. Celine and Jesse are lying on the ground together, Jesse draining the last of the wine from his glass before placing it on the grass and rolling onto his back. The pair are staring up at the full moon in the sky above them. Celine reflects that she has had many beautiful moments in her life – tiny isolated instants of beauty and significance – but was always aware that the people who were with her at the time were somehow unable to share in the wonder she felt at the time. She does, however, feel glad to be in Jesse's company on this unique night together. Jesse asks her if she feels they could ever have other similar experiences together, but she laughs his question off, asking if he has so quickly forgotten their promise to be responsible and rational about the fact that they'll never see each other again. Picking up on her earlier thought, Jesse says that he knows exactly what she means about experiencing such exceptional incidents in life, but that he always believed that he himself was an unwelcome interloper whenever they took place. He pushes himself up onto his elbow to address her directly. Jesse explains that because he is naturally such a familiar presence at all the activities in life that he participates in, he has begun to feel tired of himself, adding that if he and Celine were together over a long period of time she would also inevitably become irritated by his mannerisms and some of his character traits. Lying back again, he adds that when they are together, he finds that he can lose himself in an unusual and welcoming way that can only be matched by drugs or alcohol... or, Celine suggests, sex. Turning to face each other, she says that all she wants at that moment is to be kissed. Jesse readily agrees with her sentiment, and they embrace tenderly. After a few moments, she breaks away and sits up, saying that she feels that they shouldn't have intercourse – as they don't plan to see each other again, she'll feel a close bond with him as a result of their actions that she'll never be able to engage with again. Jesse suggests that they could ignore their pact and decide to make an attempt at keeping their relationship going, but Celine laughs it off, saying that she doesn't want to fly in the face of common sense just for the sake of making love. Seeming keen not to upset her, Jesse agrees. As she lies back again, she then asks him – half jokingly – if this means that he doesn't really want to see her again. Sitting up again, he replies that if he had the chance of never seeing her again or being forced to marry her there and then, he would choose marriage without a second thought. Celine responds that she felt that she'd made her mind up about having sex with him before she'd left the train, but now that they've got to know each other so well she's unsure about whether that is still true. Half out of frustration and half out of genuine amusement, they laugh while still drawing closer to each other. They kiss again. Celine asks Jesse why she has to make things so complex, but Jesse replies that he has no answer for that particular question. Their embrace becomes much more animated and passionate as the camera draws back.

With this sequence, any lingering doubt of the significance of the relationship between Celine and Jesse is soundly eradicated; their frank and unequivocal admission that getting to know each other has somehow transcended all of their previous expectations with regard to interpersonal relationships further bolsters the depth of feeling that has grown between them. Yet although it is implied that their unique romantic bond is now consummated, neither of them appears to consider the act to be the apex of their time together; quite the contrary, in fact, given their renewed awareness of the ever-nearing conclusion of their encounter and subsequent vain attempts to circumvent the finality that it presents.

It is now early morning. The sky, though still slightly dim, is suggestive of late dusk as we see it emerging from above the treetops. We cut to some Viennese rooftops, and then to a stretch of pavement near a slightly run-down building. Celine and Jesse are walking along this paved area in companionable silence. Jesse takes Celine's hand; she offers no resistance to the gesture. He asks her what she'll do when she finally gets home, to which she replies that she'll probably get in contact with her mother and father. When asked the same question, Jesse responds that he'll have to collect his dog from the home of his friend, who has been looking after the pet in his absence. Jesse seems pained for a moment as he realises that, with the arrival of morning, their time together is finally coming to an end. Celine is likewise unhappy about the fact. As they ruminate on this unfortunate detail, they hear the sound of someone playing a harpsichord. Tracing it to a nearby building, they quietly sneak up to a low window and look down into a beautifully furnished basement apartment. A young man is playing intently from a book of sheet music, totally oblivious to their presence. Back on the pavement, moved by the composition, Jesse takes Celine in his arms and they dance. He asks if you can, in fact, actually dance to harpsichord music, and Celine responds in the affirmative. As he spins her around, he is momentarily taken aback by her beauty, and tells her that he wants to take a photograph of her in his mind so that he will never allow himself to forget her or the moment they have found themselves in. He takes a step back, stares into her smiling face for a few seconds, and then kisses her. She puts her arms around him and they embrace warmly. Celine seems pained to let go of him. Hand in hand, they continue along the street and out of shot.

After a few shots of historical Viennese buildings, we are reunited with Celine and Jesse on the steps of a monument. Jesse is in a seated position, with Celine lying down next to him. Reflecting on the small amount of time that now remains to them, Jesse quotes a W.H. Auden poem (*As I Walked One Evening*) that he remembers hearing recited by Dylan Thomas on an old recording in the past. Celine seems to appreciate its sentiment. She says that whereas earlier Jesse had suggested that couples eventually tire of each other's quirks and characteristics, she doesn't feel that this would be true for her. Instead, she would

THE CINEMA OF RICHARD LINKLATER   229

consider such familiarity to be a positive factor, for building such an intimate knowledge of a partner would truly herald an ever more lasting love between her and them. She reaches out and affectionately strokes Jesse's hair and face. At that moment, Jesse remembers that they had completely forgotten to attend the play that they had been invited to earlier – *Bring Me the Horns of Wilmington's Cow*. Celine laughs as she remembers their encounter with the actors, though she doesn't seem too bothered at having missed the experience of their play. She and Jesse look longingly at each other once again.

The unexpected appearance of the harpsichord player in his room of impeccable historical finery, combined with the evocative words of Auden's poem, again communicates the notion of Celine and Jesse's oddly timeless encounter just as it also conveys the fact that their meeting is about to come to an end. While the essence of their time together has thus far been the beauty of its unhurried, free-wheeling quality which has given them ample opportunity to get to know each other over the course of its duration, this strangely hermetic experience is now in the process of being dispelled just as rapidly as it first took form.

We see Jesse and Celine from the back as they head along a train platform. A train is currently at a standstill near the platform, and passengers are boarding and disembarking all around them. They both have one of their hands resting on the handle of Celine's travelling bag, now back from storage. Celine and Jesse are both now beginning to seem increasingly emotional at the prospect of their imminent parting. Celine asks if Jesse is certain of all the details of his travel plans. He replies that he is. Celine spots the carriage that she wants to board, and they draw to a halt, both of them obviously dreading what has to come next.

Now unabashedly upset at their parting, they find themselves tongue-tied and unable to find a suitable way to wrap up their encounter. They hold each other, break apart and embrace each other again as they wish one another well for their respective futures. They kiss passionately one last time, heartbroken at their separation, but both aware that the train is about to depart from the platform. At the very last moment, Jesse suggests that they forget their earlier agreement and keep in touch after all. Celine agrees – she had been waiting for him to suggest it, not wanting to do so herself in case he didn't want to extend the relationship. Their dialogue begins to be accompanied by the sound of train announcements from the station's tannoy system in the distance. Jesse suggests that they meet again in Vienna, and Celine suggests they do so in five years' time. Thinking fast, Jesse feels that this is a very long period of time, and proposes they meet in a year's time instead. Happy with the arrangement, she agrees, but then he suddenly suggests making it six months instead. The both concur with the plan to meet six months from the previous day, 16th June, at 6pm at the station's ninth track. Thus they will exactly replicate the conditions of their first arrival in Vienna, half a year onwards. With this agreement in place, they both consent not to write or call each other – it can wait until they're reunited in December. The prospect of their reunion numbing the pain they feel at their severance, they kiss one final time before Celine races aboard the train with her luggage. Moments later, the platform now much quieter, the train's doors slide closed. Jesse saunters along the side of the train as Celine wanders along the corridor of her carriage. Finding an empty compartment, she stores away her baggage and takes a seat by the window. The train begins to move away. Back at the station, Jesse is alone with his own bag. He is heading from the platform onto a central concourse, and – obviously still emotional at his parting from Celine – heads down on an escalator.

Linklater's choice of the 16th of June for Jesse and Celine's meeting is noteworthy. The date is the same summer's day which provides the backdrop for the narrative of James Joyce's *Ulysses* (1922), which witnessed Joyce's protagonist Leopold Bloom traversing the city of Dublin in a similarly meandering fashion to Celine and Jesse's impromptu amble around Vienna. For Bloom, the 16th of June (or Bloomsday, as it has latterly become known) was a strangely significant day that could never be repeated, and indeed the experiences that have affected Jesse and Celine are likewise indelible even as their relationship itself may still prove to be ephemeral. Both characters leave Vienna as profoundly changed individuals, and yet the judgement lies entirely in the mind of the audience as to the likelihood of whether Jesse and Celine would actually make their December date, or indeed would ever be reunited in the future. (This issue would remain unresolved until the release of Linklater's sequel, *Before Sunset*, in 2004.)

The film closes with a montage of shots showing the various different places that Jesse and Celine had visited during their time in Vienna. Many of them seem different in daylight, having previously been seen only in the darkness of night. The bridge over the railway tracks, where they had met the two amateur actors. The floating restaurant on the Danube, and the table they had shared together. The walkway overlooking the Viennese street. The wooden pallet in the narrow alleyway where they had discussed the nature of love. The cemetery of the nameless, now deserted. The famous Wiener Prater Ferris wheel, currently not in motion. The fountain and outdoor café where they had met the fortune teller, closed at this hour, as an elderly man walks past with a carrier bag. The riverside walkway near the Danube, where the street poet (now long gone) had composed *Daydream Delusion*. The area of parkland where the couple had shared their intimate embrace; their discarded bottle of wine is still lying on the ground as a lady in her late seventies, a canvas bag in her hand, makes her way slowly through the area. All of the scenes seem strangely lifeless, and sometimes even melancholic, without the presence of Celine and Jesse to bring them alive.

On a seat in a coach, Jesse is staring out of one of the windows. His expression is distant. His baggage is laid out on the seat next to him. Abstractedly, he starts to look around, then stares ahead and closes his eyes. Perhaps in remembrance of what he has just experienced, a beatific smile spreads across his face.

We then cut to Celine on her train, the landscape hurtling past her through the adjacent window. Her Georges Bataille book is on her lap. Her expression is contemplative and a little sad as she stares ahead, though she too eventually smiles gently. She rests her head against the side of the carriage and contentedly closes her eyes and we fade to black and the credits roll.

Notes and References

CHRONOLOGICAL FILMOGRAPHY

It's Impossible to Learn to Plow by Reading Books (1988)

Production Company: Detour Filmproduction.
Director: Richard Linklater.
Producer: Richard Linklater.
Screenplay: Richard Linklater.
Film Editor: Richard Linklater.
Running Time: 85 minutes.
Main Cast: Richard Linklater, James Goodwin, Dan Kratochvil, Linda Finney, Tracy Crabtree, Linda Levine, Lisa Schiebold, Erin McAfee, D. Montgomery, Scott Van Horn, Daniel Johnston, Tammy Gomez, Keith McCormack.

Slacker (1991)

Production Company: Detour Filmproduction.
Distributor: Orion.
Director: Richard Linklater.
Producer: Richard Linklater.
Screenplay: Richard Linklater.
Film Editor: Scott Rhodes.
Cinematography: Lee Daniel.
Production Manager: Anne Walker-McBay.
Production Design: Deborah Pastor.
Casting: Anne Walker-McBay.
Graphics: Ron Marks.
Art Department: Denise Montgomery and Debbie Pastor.
Sound: D. Montgomery.
Running Time: 97 minutes.
Main Cast: Richard Linklater (Should Have Stayed at Bus Station), Rudy Basquez (Taxi Driver), Jean Caffeine (Roadkill), Jan Hockey (Jogger), Stephan Hockey (Running Late), Mark James (Hit-and-Run Son), Samuel Dietert (Grocery Grabber of Death's Bounty), Bob Boyd (Officer Bozzio), Terrence Kirk (Officer Love), Keith McCormack (Street Musician), Jennifer Schaudies (Walking to Coffee Shop), Dan Kratochvil (Espresso Czar/Masonic Malcontent), Maris Strautmanis (Giant Cappucino), Brecht Andersch (Dostoyevsky Wannabe), Tom Pallotta (Looking for Missing Friend), Jerry Delony (Been on the Moon Since the Fifties), Heather West (Tura Satana Lookalike), John Spath (Co-op Guy), Ron Marks (Bush Basher), Daniel Dugan (Comb Game Player), Brian Crockett (Sadistic Comb Game Player), Scott Marcus (Ultimate Loser),

Stella Weir (Stephanie from Dallas), Teresa Taylor (Papsmear Pusher), Greg Wilson (Anti-Traveller), Gina Lalli (Sidewalk Psychic), Lori Capp (Traumatised Yacht Owner), Louis Black (Paranoid Paper Reader), Nigel Benchoff (Budding Capitalist Youth), Kevin Whitley (Jilted Boyfriend), Steven Anderson (Guy Who Tosses Typewriter), David Haymond (Street Dweller), John Slate (Conspiracy A-Go-Go Author), Charles Gunning (Hitchhiker Awaiting "True Call"), Tamsy Ringler (Video Interviewer), Louis Mackey (Old Anarchist), Kathy McCarty (Anarchist's Daughter), Michael Laird (Burglar), Kalman Spelletich (Video Backpacker), D. Montgomery (Having a Breakthrough Day), R. Malice (Scooby Doo Philosopher), Mark Quirk (Papa Smurf), Lucinda Scott (Dairy Queen Photographer), Wammo (Anti-Artist), Joseph Jones (Old Man Recording Thoughts), Sean Coffey (Super-8 Cameraman), Greg Ward (Tosses Camera Off Cliff).

Dazed and Confused (1993)

Production Company: Detour Filmproduction/Alphaville Films.
Distributor: Universal Pictures.
Director: Richard Linklater.
Producers: Sean Daniel, James Jacks and Richard Linklater.
Co-Producer: Anne Walker-McBay.
Screenplay: Richard Linklater.
Film Editor: Sandra Adair.
Cinematography: Lee Daniel.
Production Manager: Alma Kuttruff.
Music Editor: Jeff Charbonneau.
Sound Editor: Clayton Collins
Production Design: John Frick.
Casting: Don Phillips.
Art Direction: Jenny C. Patrick.
Set Decoration: Deborah Pastor.
Costume Design: Katherine Dover.
Running Time: 103 minutes.
Main Cast: Jason London (Randall 'Pink' Floyd), Rory Cochrane (Ron Slater), Wiley Wiggins (Mitch Kramer), Sasha Jenson (Don Dawson), Michelle Burke (Jodi Kramer), Adam Goldberg (Mike Newhouse), Anthony Rapp (Tony Olson), Matthew McConaughey (David Wooderson), Marissa Ribisi (Cynthia Dunn), Shawn Andrews (Kevin Pickford), Cole Hauser (Benny O'Donnell), Milla Jovovich (Michelle Burroughs), Joey Lauren Adams (Simone Kerr), Christin Hinojosa

(Sabrina Davis), Ben Affleck (Fred O'Bannion), Jason O. Smith (Melvin Spivey), Deena Martin (Shavonne Wright), Parker Posey (Darla Marks), Nicky Katt (Clint Bruno).

Before Sunrise (1995)

Production Company: Detour Filmproduction / Castle Rock Entertainment / Filmhaus Wien
Universa Filmpro / Sunrise Production / Columbia Pictures.
Distributor: Columbia Pictures.
Director: Richard Linklater.
Producer: Anne Walker-McBay.
Co-Producers: Wolfgang Ramml, Gernot Schaffler and Ellen Winn Wendl.
Associate Producer: Gregory Jacobs.
Executive Producer: John Sloss.
Screenplay: Richard Linklater and Kim Krizan.
Film Editors: Sandra Adair and Sheri Galloway.
Cinematography: Lee Daniel.
Production Manager: Bernhard Schmatz.
Original Score: Fred Frith.
Production Design: Florian Reichmann.
Casting: Alycia Aumuller.
Costume Design: Florentina Welley.
Running Time: 105 minutes.
Main Cast: Ethan Hawke (Jesse), Julie Delpy (Celine), Andrea Eckert (Wife on Train), Hänno Poschl (Husband on Train), Karl Bruckschweaiger (Guy on Bridge), Tex Rubinowitz (Guy on Bridge), Erni Mangold (Palm Reader), Dominik Castell (Street Poet), Haymon Maria Buttinger (Bartender), Harold Waiglein (Guitarist in Club), Bilge Jeschim (Belly Dancer), Wolfgang Glüxam (Harpsichord Player).

SubUrbia (1996)

Production Company: Detour Filmproduction / Castle Rock Entertainment.
Distributor: Sony Pictures Classics / Warner Brothers Pictures.
Director: Richard Linklater.
Producer: Anne Walker-McBay.
Line Producer: Ginger Sledge.
Executive Producer: John Sloss.

Screenplay: Eric Bogosian, from the play by Eric Bogosian.
Film Editor: Sandra Adair.
Director of Photography: Lee Daniel.
Post-Production Supervisor: Amy Lowrey.
Production Design: Catherine Hardwicke.
Casting: Alycia Aumuller and Judy Henderson.
Art Direction: Seth Reed.
Set Decoration: Keith Fletcher.
Costume Design: Melanie Armstrong Fletcher.
Running Time: 121 minutes.
Main Cast: Jayce Bartok (Pony), Amie Carey (Sooze), Nicky Katt (Tim), Ajay Naidu (Nazeer Choudhury), Parker Posey (Erica), Giovanni Ribisi (Jeff), Samia Shoaib (Pakeesa Choudhury), Dina Spybey (Bee-Bee), Steve Zahn (Buff), Kitt Brophy (Sooze's Mom), Jonn Cherico (Shopping Channel Host), Keith Preusse (Officer Chip), Eric Park (Officer Gary), William Martin Hayes (Scuff), Bill Wise (George the Limo Driver), M.J. Lin (Restaurant Hostess).

The Newton Boys (1998)

Production Company: Detour Filmproduction / Twentieth Century Fox / Newton Boys Ventures Inc.
Distributor: Twentieth Century Fox Film Corporation.
Director: Richard Linklater.
Producer: Anne Walker-McBay.
Co-Producer: Clark Lee Walker.
Associate Producer: Keith Fletcher.
Executive Producer: John Sloss.
Screenplay: Richard Linklater, Claude Stanush and Clark Lee Walker, from the book by Claude Stanush.
Film Editor: Sandra Adair.
Director of Photography: Peter James.
Unit Production Manager: Bill Scott.
Original Score: Edward D. Barnes.
Production Design: Catherine Hardwicke.
Casting: Don Phillips.
Art Direction: Andrea Dopaso, John Frick and Randy Moore.
Set Decoration: Jeanette Scott.
Costume Design: Shelley Komarov.
Running Time: 113 minutes.
Main Cast: Matthew McConaughey (Willis Newton), Skeet Ulrich (Joe

Newton), Ethan Hawke (Jess Newton), Gail Cronauer (Ma Newton), Vincent D'Onofrio (Dock Newton), Julianna Margulies (Louise Brown), Dwight Yoakam (Brentwood Glasscock), Charles Gunning (Slim), Becket Gremmels (Lewis), Glynn Williams (Farmer Williams), Chloe Webb (Avis Glasscock), Jennifer Miriam (Catherine), Angie Chase (Kat), Lynn Mathis (Arthur Adams), Bo Hopkins (K.P. Aldrich), Tommy Townsend (Omaha Detective), Joe Stevens (Bank Association President), Ken Farmer (Frank Hamer), Daniel Tucker Kamin (District Attorney), David Jensen (William Fahy), Luke Askew (Chief Schoemaker).

Waking Life (2001)

Production Company: Detour Filmproduction / Fox Searchlight Pictures / Independent Film Channel / Thousand Words / Flat Black Films / Line Research.

Distributor: Twentieth Century Fox Film Corporation.

Director: Richard Linklater.

Producers: Tommy Pallotta, Jonah Smith, Anne Walker-McBay and Palmer West.

Executive Producers: Caroline Kaplan, Jonathan Sehring and John Sloss.

Screenplay: Richard Linklater.

Film Editor: Sandra Adair.

Cinematography: Richard Linklater and Tommy Pallotta.

Post-Production Supervisor: Patrick Lindenmaier.

Original Score: Glover Gill.

Casting: Lizzie Curry Martinez.

Art Direction: Bob Sabiston.

Running Time: 99 minutes.

Main Voice Cast: Wiley Wiggins (Main Character), Trevor Jack Brooks (Young Boy Playing Paper Game), Lorelei Linklater (Young Girl Playing Paper Game), Bill Wise (Boat Car Guy), Robert C. Solomon (Philosophy Professor), Kim Krizan (Herself), Eamonn Healy (Shape-Shifting Man), J.C. Shakespeare (Self-Burning Man), Ethan Hawke (Jesse), Julie Delpy (Celine), Charles Gunning (Angry Man in Jail), David Sosa (Himself), Alex Jones (Man in Car with P.A.), Otto Hofmann (Himself), Aklilu Gebrewold (Himself), Steve Fitch (Chimpanzee), Louis Mackey (Himself), Alex Nixon (Man Writing Novel at the Bar), Violet Nichols (Woman Talking to the Novel Writer), Steven Prince (Man Talking to the Bartender), Ken Webster (Bartender), Jason T. Hodge (Man with the Long Hair), Guy Forsyth (Himself), John Christensen (Guy Talking about

Turning the Light on in Dreams), Caveh Zahedi (Himself), David Jewell (Man Talking to Caveh), R.C. Whittaker (Man on the Lamppost), Hymie Samuelson (Mr Debord), David Martinez (Man on the Train), Speed Levitch (Himself), Marta Banda (Friendly Girl), Steven Soderbergh (Interviewed on Television), Charles Murdock (Old Man), Mona Lee (Quiet Woman at Restaurant), Louis Black (Kierkegaard Disciple), Richard Linklater (Pinball Playing Man).

Tape (2001)

Production Company: Detour Filmproduction / IFC Productions / InDigEnt / The Independent Film Channel Productions / Tape Productions Inc.
Distributor: Bir Film / Lions Gate Films / Metrodome Distribution / Media Suits / Upstream Pictures.
Director: Richard Linklater.
Producers: Alexis Alexanian, Anne Walker-McBay and Gary Winick.
Co-Producers: Robert Cole and David Richenthal.
Executive Producers: Caroline Kaplan, Jonathan Sehring and John Sloss.
Screenplay: Stephen Belber, from the play by Stephen Belber.
Film Editor: Sandra Adair.
Cinematography: Maryse Alberti.
Production Supervisor: Jake Abraham.
Production Design: Stephen J. Beatrice.
Set Decoration: Christopher P. Peroni.
Costume Design: Catherine Thomas.
Running Time: 86 minutes.
Main Cast: Ethan Hawke (Vince), Robert Sean Leonard (Jon Salter), Uma Thurman (Amy Randall).

The School of Rock (2003)

Production Company: Paramount Pictures / Scott Rudin Productions / MFP Munich Film Partners GmbH & Company I. Produktions KG.
Distributor: Paramount Pictures / United International Pictures.
Director: Richard Linklater.
Producer: Scott Rudin.
Executive Producers: Scott Aversano and Steve Nicolaides.
Screenplay: Mike White.
Film Editor: Sandra Adair.

Cinematography: Rogier Stoffers.
Unit Production Manager: Joseph E. Iberti.
Original Score: Craig Wedren.
Production Design: Jeremy Conway.
Casting: Ilene Starger.
Art Direction: Adam Scher.
Set Decoration: Karin Wiesel Holmes.
Costume Design: Karen Patch.
Running Time: 108 minutes.
Main Cast: Jack Black (Dewey Finn), Adam Pascal (Theo), Lucas Papaelias (Neil), Chris Stack (Doug), Sarah Silverman (Patty Di Marco),Mike White (Ned Schneebly), Lucas Babin (Spider), Joan Cusack (Rosalie Mullins), Jordan-Claire Green (Michelle), Veronica Afflerbach (Eleni), Miranda Cosgrove (Summer Hathaway), Joey Gaydos Jr. (Zack Mooneyham), Robert Tsai (Lawrence), Angelo Massagli (Frankie), Kevin Clark (Freddy Jones), Maryam Hassan (Tomika), Caitlin Hale (Marta), Cole Hawkins (Leonard), Brian Falduto (Billy), James Hosey (Marco), Aleisha Allen (Alicia), Zachary Infante (Gordon), Rebecca Brown (Katie), Jaclyn Neidenthal (Emily).

Before Sunset (2004)

Production Company: Detour Filmproduction / Castle Rock Entertainment.
Distributor: Warner Brothers Pictures.
Director: Richard Linklater.
Producers: Anne Walker-McBay and Richard Linklater.
Co-Producer: Isabelle Coulet.
Executive Producer: John Sloss.
Screenplay: Richard Linklater, Julie Delpy and Ethan Hawke, from a story by Richard Linklater and Kim Krizan.
Film Editor: Sandra Adair.
Cinematography: Lee Daniel.
Unit Production Manager: Jean-Marc Abbou.
Post-Production Supervisor: Sara Johnson.
Production Design: Baptiste Glaymann.
Costume Design: Thierry Delettre.
Running Time: 77 minutes.
Main Cast: Ethan Hawke (Jesse), Julie Delpy (Celine), Vernon Dobtcheff (Bookstore Manager), Louise Lemoine Torres (Journalist #1), Rodolphe Pauly (Journalist #2), Mariane Plasteig (Waitress), Diabolo

(Philippe), Denis Evrard (Boat Attendant), Albert Delpy (Man at Grill), Marie Pillet (Woman in Courtyard).

Bad News Bears (2005)

Production Company: Detour Filmproduction / Geyer Kosinski / Media Talent Group.
    Distributor: Paramount Pictures / United International Pictures.
    Director: Richard Linklater.
    Producer: J. Geyer Kosinski and Richard Linklater.
    Co-Producers: Bruce Heller.
    Associate Producers: Adam Ellison, Sara Greene and Brad Marks.
    Executive Producer: Marcus Viscidi.
    Screenplay: Bill Lancaster, Glenn Ficarra and John Requa.
    Film Editor: Sandra Adair.
    Cinematography: Rogier Stoffers.
    Production Supervisor: Eileen Malyszko Lee.
    Original Score: Ed Shearmur.
    Production Design: Bruce Curtis.
    Casting: Joseph Middleton.
    Art Direction: David Lazan.
    Set Decoration: Brana Rosenfeld.
    Costume Design: Karen Patch.
    Running Time: 113 minutes.
    Main Cast: Billy Bob Thornton (Morris Buttermaker), Greg Kinnear (Roy Bullock), Marcia Gay Harden (Liz Whitewood), Sammi Kane Kraft (Amanda Whurlitzer), Ridge Canipe (Toby Whitewood), Brandon Craggs (Mike Engelberg), Jeffrey Davies (Kelly Leak), Timmy Deters (Tanner Boyle), Carlos Estrada (Miguel Agilar), Emmanuel Estrada (Jose Agilar), Troy Gentile (Matthew Hooper), Kenneth 'K.C.' Harris (Ahmad Abdul Rahim), Aman Johal (Prem Lahiri), Tyler Patrick Jones (Timothy Lupus), Jeffrey Tedmori (Garo Daragebrigadian), Carter Jenkins (Joey Bullock), Seth Adkins (Jimmy), Chase Winton (Ms Cleveland), Arabella Holzbog (Shari Bullock).

A Scanner Darkly (2006)

Production Company: Detour Filmproduction / Warner Independent Pictures / Thousand Words / 3 Arts Entertainment / Section Eight Ltd.
    Distributor: Warner Independent Films.
    Director: Richard Linklater.

Producers: Tommy Pallotta, Jonah Smith, Erwin Stoff, Anne Walker-McBay and Palmer West.

Co-Producers: Erin Ferguson.

Associate Producer: Sara Greene.

Executive Producers: George Clooney, Ben Cosgrove, Jennifer Fox, John Sloss and Steven Soderbergh.

Screenplay: Richard Linklater, from the novel by Philip K. Dick.

Film Editor: Sandra Adair.

Cinematography: Shane F. Kelly.

Unit Production Manager: Susan Kirr.

Executive in Charge of Production: Ravi D. Mehta.

Original Score: Graham Reynolds.

Production Design: Bruce Curtis.

Casting: Denise Chamian and Beth Sepko.

Set Decoration: Joaquin A. Morin.

Costume Design: Kari Perkins.

Running Time: 100 minutes.

Main Cast: Keanu Reeves (Bob Arctor), Robert Downey Jr (James Barris), Woody Harrelson (Ernie Luckman), Rory Cochrane (Charles Freck), Winona Ryder (Donna), Sean Allen (Additional Fred Scramble Suit Voice), Mitch Baker (Brown Bear Lodge Host), Cliff Haby (Voice from Headquarters), Steven Chester Prince (Cop), Natasha Valdez (Waitress), Mark Turner (Additional Hank Scramble Suit Voice), Melody Chase (Arctor's Wife), Alex Jones (Arrested Protester).

Fast Food Nation (2006)

Production Company: BBC Films / HanWay Films / Recorded Picture Company / Participant Productions.

Distributor: Twentieth Century Fox Film Corporation.

Director: Richard Linklater.

Producers: Malcolm McLaren and Jeremy Thomas.

Co-Producer: Ann Carli.

Associate Producers: Sara Greene and Alexandra Stone.

Executive Producer: Jeff Skoll and Peter Watson.

Screenplay: Richard Linklater and Eric Schlosser, from the book by Eric Schlosser.

Film Editor: Sandra Adair.

Cinematography: Lee Daniel.

Unit Production Manager: Victor Ho.

Post-Production Supervisor: Dan Genetti.

Original Score: Friends of Dean Martinez.
Production Design: Bruce Curtis.
Art Direction: Joachin A. Morin.
Set Decoration: Phil Shirey.
Costume Design: Kari Perkins.
Running Time: 116 minutes.
Main Cast: Wilmer Valderrama (Raul), Catalina Sandino Moreno (Sylvia), Ana Claudia Talancón (Coco), Juan Carlos Serrán (Esteban), Armando Hernández (Roberto), Greg Kinnear (Don Henderson), Frank Ertl (Jack Deavers), Michael Conway (Phil), Mitch Baker (Dave), Ellar Salmon (Jay), Dakota Edwards (Stevie), Dana Wheeler-Nicholson (Debi), Luis Guzmán (Benny), Bobby Cannavale (Mike), Francisco Rosales (Jorge), Ashley Johnson (Amber), Paul Dano (Brian), Patricia Arquette (Cindy), Roger Cudney (Terry), Glen Powell (Steve), Cherami Leigh (Kim), Esai Morales (Tony), Yareli Arizmendi (Gloria), Matt Hensarling (Kevin), Mileidy Moron Marchant (Vicky), Kris Kristofferson (Rudy Martin), Raquel Gavia (Rita), Hugo Perez (Francisco), Bruce Willis (Harry Rydell), Helen Merino (Lisa), Erinn Allison (Hotel Desk Clerk), Barbara Chisholm (Waitress), Larizza Salcido Gameros (Maria), Lana Dieterich (UMP Nurse), John Scott Horton (Greg), Ethan Hawke (Pete), Aaron Himelstein (Andrew), Avril Lavigne (Alice), Marco Perella (Tom Watson), Lou Taylor Pucci (Paco), Mónica Cano Mascorro (Magdalene), Cora Cardona (UMP Translator), Humberto Velez (Cesar), Derek Chase Hickey (Restaurant Customer).

Inning By Inning: A Portrait of a Coach (2008)

Production Company: Detour Filmproduction.
Distributor: ESPN Original Entertainment.
Director: Richard Linklater.
Producer: Brian Franklin.
Associate Producers: Sandra Adair and Sara Greene.
Executive Producers: Connor Schell and John Sloss.
Senior Producer: Daniel Silver.
Film Editor: Sandra Adair.
Cinematography: Brian Franklin.
Original Score: Michael McLeod.
Music Editor: Lesley Langs.
Running Time: 106 minutes.
Main Cast: Augie Garrido, Ben Barnes, Bob Bennett, Stan Bush, Bobby Campo, Cathy Clark, Dick Clark, Roger Clemens, Buck Cody, Kevin

Costner, J. Brent Cox, Steve Ditolla, Deloss Dodds, Pete Donovan, Jason Gill, Cliff Hatter, George Horton, Ryan Hueble, Clyde Huyck, Joe Jamail, Seth Johnston, Bill Kernan, Mark Kotsay, Bill Little, Dustin Majewski, Joe Martelli, Mike Mathieson, Clark Millholland, Jose Mota, Phil Nevin, Omar Quintanilla, Jack Reinholtz, Darrell Royal, Ted Silva, Tom Sommers, Neale Stoner, Huston Street, Taylor Teagarden, Curtis Thigpen, Rick Vanderhook, Tim Wallach, Dave Weatherman, Scott Wright.

Me and Orson Welles (2008)

Production Company: Detour Filmproduction / CinemaNX / Cinetic Media / Framestore / Fuzzy Bunny Films.
Distributor: Freestyle Releasing / New Line Cinema.
Director: Richard Linklater.
Producers: Richard Linklater, Mark Samuelson and Ann Carli.
Co-Producers: Holly Gent Palmo and Vincent Palmo Jr.
Associate Producers: Sara Greene and Jessica Parker.
Executive Producers: Steve Christian, Steve Norris and John Sloss.
Line Producer: Richard Hewitt.
Screenplay: Holly Gent Palmo and Vincent Palmo Jr., adapted from the novel by Robert Kaplow.
Film Editor: Sandra Adair.
Cinematography: Dick Pope.
Production Manager: Emily Stillman.
Post-Production Supervisor: Miranda Jones.
Original Score: Michael J. McEvoy.
Casting: Lucy Bevan.
Production Design: Laurence Dorman.
Art Direction: Bill Crutcher, David Doran and Stuart Rose.
Set Decoration: Richard Roberts.
Costume Design: Nic Ede.
Running Time: 107 minutes.
Main Cast: Zac Efron (Richard Samuels), Christian McKay (Orson Welles), Claire Danes (Sonja Jones), Ben Chaplin (George Coulouris), Zoe Kazan (Gretta Alder), Eddie Marsan (John Houseman), Kelly Reilly (Muriel Brassler), James Tupper (Joseph Cotton), Thomas Arnold (George Duthie), Leo Bill (Norman Lloyd), Shane James Bordas (Elliott Reid), Michael Brandon (Les Tremayne), Aaron Brown (Longchamps Kid), Janie Dee (Mrs Samuels), Alessandro Giuggioli (Hiram Sherman), Garrick Hagon (Dr Mewling), Patrick Kennedy (Grover Burgess), Lexie Lambert (Lizzy), Harry Macqueen (John A Willard), Megan Maczko (Evelyn

Allen), Michael J. McEvoy (Epstein), Jo McInnes (Jeannie Rosenthal), Iain McKee (Vakhtangov), Simon Nehan (Joe Holland), Travis Oliver (John Hoyt), Rhodri Neil Orders (Stefan Schnabel), Nathan Osgood (Radio Announcer), Simon Lee Phillips (Walter Ash), Imogen Poots (Lorelei Lathrop), Saskia Reeves (Barbara Luddy), Marlene Sidaway (Grandmother Samuels), Daniel Tuite (William Mowry), Al Weaver (Sam Leve), Robert Wilfort (Radio Director).

NOTES

1. IT'S IMPOSSIBLE TO LEARN TO PLOW BY READING BOOKS (1988)

1. For an interesting discussion of Linklater's early career, including his departure from Sam Houston State University and his employment prior to his directorial debut, Michael Koresky and Jeff Reichert's interview 'A Conversation with Richard Linklater', in the Summer 2004 edition of *Reverse Shot Online*, is of great value. The feature also discusses Linklater's role in establishing the highly respected Austin Film Society along with cinematographer Lee Daniel: Michael Koresky and Jeff Reichert, 'A Conversation with Richard Linklater', in *Reverse Shot Online*, Summer 2004.

<http://www.reverseshot.com/legacy/summer04/linklater1.html>

An article which discusses Linklater's career in film in detail, including its early stages, is Brian Price's 'Richard Linklater', which appears in *Senses of Cinema*'s June 2003 edition: Brian Price, 'Richard Linklater', in *Senses of Cinema*, June 2003.

<http://www.sensesofcinema.com/contents/directors/03/linklater.html>

2. Various Contributors, *Slacker: The Criterion Edition* (New York: The Criterion Collection, 2004).

3. In his evaluation of the film for *DVD Critic*, as part of a wider review of *Slacker: The Criterion Edition* on 27 September 2004, Bill Gibron considered *It's Impossible to Learn to Plow* to be interesting to watch in relation to Linklater's later work: Bill Gibron, '*Slacker: Criterion Collection*' , in *DVD Verdict*, 27 September 2004.

<http://www.dvdverdict.com/reviews/slacker.php>

Christopher Null's short 2004 review of *It's Impossible to Learn to Plow* on *FilmCritic.com* likewise draws comparisons between the film and the later *Slacker*, and also notes the influence of Jim Jarmusch's filmic style on Linklater's choice of narrative structure: Christopher Null, '*It's Impossible to Learn to Plow by Reading Books*', in *FilmCritic.com*, 2004.

<http://filmcritic.com/misc/emporium.nsf/84dbbfa4d71014498625 6c290016f76e/54304a02c3c6849088256f050001d05a?OpenDocument>

2. SLACKER (1991)

4. For an interesting assessment of Generation X-influenced films of the early 1990s, it is worth referring to John Ottenhoff's 'Movie Reviews' feature in the 15 June 1994 issue of *Christian Century*.

5. Steven Brown and Ulrik Volgsten, *Music and Manipulation: On the*

Social Uses and Social Control of Music (New York: Berghahn Books, 2005), p.204.

6. One helpful comparison between the Generation X of Linklater's era and the term's earliest mid-sixties roots can be found in Anushka Asthana and Vanessa Thorpe's article 'Whatever happened to the original Generation X?' in the 23 January 2005 issue of *The Observer*.

7. Douglas Coupland, *Generation X: Tales for an Accelerated Culture* (New York: St Martin's Press, 1991).

8. Coupland was also to contribute the Foreword for Linklater's illustrated screenplay of *Slacker*: Richard Linklater, *Slacker* (New York: St Martin's Press, 1992), pp.1-2.

9. James Annesley, *Blank Fictions: Consumerism, Culture and the Contemporary American Novel* (London: Pluto Press, 1998), p.126.

10. Henry A. Giroux, 'Doing Cultural Studies: Youth and the Challenge of Pedagogy', in *Harvard Educational Review*, 64:3, Fall 1994.

11. Brian Raftery, '*Slacker*: 15 years later', in *Salon*, 5 July 2006.

12. Richard Linklater, *Slacker* (New York: St Martin's Press, 1992), pp.3-4; pp.16-24.

13. Grant McCracken, *Flock and Flow: Predicting and Managing Change in a Dynamic Marketplace* (Bloomington: Indiana University Press, 2006), p.78.

14. Matthew Pustz, *Comic Book Culture: Fanboys and True Believers* (Jackson: University of Mississippi Press, 2000), p.96.

15. Jeffrey Slonin, 'A Thousand Words', in *ArtForum*, December 1993.

16. Richard Porton, *Film and the Anarchist Imagination* (New York: Verso, 1999), p.168.

17. Roger Ebert, '*Slacker*', in *The Chicago Sun-Times*, 23 August 1991.

18. Dana Thomas, '*Slacker*', in *The Washington Post*, 23 August 1991.

19. Chris Hicks, '*Slacker*', in *Deseret News*, 19 October 1991.

20. Jonathan Carter, 'Richard Linklater', in *BBC Collective*, 17 June 2002. <http://www.bbc.co.uk/dna/collective/A818778>

21. Carolina A. Miranda, 'Slack is Back', in *Time*, 13 September 2004.

22. Hal Hinson, '*Slacker*', in *The Washington Post*, 23 August 1991.

23. Ben Thompson, 'The Return of the Talkies', in *The Independent*, 22 January 1996.

3. DAZED AND CONFUSED (1993)

24. The film's uncompromising presentation of the pains of adolescence is discussed in detail by Roger Ebert in his review of the film in the 24 September 1993 edition of *The Chicago Sun-Times*.

25. Richard Corliss, 'A Toke of Our Esteem', in *Time*, 11 October 1993.

26. For an interesting discussion of Parker Posey's prominence in American independent film, which also briefly mentions Linklater, it is worth referring to the following: Chris Holmlund, *Contemporary American Independent Film: From the Margins to the Mainstream* (Oxford: Routledge, 2004), p.75.

27. Desson Howe, '*Dazed and Confused*', in *The Washington Post*, 22 October 1993.

28. Jon Lebkowsky, 'Interview with Richard Linklater', in *Mindjack*, 1992. <http://www.mindjack.com/interviews/linklater1.html>

29. ibid.

30. Particularly favourable reviews can be found in Marjorie Baumgarten's feature on the film in the 24 September 1993 edition of *The Austin Chronicle*, Peter Travers's evaluation in the *Rolling Stone* of 14 October 1993, and Scott Tobias's retrospective review posted to *The Onion A.V. Club* on 7 June 2006:

<http://www.avclub.com/content/node/49276/>

31. Jim DeRogatis, 'The '70s Obviously Sucked – Not! (Or at Least Not the Music, Anyway)', in *Dazed and Confused: The Criterion Edition* (New York: The Criterion Collection, 2006).

32. The stylistic differences between *Slacker* and *Dazed and Confused* are discussed with Richard Linklater in Lane Relyea's interview 'What, me work? Interview with director Richard Linklater', which appeared in the April 1993 issue of *ArtForum*.

4. BEFORE SUNRISE (1995)

33. Among the critics who favourably drew attention to this sequence were Sheila Johnston's review 'Ships that pass in the night' in the 20 April 1995 issue of *The Independent*, Roger Ebert's review of the film in the 27 January 1995 edition of *The Chicago Sun-Times*, and Quentin Curtis's 'Perfect love on the night train', in *The Independent*'s 23 April 1995 issue.

34. Peter Rainer, '*Before Sunrise*', in *The Los Angeles Times*, 6 April 1996.

35. For an interesting discussion of spiritual themes in *Before Sunrise*, it is worth referring to Steven Taylor's *The Out of Bounds Church?: Learning to Create a Community of Faith in a Culture of Change* (Grand Rapids: Zondervan Press, 2005), pp.82-84.

36. There is a valuable comparison of Hawke's roles in *Before Sunrise* and *Reality Bites*, and how they fit into the broader picture of Generation

X film-making, to be found in Peter Hanson's *The Cinema of Generation X: A Critical Study of Films and Directors* (Jefferson: McFarland and Company, 2002), pp.16-17.

37. A valuable interview with Delpy, in which she discusses her early career as well as her appearance in *Before Sunrise*, appears in Sophie Barker's 'Darling of the Slacker Generation', in the 16 April 1995 issue of *The Independent*.

38. John Simon, '*Before Sunrise*', in *National Review*, 6 March 1995.

39. Marjorie Baumgarten, '*Before Sunrise*', in *The Austin Chronicle*, 27 January 1995.

40. Mick LaSalle, 'An Extraordinary Day Dawns *Before Sunrise*', in *The San Francisco Chronicle*, 27 January 1995.

5. SUBURBIA (1996)

41. Godfrey Cheshire, '*subUrbia*', in *Variety*, 11 October 1996.

42. Roger Ebert, '*subUrbia*', in *The Chicago Sun-Times*, 7 March 1997.

43. Linklater gives a rewarding account of his approach to *subUrbia*, and how it related to his body of work thus far, in: Tim Ryhs, 'Hanging Out with Richard Linklater', in *MovieMaker*, February 1997.

<http://www.industrycentral.net/director_interviews/RL04.htm>

44. Of particular value is Grant McCracken's interesting discussion of modern film-makers' interpretations of consumer culture and manufacturing modernisation in: Grant McCracken, *Culture and Consumption II: Markets, Meaning and Brand Management* (Bloomington: Indiana University Press, 2005), pp.14-15.

45. Eric Bogosian, *subUrbia* (New York: Theatre Communications Group, 1995), p.2.

46. Jack Mathews, '*subUrbia: subUrbia* Goes Back to Confused Days', in *The Los Angeles Times*, 7 February 1997.

47. Rita Kempley, 'Suburban Bawl', in *The Washington Post*, 7 March 1997.

48. Jack Garner, '*subUrbia*', in *The Rochester Democrat and Chronicle*, 2 May 1997.

6. THE NEWTON BOYS (1998)

49. Willis Newton and Joe Newton, as told to Claude I. Stanush and David Middleton, *The Newton Boys: Portrait of an Outlaw Gang* (Abilene: State House Press, 1994).

50. A valuable account of the making of the film can be found in Lewis

Black's article 'The Newton Boys' in the 30 March 1998 edition of The Austin Chronicle.

51. Jonathan Rosenbaum, Essential Cinema: On the Necessity of Film Canons (Baltimore: Johns Hopkins University Press, 2004), p.115; p.118.

52. Peter Stack's review of the film in The San Francisco Chronicle's 27 March 1998 issue is particularly complimentary in this regard.

53. Emanuel Levy, for instance, drew such comparisons between The Newton Boys and several other historical crime movies in his review of 13 March 1998 for Variety, but noted that in his opinion Linklater's film lacked the potent appeal which had lent the other films their long-running success with audiences.

54. Tom McCarthy, '"Formula" makes Newton Boys shine', in The Daily Beacon, 9 April 1998.

55. Laura Miller, 'The Mild Bunch: Richard Linklater takes a stab at a stale genre with The Newton Boys', in Salon, 27 March 1998.

56. Jeff Millar gives a notably damning assessment of the film's pace in the 25 March 1998 issue of The Houston Chronicle.

57. One of the most favourable reviews can be found in Duane Dudek's review in the 27 March 1998 edition of The Milwaukee Journal Sentinel.

58. Jesse Sublett, 'Another Day, Another Dollar', in Texas Monthly, 1 April 1998.

59. Linklater discusses The Newton Boys and its relationship to his wider body of work in an interview with David Walsh, 'You can't hold back the human spirit', which was posted to the World Socialist Web Site on 27 March 1998:
<http://www.wsws.org/arts/1998/mar1998/link-m27.shtml>

7. WAKING LIFE (2001)

60. Erica Abeel, 'Dream Project', in Film Journal, November 2001. See also: J.Hoberman, 'Sleep With Me: Intimacy; Waking Life; Focus', in The Village Voice, 17-23 October 2001.

61. George Santayana, Interpretations of Poetry and Religion (Whitefish: Kessinger Publishing, 2005) [1900]. The section under consideration is Chapter X: 'The Elements and Function on Poetry'.

62. The memorably articulate, subversive and dryly cynical views of Bill Hicks (1961-94) on the subject of political philosophy featured prominently in a number of his stand-up performances, many of which mirrored the disdain that the 'Self-Burning Man' expresses towards the effectiveness of America's democratic system. For just a few examples, see:

Bill Hicks, *Love All the People*, rev. edn. (London: Constable, 2005), pp.122-24; pp.154-55; pp.342-46.

63. An illuminating discussion of Bazin's theories can be found in Peter Hutchings's 'Genre theory and criticism', in *Approaches to Popular Film*, ed. by Joanne Hollows and Mark Jancovich (Manchester: Manchester University Press, 1995), pp.61-63.

64. For interesting analysis of the discussion between Caveh Zahedi and David Jewell on the subject of Andre Bazin, Chris Chang's feature 'Cosmic Babble: *Waking Life*', in *Film Comment*'s September/October 2001 edition is well worth a look.

65. Todd McCarthy, '*Waking Life*', in *Variety*, 25 January 2001.

66. Among the most approving reviews at the time were Kirk Honeycutt's review for the 29 January 2001 edition of *The Hollywood Reporter*, Steven Rea's review of the film for *The Philadelphia Inquirer*'s 26 October 2001 edition, and Roger Ebert's particularly positive assessment in *The Chicago Sun-Times* of 19 October 2001.

67. Peter Rainer, 'Dreams Work', in *New York Magazine*, 29 October 2001.

68. Kirk Honeycutt, '*Waking Life*' , in *The Hollywood Reporter*, 29 January 2001.

69. Kevin Thomas, '*Waking Life*' , i n *The Los Angeles Times*, 19 October 2001.

70. Sean Axmaker, '*Slacker* director sleepwalks through *Waking Life*', in *The Seattle Post-Intelligencer*, 26 October 2001.

71. Rene Rodriguez, 'Talking heads fill *Waking Life*', in *The Miami Herald*, 9 November 2001. For an interesting alternative take on this argument, see also: Peter Bradshaw, '*Waking Life*', in *The Guardian*, 19 April 2002.

8. TAPE (2001)

72. Geoff King, *American Independent Cinema* (London: I.B. Tauris, 2005), p.53.

73. Linklater gives a detailed interview about the creation of *Tape* and his adoption of digital film-making techniques in an interview with Anlee Ellingson in the November 2001 issue of *BoxOffice Online*:
<http://www.boxoffice.com/issues/nov01/linklater.html>

74. Stephen Belber, *Tape* (London: Nick Hern Books, 2003), p.i.

75. Roger Ebert, '*Tape*', in *The Chicago Sun-Times*, 16 November 2001.

76. Ryan Gilbey, '*Tape*', in *The Observer*, 14 July 2002.

77. Dennis Lim, 'Uncertainty Principles: *Tape; K-Pax*', in *The Village*

Voice, 31 October-6 November 2001.

78. Peter Bradshaw, '*Tape*', in *The Guardian*, 12 July 2002.

79. Stephen Phelan, 'Auteur State: *Tape*', in *The Sunday Herald*, 9 June 2002.

80. Peter Rainer, 'Grudge Report', in *New York Magazine*, 12 November 2001.

81. Sam Adams, '*Tape*', in *The Philadelphia City Paper*, 15-22 November 2001.

82. Michael O'Sullivan, '*Tape* Eventually Unravels', in *The Washington Post*, 16 November 2001.

83. Mike Clark, '*Tape* won't stick in viewers' minds', in *USA Today*, 2 November 2001.

84. Dennis Harvey, '*Tape*', in *Variety*, 29 January 2001.

9. SCHOOL OF ROCK (2003)

85. Jack Black takes part in a full and frank discussion of how he came to choose the role of Dewey Finn in an interview with Jim DeRogatis in the 28 September 2003 issue of *The Chicago Sun-Times*.

86. J. Hoberman, 'Hear My Song: A Slacker Musician Teaches Preppie Tykes a Lesson in Unleashing Their Inner Rockers', in *The Village Voice*, 24-30 September 2003.

87. Kirk Honeycutt, '*The School of Rock*', in *The Hollywood Reporter*, 10 September 2003.

88. Peter Hartlaub, 'Black's 3 R's: reading, writing, rocking', in *The San Francisco Chronicle*, 5 March 2004.

89. Andrew O'Hehir, '*School of Rock*', in *Salon*, 3 October 2003.

90. Jeff Vice, '*The School of Rock* is messy, but hilarious', in *Deseret News*, 3 October 2003.

91. Bruce Westbrook, '*School of Rock*', in *The Houston Chronicle*, 12 May 2004.

92. Sean Axmaker, 'Performances make *School of Rock* sing', in *The Seattle Post-Intelligencer*, 3 October 2003.

93. Roger Ebert, '*School of Rock*', in *The Chicago Sun-Times*, 3 October 2003.

94. Linklater discusses *School of Rock*, and the way that the film fits into his wider oeuvre, in an interview with Rebecca Winters for *Time* magazine's 13 October 2003 edition.

10. BEFORE SUNSET (2004)

95. Alex Field, *The Hollywood Project: A Look into the Minds of the Makers of Spiritually Relevant Films* (Orlando: Relevant Books, 2004), pp.124-25.

96. Delpy explains her approach to reviving the character of Celine for the film in an interview with Charlotte O'Sullivan in *The Independent*'s 23 July 2004 issue.

97. Philip French, '*Before Sunset*', in *The Observer*, 25 July 2004.

98. Delpy conducts an interesting interview with Hawke on the subject of his film adaptation of *The Hottest State* in the October 2006 edition of *Interview* magazine.

99. Hawke briefly deliberates upon his writing career and the autobiographical aspects of *Before Sunset* in an interview with Leslie Felperin for the 18 June 2004 issue of *The Independent*.

100. The political themes which run through *Before Sunset* are discussed at length by Kevin Lee in his article 'Finding Freedom the Second Time Around: The Politics of *Before Sunset*', in the October 2004 edition of *Senses of Cinema*:
<http://www.sensesofcinema.com/contents/04/33/before_sunset.html>

101. Linklater talks about the challenges of setting a narrative within a real-time framework in Dennis Lim's feature 'From Dawn Till Dusk', in the 29 June 2004 issue of *The Village Voice*.

102. Steve Persall, 'The Perfect *Sunset*', in *The St. Petersburg Times*, 22 July 2004.

103. Jonathan Romney, 'Haven't I seen you somewhere before?', in *The Independent on Sunday*, 25 July 2004.

104. Philip French, '*Before Sunset*', in *The Observer*, 25 July 2004.

105. Scott Tobias, '*Before Sunset*', in *The Onion A.V. Club*, 29 June 2004. <http://www.avclub.com/content/node/17850/>

106. Mike Clark, '*Before Sunset* awakens a love long sleeping', in *USA Today*, 1 July 2004.

107. Marjorie Baumgarten, '*Before Sunset*', in *The Austin Chronicle*, 9 July 2004.

108. Michael Wilmington, '*Before Sunset*', in *The Chicago Tribune*, 28 June 2004.

109. David Germain, 'New day dawns for Hawke, Delpy in *Before Sunset*', in *The Oakland Tribune*, 2 July 2004.

110. Roger Ebert, '*Before Sunset*', in *The Chicago Sun-Times*, 2 July 2004.

111. David Denby, 'Wanderers: *Before Sunset* and *The Terminal*', in *The New Yorker*, 5 July 2004.

112. Nick James, 'Debrief Encounter', in *Sight and Sound*, August 2004.

11. BAD NEWS BEARS (2005)

113. A valuable retrospective of Linklater's directorial career leading up to the release of *Bad News Bears* can be found in Joel Stein's article 'He's Having a Ball', which appears in *Time* Magazine's 11 July 2005 issue.

114. Bruce Westbrook, '*School of Rock*', in *The Houston Chronicle*, 12 May 2004.

115. A detailed comparison of the two different incarnations of *Bad News Bears* can be found in Michael Wilmington's review in *The Chicago Tribune*'s 14 July 2005 edition.

116. Peter Travers, '*Bad News Bears*', in *Rolling Stone*, 22 July 2005.

117. Thornton discusses his approach to the role of Morris Buttermaker in an interview with Cindy Pearlman for the 17 July 2005 issue of *The Chicago Sun-Times*.

118. Philip French, '*Bad News Bears*', in *The Observer*, 14 August 2005.

119. Scott Tobias, '*Bad News Bears*', in *The Onion A.V. Club*, 19 July 2005. <http://www.avclub.com/content/node/24938/>

120. Marc Savlov, '*Bad News Bears*', in *The Austin Chronicle*, 22 July 2005.

121. Brian Lowry, '*Bad News Bears*', in *Variety*, 17 July 2005.

122. Michael Atkinson, 'Bush League', in *The Village Voice*, 26 July 2005.

123. Chris Vognar, '*Bad News Bears*', in *The Dallas Morning News*, 22 July 2005.

124. Mick LaSalle, '*Bad News Bears* drops the ball', in *The San Francisco Chronicle*, 22 July 2005.

12. A SCANNER DARKLY (2006)

125. Linklater discusses Sabiston's processing technique, and many other aspects of the production, in Marc Savlov's interview 'Securing the Substance' which appears in the 7 July 2006 issue of *The Austin Chronicle*.

126. Linklater has an interesting dialogue with Rob Nelson in the 30 May 2006 edition of *The Village Voice*, where he explains his selection of

subject matter in choosing *A Scanner Darkly* for adaptation, as well as relating it to his other major film project being released that year.

127. A summarised account of Dick's many novels and other works can be found in: John Clute and Peter Nicholls, *The Encyclopedia of Science Fiction*, rev. edn. (New York: St Martin's Press, 1995), pp.328-330. Also well worth consulting is 'The Men in Their High Castles: Dick and Other Visionaries', a chapter which appears in the following invaluable reference work: Brian Aldiss, with David Wingrove, *Trillion Year Spree* (London: Paladin, 1988) [1986], pp.390-426.

128. Cochrane talks about the role of Charles Freck, as well as his experience of working with Richard Linklater, in an interview with Cassie Carpenter in the 21 July 2006 edition of *The Chicago Sun-Times*.

129. Philip French, '*A Scanner Darkly*', in *The Observer*, 20 August 2006.

130. Justin Chang, '*A Scanner Darkly*', in *Variety*, 25 May 2006.

131. Marjorie Baumgarten, '*A Scanner Darkly*', in *The Austin Chronicle*, 7 July 2006.

132. Duane Byrge, 'Animation wasted in static *Scanner Darkly*', in *The Chicago Sun-Times*, 7 July 2006.

133. Michael Wilmington, '*A Scanner Darkly*', in *The Chicago Tribune*, 7 July 2006.

134. Peter Travers, '*A Scanner Darkly*', in *Rolling Stone*, 23 June 2006.

135. Keith Phipps, '*A Scanner Darkly*', in *The Onion A.V. Club*, 5 July 2006. <http://www.avclub.com/content/node/50156/>

136. J. Hoberman, 'Brain Candy: Richard Linklater's literate Dick adaptation is a brain-bending D-light', in *The Village Voice*, 5 July 2006.

137. For an interesting discussion of Linklater's interest in the works of Philip K. Dick, his interview with Mike Russell of the *CulturePulp* website is both valuable and very detailed. The site also contains an illustrated summary of the interview in a cartoon style, as well as both a truncated and unexpurgated transcript of Linklater's detailed conversation with Russell, and is not to be missed: Mike Russell, 'The *CulturePulp* Q&A: Richard Linklater', in *CulturePulp*, 54, 16 July 2006.

<http://homepage.mac.com/merussell/iblog/B835531044/C159267 8312/E20060701140745/index.html>

See also: Mike Russell, 'The Richard Linklater Interview', in *CulturePulp*, 54, 16 July 2006.

<http://homepage.mac.com/merussell/iblog/B835531044/C116216 2177/E20060717001411/index.html>

13. FAST FOOD NATION (2006)

138. A very rewarding discussion of Linklater's approach to directing *Fast Food Nation* and the way that the film fits into his wider canon of work can be found in: Tim Robey, 'The Best Years in the Life of Richard Linklater', in *Sight and Sound*, April 2007. See also: Rob Nelson, 'Richard Linklater: Grazed and Abused', in *Mother Jones*, November-December 2006.

139. Jeff Vice, 'Author insisted on fictionalized *Fast Food*', in *Deseret News*, 19 November 2006. See also: Andrew Wineke, '*Fast Food Nation* author notes change, good and bad, since book', in *The Colorado Springs Gazette*, 19 July 2006.

140. Linklater and Schlosser describe the relationship between the book and the film in Mary Houlihan's article 'Author, director turn facts into *Food* for thought', which appears in the 17 November 2006 edition of *The Chicago Sun-Times*.

141. Carina Chocano, '*Fast Food Nation*', in *The Los Angeles Times*, 17 November 2006.

142. David Gritten, 'This film may make you sick', in *The Daily Telegraph*, 4 May 2007.

143. Stephen Applebaum, 'Fries and Lies', in *The Scotsman*, 10 February 2007.

144. Ruthe Stein, 'A plentiful serving of diet don'ts', in *The San Francisco Chronicle*, 17 November 2006.

145. Peter Travers, '*Fast Food Nation*', in *Rolling Stone*, 13 November 2006.

146. Todd McCarthy, '*Fast Food Nation*', in *Variety*, 19 May 2006.

147. Marc Savlov, '*Fast Food Nation*', in *The Austin Chronicle*, 17 November 2006.

148. Kirk Honeycutt, '*Fast Food Nation*', in *The Hollywood Reporter*, 20 May 2006.

149. Jeff Vice, 'Lose appetite at *Food*', in *Deseret News*, 17 November 2006.

150. David Noh, '*Fast Food Nation*', in *Film Journal*, 17 November 2006.

151. Richard Corliss and Mary Corliss, 'Getting Indigestion Over *Fast Food Nation*', in *Time*, 19 May 2006.

152. Sam Adams, 'Takeout Order: Richard Linklater and Eric Schlosser set their sights on *Fast Food Nation*', in *The Philadelphia City Paper*, 15 November 2006.

153. Scott Tobias, '*Fast Food Nation*', in *The Onion A.V. Club*, 16

November 2006. <http://www.avclub.com/content/node/55385/>

154. Warren Epstein, '*Fast Food* lacks flavor', in *The Colorado Springs Gazette*, 17 November 2006.

155. Kyle Smith, 'Stick it in your bun', in *The New York Post*, 17 November 2006.

156. Bill Vourvoulias, '*Fast Food Nation*', in *Interview*, November 2006.

14. INNING BY INNING (2008)

157. Ashley Moreno, 'Zen and the Art of Winning Championships: Richard Linklater profiles living legend Augie Garrido in *Inning by Inning*', in *The Austin Chronicle*, 30 May 2008.

158. John DeFore, 'Richard Linklater's *Inning by Inning* follows coach Augie Garrido', in *The American-Statesman*, 2 June 2008.

159. Scott Tobias, '*Inning By Inning: A Portrait Of A Coach*', in *The Onion A.V. Club*, 17 June 2009.
<http://www.avclub.com/articles/inning-by-inning-a-portrait-of-a-coach,29316/>

15. ME AND ORSON WELLES (2008)

160. Catherine Shoard, 'Zac Efron is a revelation in Richard Linklater's *Me and Orson Welles*', in *The Guardian*, 18 September 2009.

161. Todd McCarthy, '*Me and Orson Welles*', in *Variety*, 8 September 2008. See also: Kirk Honeycutt, '*Me and Orson Welles*', in *The Hollywood Reporter*, 7 September 2008.

162. Allan Hunter, '*Me and Orson Welles*', in *Screen Daily*, 6 September 2008.

163. James Rocchi, 'TIFF Review: *Me and Orson Welles*', in *Cinematical*, 11 September 2008.
<http://www.cinematical.com/2008/09/11/tiff-review-meand-orson-welles/> See also: Roger Ebert, 'Some real eye-openers', in *The Chicago Sun-Times*, 14 September 2008.

CONCLUSION

164. Although Linklater's respect for European cinema is evident from a great many of his interviews and commentaries, one text that is particularly worth seeking out is his short chapter on Robert Bresson's *L'Argent* (1983) which, in spite of its relative brevity, speaks volumes

about his undeniable passion for films the world over: Richard Linklater, 'L'Argent', in *Projections 4 1/2: In Association with Positif*, ed. by John Boorman and Walter Donohue (London: Faber and Faber, 1995), pp.243-45. Linklater's approach to film, and similarities between *L'Argent* and *Slacker*, are also discussed in Brian Price's insightful analysis which can be found in: Brian Price, 'Richard Linklater', in *Senses of Cinema*, June 2003.

<http://www.sensesofcinema.com/contents/directors/03/linklater.html>

165. It is interesting to consider the following discussion of the *Cahiers du Cinema* and then relate it to the nature of Linklater's work, particularly with regard to his position as one of the most prominent postmodern independent American auteurs: Helen Stoddart, 'Auteurism and film authorship theory', in *Approaches to Popular Film*, ed. by Joanne Hollows and Mark Jancovich (Manchester: Manchester University Press, 1995), pp.37-57.

166. Jeff Vice, '*Bears* is funny, but it's not for all', in *Deseret News*, 22 July 2005.

167. Linklater discusses his views on the role of corporations, the culture of unconstrained consumerism and a great many other topics in the following detailed interview: Jon Lebkowsky, 'Interview with Richard Linklater', in *Mindjack*, 1992.

<http://www.mindjack.com/interviews/linklater1.html>

168. Gavin Smith, 'Gavin Smith on Richard Linklater's *Waking Life*', in *Film Comment*, March 2001.

169. Roger Ebert, '*Before Sunrise*', in *The Chicago Sun-Times*, 27 January 1995.

170. Michael Wilmington, '*Bad News Bears*', in *The Chicago Tribune*, 14 July 2005.

171. Kevin Smith has acknowledged the influence of Linklater's early work on his film-making in a number of interviews. The following article is particularly worth reading: Suzanne Ely, 'Kevin Smith Talks Screenwriting, *Slacker* and *Superman*', in *IndieWIRE*, 12 December 2000.

<http://www.indiewire.com/biz/biz_001212_K.Smith.html>

See also: Anon., 'The Monster That Ate Hollywood: Interview – Kevin Smith', in *PBS Frontline*, May 2001.

<http://www.pbs.org/wgbh/pages/frontline/shows/hollywood/interviews/smith.html>

172. A very valuable overview of the Mumblecore film phenomenon can be found in J. Hoberman's article 'It's Mumblecore!' in the 17 August 2007 edition of *The Village Voice*. See also: Michael Koresky, 'The

Mumblecore Movement? Andrew Bujalski on his *Funny Ha Ha'*, in *IndieWIRE*, 2 May 2005.

    <http://www.indiewire.com/people/people_050502bujalski.html>

173. Larry Carroll, 'Got Plans For 2013? Check Out Richard Linklater's "12 Year Movie"', in *MTV.com*, 28 November 2006.

    <http://www.mtv.com/movies/news/articles/1546688/11282006/story.jhtml

174. David T. Johnson, 'Directors on Adaptation: A Conversation with Richard Linklater', in *Literature Film Quarterly*, Spring 2007.

175. Paul Simpson, ed., *The Rough Guide to Cult Movies* (London: Haymarket Customer Publishing, 2001), p.65.

SELECT BIBLIOGRAPHY

Books and Reference Guides

Aldiss, Brian, with David Wingrove, *Trillion Year Spree* (London: Paladin, 1988) [1986].

Annesley, James, *Blank Fictions: Consumerism, Culture and the Contemporary American Novel* (London: Pluto Press, 1998).

Armes, Roy, *Film and Reality: An Historical Survey* (Harmondsworth: Penguin, 1974).

Austin, Joe, and Michael Nevin Willard, eds, *Generations of Youth: Youth Cultures and History in Twentieth-Century America* (New York: NYU Press, 1998).

Baudrillard, Jean, *Simulacra and Simulation*, trans. by Sheila Faria Glaser (Ann Arbor: University of Michigan Press, 1994) [1981].

Belber, Stephen, *Tape* (London: Nick Hern Books, 2003).

Bogosian, Eric, *subUrbia* (New York: Theatre Communications Group, 1995).

Boorman, John, and Walter Donohue, eds, *Projections 41/2: In Association with Positif* (London: Faber and Faber, 1995).

Brown, Steven, and Ulrik Volgsten, *Music and Manipulation: On the Social Uses and Social Control of Music* (New York: Berghahn Books, 2005).

Bryanton, Rob, *Imagining the Tenth Dimension: A New Way of Thinking About Time and Space* (Oxford: Trafford Publishing, 2007).

Clifford, James, *The Predicament of Culture: Twentieth-Century Ethnography, Literature and Art* (Cambridge, Massachusetts: Harvard University Press, 1988).

Clute, John, and Peter Nicholls, *The Encyclopedia of Science Fiction*, rev. edn. (New York: St Martin's Press, 1995).

Coupland, Douglas, *Generation X: Tales for an Accelerated Culture* (New York: St Martin's Press, 1991).

Descartes, René, *A Discourse on Method*, trans. by John Veitch (London: J.M. Dent and Sons, 1957) [1637].

Dick, Philip K., *Five Great Novels: The Three Stigmata of Palmer Eldritch, Martian Time-Slip, Do Androids Dream of Electric Sheep?, Ubik, A Scanner Darkly* (London: Gollancz, 2004).

Docker, John, *Postmodernism and Popular Culture: A Cultural History* (Cambridge: Cambridge University Press, 1994).

Duncombe, Stephen, *Notes from Underground: Zines and the Politics of Alternative Culture* (New York: Verso, 1997).

Ellis, John, *Visible Fictions: Cinema, Television, Video* (London: Routledge, 1989) [1982].

Field, Alex, *The Hollywood Project: A Look into the Minds of the Makers of*

Spiritually Relevant Films (Orlando: Relevant Books, 2004).

Graham, Don, *Giant Country: Essays on Texas* (Fort Worth: TCU Press, 1999).

Halpern, Leslie, *Dreams on Film: The Cinematic Struggle Between Art and Science* (Jefferson: McFarland and Company, 2003).

Hanson, Peter, *The Cinema of Generation X: A Critical Study of Films and Directors* (Jefferson: McFarland and Company, 2002).

Helton, J.R., *Below the Line* (San Francisco: Last Gasp, 2000).

Hicks, Bill, *Love All the People*, rev. edn. (London: Constable, 2005).

Hollows, Joanne, and Mark Jancovich, eds, *Approaches to Popular Film* (Manchester: Manchester University Press, 1995).

Holmlund, Chris, *Contemporary American Independent Film: From the Margins to the Mainstream* (Oxford: Routledge, 2004).

Kaplow, Robert, *Me and Orson Welles* (London: Penguin, 2005).

King, Geoff, *American Independent Cinema* (London: I.B. Tauris, 2005).

Kolya, Nicholas, *You Never Ate Lunch in This Town to Begin With: An Outsider's Inside Look at the Outside of Hollywood* (Lincoln: Writers Club Press, 2002).

Levy, Emanuel, *Cinema of Outsiders: The Rise of American Independent Film* (New York: NYU Press, 1999).

Lewis, Jon, *New American Cinema* (Durham: Duke University Press, 1998).

Linklater, Richard, *Slacker* (New York: St Martin's Press, 1992).

Linklater, Richard, Denise Montgomery and Friends, *Dazed and Confused: Teenage Nostalgia, Instant and Cool 70's Memorabilia, A Celebration of the Hit Movie* (New York: St Martin's Press, 1993).

Linklater, Richard, Kim Krizan, Ethan Hawke and Julie Delpy, *Before Sunrise and Before Sunset* (New York: Vintage Books, 2005).

Macko, Lia, and Kerry Rubin, *Mid Life Crisis at 30: How the stakes have changed for a new generation – and what to do about it* (New York: Rodale Press, 2004).

McCracken, Grant, *Culture and Consumption II: Markets, Meaning and Brand Management* (Bloomington: Indiana University Press, 2005).

McCracken, Grant, *Flock and Flow: Predicting and Managing Change in a Dynamic Marketplace* (Bloomington: Indiana University Press, 2006).

Merchey, Jason A., *Building a Life of Value: Timeless Wisdom to Inspire and Empower Us* (Beverly Hills: Little Moose Press, 2005).

Miller, Toby, and Robert Stam, eds., *A Companion to Film Theory* (Oxford: Blackwell, 2004) [1999].

Mitchell, Jeremy, and Richard Maidment, eds., *The United States in the Twentieth Century: Culture* (London: Hodder and Stoughton, 1994).

Natoli, Joseph P., *This is a Picture and Not the World: Movies and a Post-9/11 America* (Albany: State University of New York Press, 2007).

Newton, Willis and Joe Newton as told to Claude I. Stanush and David Middleton, *The Newton Boys: Portrait of an Outlaw Gang* (Abilene: State House Press, 1994).

Porton, Richard, *Film and the Anarchist Imagination* (New York: Verso, 1999).

Pringle, David, *The Ultimate Guide to Science Fiction: An A-Z of Books* (London: Grafton,
1990).

Pustz, Matthew, *Comic Book Culture: Fanboys and True Believers* (Jackson: University of Mississippi Press, 2000).

Rosenbaum, Jonathan, *Essential Cinema: On the Necessity of Film Canons* (Baltimore: Johns Hopkins University Press, 2004).

Ryan, Michael, and Douglas Kellner, *Camera Politica: The Politics and Ideology of Contemporary Hollywood* (Indianapolis: Indiana University Press, 1988).

Santayana, George, *Interpretations of Poetry and Religion* (Whitefish: Kessinger Publishing, 2005) [1900].

Schlosser, Eric, *Fast Food Nation: What the All-American Meal is Doing to the World* (London: Penguin, 2002) [2001].

Shiach, Morag, *Discourse on Popular Culture: Class, Gender and History in Cultural Analysis, 1730 to the Present* (Stanford: Stanford University Press, 1989).

Simpson, Paul, ed., *The Rough Guide to Cult Movies* (London: Haymarket Customer Publishing, 2001).

Stanush, Claude, and Michele Stanush, *All Honest Men* (New York: Permanent Press, 2003).

Stringer, Julian, *Movie Blockbusters* (Oxford: Routledge, 2003).

Taylor, Steven, *The Out of Bounds Church?: Learning to Create a Community of Faith in a Culture of Change* (Grand Rapids: Zondervan Press, 2005).

Various Contributors, *Dazed and Confused: The Criterion Edition* (New York: The Criterion Collection, 2006).

Various Contributors, *Slacker: The Criterion Edition* (New York: The Criterion Collection, 2004).

Wilson, Elizabeth, *Bohemians: The Glamorous Outcasts* (London: Tauris Parke, 2002).

Articles, Interviews and Reviews

Abeel, Erica, 'Dream Project', in *Film Journal*, November 2001.

Adams, Mark, 'What a clever Dick', in *The Sunday Mirror*, 13 August 2006.

Adams, Sam, 'Takeout Order: Richard Linklater and Eric Schlosser set their sights on *Fast Food Nation*', in *The Philadelphia City Paper*, 5 November 2006.

Adams, Sam, '*Tape*', in *The Philadelphia City Paper*, 15-22 November 2001.

Adams, Sam, '*The Newton Boys*' , i n *The Philadelphia City Paper*, 26 March-2 April 1998.

Addiego, Walter, 'Brother, Can You Spare a Crime?', in *The San Francisco Examiner*, 27 March 1998.

Alvarez, Max J., 'Delpy outshines Hawke in beguiling *Sunrise*', in *The Milwaukee Journal*, 27 January 1995.

Anderson, Jeffrey M., '*Scanner Darkly*: Brains, visuals beat thrills', in *The Oakland Tribune*, 7 July 2006.

Anon., 'The Monster That Ate Hollywood: Interview – Kevin Smith', in *PBS Frontline*, May 2001.

<http://www.pbs.org/wgbh/pages/frontline/shows/hollywood/intervi ews/smith.html>

Arnold, Andrew D., 'A First Base Hit and a Guilty Pleasure', in *Time*, 28 May 2005.

Applebaum, Stephen, 'Fries and Lies', in *The Scotsman*, 10 February 2007.

Asthana, Anoushka, and Vanessa Thorpe, 'Whatever happened to the original Generation X?', in *The Observer*, 23 January 2005.

Atkinson, Michael, 'Bush League', in *The Village Voice*, 26 July 2005.

Axmaker, Sean, 'Lovers' reunion reveals regrets and stirs emotions', in *The Seattle Post-Intelligencer*, 2 July 2004.

Axmaker, Sean, 'Performances make *School of Rock* sing', in *The Seattle Post-Intelligencer*, 3 October 2003.

Axmaker, Sean, '*Slacker* director sleepwalks through *Waking Life*', in *The Seattle Post-Intelligencer*, 26 October 2001.

Axmaker, Sean, 'Unsettling *Scanner* tends to lose its way', in *The Seattle Post-Intelligencer*, 7 July 2006.

Badt, Karin Luisa, 'What's Wrong with Fast Food? A Conversation with Richard Linklater and Eric Schlosser on *Fast Food Nation*', in *Bright Lights Film Journal*, 54, November 2006.

Barker, Sophie, 'Darling of the Slacker Generation', in *The Independent*, 16 April 1995.

Barsanti, Chris, 'Waking Life', in Film Threat, 1 November 2001.

Baumgarten, Marjorie, 'A Scanner Darkly', in The Austin Chronicle, 7 July 2006.

Baumgarten, Marjorie, 'Before Sunrise', in The Austin Chronicle, 27 January 1995.

Baumgarten, Marjorie, 'Before Sunset', in The Austin Chronicle, 9 July 2004.

Baumgarten, Marjorie, 'Dazed and Confused', in The Austin Chronicle, 24 September 1993.

Baumgarten, Marjorie, 'The Newton Boys', in The Austin Chronicle, 27 March 1998.

Bellafante, Ginia, 'Generation X-cellent', in Time, 27 February 1995.

Billington, Alex, 'Toronto Review: Richard Linklater's Me and Orson Welles', in FirstShowing.net, 6 September 2008.

<http://www.firstshowing.net/2008/09/06/toronto-reviewrichard-linklaters-me-and-orson-welles/>

Black, Lewis, 'The Newton Boys', in The Austin Chronicle, 30 March 1998.

Booth, Michael, 'Too many items on the menu', in The Denver Post, 15 November 2006.

Bradshaw, Peter, 'Bad News Bears', in The Guardian, 12 August 2005.

Bradshaw, Peter, 'Before Sunset', in The Guardian, 23 July 2004.

Bradshaw, Peter, 'Fast Food Nation', in The Guardian, 18 August 2006.

Bradshaw, Peter, 'School of Rock', in The Guardian, 6 February 2004.

Bradshaw, Peter, 'Tape', in The Guardian, 12 July 2002.

Bradshaw, Peter, 'Waking Life', in The Guardian, 19 April 2002.

Budasi, Teresa, 'Star-struck Fast Food little more than filler', in The Chicago Sun-Times, 17 November 2006.

Burr, Ty, 'Before Sunset: French Kiss' in The Boston Globe, 2 July 2004.

Byrge, Duane, 'Animation wasted in static Scanner Darkly', in The Chicago Sun-Times, 7 July 2006.

Caine, Barry, 'Not Half Bad Grin and Bear It: The good news in Bad News', in The Oakland Tribune, 21 July 2005.

Caine, Barry, 'Tweens sure to love Black's School of Rock', in The Oakland Tribune, 3 October 2003.

Caro, Mark, 'School of Rock', in The Chicago Tribune, 2 October 2003.

Carpenter, Cassie, 'Cochrane not dazed by playing Scanner addict', in The Chicago Sun-Times, 21 July 2006.

Carroll, Larry, 'Got Plans For 2013? Check Out Richard Linklater's "12 Year Movie"', in MTV.com, 28 November 2006.

<http://www.mtv.com/movies/news/articles/1546688/11282006/story.jhtml>

Carter, Jonathan, 'Richard Linklater', in *BBC Collective*, 17 June 2002. <http://www.bbc.co.uk/dna/collective/A818778>

Chang, Chris, 'Cosmic Babble: *Waking Life*', in *Film Comment*, September/October 2001.

Chang, Justin, '*A Scanner Darkly*', in *Variety*, 25 May 2006.

Cheshire, Godfrey, '*subUrbia*', in *Variety*, 11 October 1996.

Chocano, Carina, '*A Scanner Darkly*', in *The Los Angeles Times*, 7 July 2006.

Chocano, Carina, '*Fast Food Nation*', in *The Los Angeles Times*, 17 November 2006.

Chocano, Carina, 'The *Bad News Bears*', in *The Los Angeles Times*, 22 July 2005.

Clark, Mike, '*Before Sunset* awakens a love long sleeping', in *USA Today*, 1 July 2004.

Clark, Mike, 'For those about to laugh, we salute *School of Rock*', in *USA Today*, 2 October 2003.

Clark, Mike, '*Tape* won't stick in viewers' minds', in *USA Today*, 2 November 2001.

Clark, Mike, '*Waking Life* is a fitful sleepwalk', in *USA Today*, 17 October 2001.

Corliss, Richard, 'A Toke of Our Esteem', in *Time*, 11 October 1993.

Corliss, Richard, and Mary Corliss, 'Getting Indigestion Over *Fast Food Nation*', in *Time*, 19 May 2006.

Curtis, Quentin, 'Perfect love on the night train', in *The Independent*, 23 April 1995.

Dargis, Manohla, '*Before Sunset*: After nine years, did their hearts grow fonder?', in *The Los Angeles Times*, 2 July 2004.

DeFore, John, 'Richard Linklater's *Inning by Inning* follows coach Augie Garrido', in *The American-Statesman*, 2 June 2008.

Delpy, Julie, 'Ethan Hawke: He may be affable, approachable and determined to fly under the radar, but look out – Ethan Hawke is spreading his wings again and ready to soar', in *Interview*, October 2006.

Denby, David, 'Liberal Education: *Bobby*, *Fast Food Nation* and *The History Boys*', in *The New Yorker*, 27 November 2006.

Denby, David, 'Wanderers: *Before Sunset* and *The Terminal*', in *The New Yorker*, 5 July 2004.

DeRogatis, Jim, 'High Fidelity: Jack Black stays true to his *School*', in *The Chicago Sun-Times*, 28 September 2003.

DeRogatis, Jim, 'The kids are all right in their movie debut', in *The Chicago Sun-Times*, 28 September 2003.

Didcock, Barry, 'Film-maker sickened by scale of food industry slaughter', in *The Sunday Herald*, 18 February 2007.

Drozdz, Maya, 'Waiting for Instantaneity', in *M/C: A Journal of Media and Culture*, 3:3, June 2000.

<http://journal.media-culture.org.au/0006/ intantaneity.php>

Dudek, Duane, 'Film puts our dreams and ideas in motion', in *The Milwaukee Journal Sentinel*, 9 November 2001.

Dudek, Duane, 'Neon-lit vampires biting society's neck', in *The Milwaukee Journal Sentinel*, 4 April 1997.

Dudek, Duane, '*Newton Boys* steal some hearts', in *The Milwaukee Journal Sentinel*, 27 March 1998.

Dudek, Duane, 'Sophisticated cousin of *Slacker* makes up at Sundance', in *The Milwaukee Journal Sentinel*, 2 February 2001.

Dudek, Duane, '*Tape* explores grudges of past', in *The Milwaukee Journal Sentinel*, 7 December 2001.

Ebert, Roger, '*Bad News Bears*', in *The Chicago Sun-Times*, 22 July 2005.

Ebert, Roger, '*Before Sunrise*', in *The Chicago Sun-Times*, 27 January 1995.

Ebert, Roger, '*Before Sunset*', in *The Chicago Sun-Times*, 2 July 2004.

Ebert, Roger, '*Dazed and Confused*' , in *The Chicago Sun-Times*, 24 September 1993.

Ebert, Roger, '*Fast Food Nation*', in *The Chicago Sun-Times*, 21 May 2006.

Ebert, Roger, '*School of Rock*', in *The Chicago Sun-Times*, 3 October 2003.

Ebert, Roger, '*Slacker*', in *The Chicago Sun-Times*, 23 August 1991.

Ebert, Roger, 'Some real eye-openers', in *The Chicago Sun-Times*, 14 September 2008.

Ebert, Roger, '*subUrbia*', in *The Chicago Sun-Times*, 7 March 1997.

Ebert, Roger, '*Tape*', in *The Chicago Sun-Times*, 16 November 2001.

Ebert, Roger, '*The Newton Boys*', in *The Chicago Sun-Times*, 27 March 1998.

Ebert, Roger, '*Waking Life*', in *The Chicago Sun-Times*, 19 October 2001.

Ellingson, Annlee, 'Director's Chair: Richard Linklater', in *BoxOffice Online*, November 2001.

<http://www.boxoffice.com/issues/nov01/linklater.html>

Ely, Suzanne, 'Kevin Smith Talks Screenwriting, *Slacker* and *Superman*', in *IndieWIRE*, 12 December 2000.

<http://www.indiewire.com/biz/biz_001212_K.Smith.html>

Epstein, Warren, '*Fast Food* lacks flavor', in *The Colorado Springs Gazette*, 17 November 2006.

Eyre, Hermione, 'My Secret Life: Eric Schlosser, Novelist', in *The Independent*, 13 May 2006.

Felperin, Leslie, 'Real-life relationships aren't clean and simple', in *The*

Independent, 18 June 2004.

French, Philip, '*A Scanner Darkly*', in *The Observer*, 20 August 2006.

French, Philip, '*Bad News Bears*', in *The Observer*, 14 August 2005.

French, Philip, '*Before Sunset*', in *The Observer*, 25 July 2004.

French, Philip, '*School of Rock*', in *The Observer*, 8 February 2004.

Garner, Jack, '*subUrbia*', in *The Rochester Democrat and Chronicle*, 2 May 1997.

Germain, David, 'New day dawns for Hawke, Delpy in *Before Sunset*', in *The Oakland Tribune*, 2 July 2004.

Germain, David, 'Whatever happened after *Sunrise*? Catch up in *Before Sunset*', in *The Chicago Sun-Times*, 23 July 2004.

Gibron, Bill, '*Slacker: Criterion Collection*', in *DVD Verdict*, 27 September 2004. <http://www.dvdverdict.com/reviews/slacker.php>

Gilbey, Ryan, 'Choice', in *The Independent*, 29 December 1994.

Gilbey, Ryan, '*SubUrbia*', in *The Independent*, 18 October 1997.

Gilbey, Ryan, '*Tape*', in *The Observer*, 14 July 2002.

Giroux, Henry A., 'Doing Cultural Studies: Youth and the Challenge of Pedagogy', in *Harvard Educational Review*, 64:3, Fall 1994.

Gleiberman, Owen, '*Before Sunset*', in *Entertainment Weekly*, 15 January 2005.

Gleiberman, Owen, '*Tape*', in *Entertainment Weekly*, 2 November 2001.

Gritten, David, 'This film may make you sick', in *The Daily Telegraph*, 4 May 2007.

Halpern, Dan, 'Another sunrise', in *The Guardian*, 8 October 2005.

Hanks, Robert, 'The Light Fantastic: *A Scanner Darkly*' , in *The Independent*, 18 August 2006.

Hartlaub, Peter, 'Black's 3 R's: reading, writing, rocking', in *The San Francisco Chronicle*, 5 March 2004.

Hartlaub, Peter, '*Scanner* stays true to Dick's novel – plus psychedelic animation', in *The San Francisco Chronicle*, 7 July 2006.

Harvey, Dennis, '*School of Rock*', in *Variety*, 9 September 2003.

Harvey, Dennis, '*Tape*', in *Variety*, 29 January 2001.

Hicks, Chris, '*Dazed and Confused*', in *Deseret News*, 16 November 2003.

Hicks, Chris, '*Slacker*', in *Deseret News*, 19 October 1991.

Hinson, Hal, '*Before Sunrise*', in *The Washington Post*, 27 January 1995.

Hinson, Hal, '*Slacker*', in *The Washington Post*, 23 August 1991.

Hoberman, J., 'Aching Life: *Before Sunrise*'s Gen X lovers walk, talk, and catch up in a romantic real-time sequel', in *The Village Voice*, 28 June 2004.

Hoberman, J., 'Brain Candy: Richard Linklater's literate Dick adaptation is a brain-bending Dlight', in *The Village Voice*, 5 July 2006.

Hoberman, J., 'Code Unknown: In the shadow of *Da Vinci*, Cannes '06's first great film', in *The Village Voice*, 23 May 2006.

Hoberman, J., 'Hear My Song: A Slacker Musician Teaches Preppie Tykes a Lesson in Unleashing Their Inner Rockers', in *The Village Voice*, 24-30 September 2003.

Hoberman, J., 'It's Mumblecore!: Films by, for, and about twenty-somethings are having a moment. IM someone about it', in *The Village Voice*, 17 August 2007.

Hoberman, J., 'Sleep With Me: *Intimacy*; *Waking Life*; *Focus*', in *The Village Voice*, 17-23 October 2001.

Hoberman, J., 'Welcome to the Jungle: Two movies, one point', in *The Village Voice*, 14 November 2006.

Hodgkinson, Tom, 'Conversations: Richard Linklater', in *The Idler*, 6 September 1994.

Honeycutt, Kirk, '*Fast Food Nation*', in *The Hollywood Reporter*, 20 May 2006.

Honeycutt, Kirk, '*Me and Orson Welles*', in *The Hollywood Reporter*, 7 September 2008.

Honeycutt, Kirk, '*The School of Rock*' , in *The Hollywood Reporter*, 10 September 2003.

Honeycutt, Kirk, '*Waking Life*', in *The Hollywood Reporter*, 29 January 2001.

Houlihan, Mary, 'Author, director turn facts into *Food* for thought', in *The Chicago Sun-Times*, 17 November 2006.

Howe, Desson, 'Aroused by *Waking Life*', in *The Washington Post*, 26 October 2001.

Howe, Desson, '*Before Sunrise*', in *The Washington Post*, 27 January 1995.

Howe, Desson, '*Dazed and Confused*', in *The Washington Post*, 22 October 1993.

Howe, Desson, '*Slacker*', in *The Washington Post*, 23 August 1991.

Hunter, Allan, '*Me and Orson Welles*', in *Screen Daily*, 6 September 2008.

Hunter, Stephen, 'Linklater's *Waking Life*: Noodling in Nod', in *The Washington Post*, 26 October 2001.

James, Nick, 'Debrief Encounter', in *Sight and Sound*, August 2004.

Johnson, David T., 'Directors on Adaptation: A Conversation with Richard Linklater', in *Literature Film Quarterly*, Spring 2007.

Johnston, Sheila, 'Old World without end', in *The Independent*, 20 April 1995.

Johnston, Sheila, 'Ships that pass in the night', in *The Independent*, 20 April 1995.

Jones, Kent, 'Dream Whirl – filmmaker Richard Linklater's *Waking Life*', in *ArtForum*, September 2001.

Jones, Kent, 'To Live or Clarify the Moment: Rick Linklater's *Waking Life*', in *Senses of Cinema*, March 2002.
<http://www.sensesofcinema.com/contents/01/19/waking.html>

Kempley, Rita, 'Richard Linklater's Waste of *Tape*: Director's latest is a little too independent', in *The Washington Post*, 16 November 2001.

Kempley, Rita, 'Suburban Bawl', in *The Washington Post*, 7 March 1997.

Kerr, Sarah, 'Whatever: *subUrbia* rehashes the clichés of youth', in *Slate*, 6 February 1997. <http://www.slate.com/id/3206/>

Koresky, Michael, 'The Mumblecore Movement? Andrew Bujalski on his *Funny Ha Ha*', in *IndieWIRE*, 2 May 2005.
<http://www.indiewire.com/people/people_050502bujalski.html>

Koresky, Michael, and Jeff Reichert, 'A Conversation with Richard Linklater', in *Reverse Shot Online*, Summer 2004.
<http://www.reverseshot.com/legacy/summer04/linklater1.html>

LaSalle, Mick, 'An Extraordinary Day Dawns *Before Sunrise*', in *The San Francisco Chronicle*, 27 January 1995.

LaSalle, Mick, '*Bad News Bears* drops the ball', in *The San Francisco Chronicle*, 22 July 2005.

LaSalle, Mick, 'Beautiful *Sunrise* Over Vienna', in *The San Francisco Chronicle*, 21 July 1995.

LaSalle, Mick, 'Tense Reunion of Old Friends: Linklater's *Tape* a chamber piece', in *The San Francisco Chronicle*, 16 November 2001.

LaSalle, Mick, 'They'll always have Paris – once more', in *The San Francisco Chronicle*, 2 July 2004.

LaSalle, Mick, '*Waking Life* a mess: Original but disjointed film', in *The San Francisco Chronicle*, 26 October 2001.

Lebkowsky, Jon, 'Interview with Richard Linklater', in *Mindjack*, 1992. <http://www.mindjack.com/interviews/linklater1.html>

Lee, Kevin, 'Finding Freedom the Second Time Around: The Politics of *Before Sunset*', in *Senses of Cinema*, October 2004.
<http://www.sensesofcinema.com/contents/04/33/before_sunset.html>

Levy, Emanuel, '*The Newton Boys*', in *Variety*, 13 March 1998.

Lieberman, Rhonda, '*The GenX Reader*: Book Reviews', in *ArtForum*, November 1994.

Lim, Dennis, 'From Dawn Till Dusk: Nine years later, the director and stars of *Before Sunrise* reunite for a stunning real-time sequel', in *The Village Voice*, 29 June 2004.

Lim, Dennis, 'Uncertainty Principles: *Tape*; *K-Pax*', in *The Village Voice*, 31 October-6 November 2001.

Lowry, Brian, '*Bad News Bears*', in *Variety*, 17 July 2005.

Matheou, Demetrios, 'Bad News Bears', in The Independent on Sunday, 14 August 2005.

Mathews, Jack, 'subUrbia: subUrbia Goes Back to Confused Days', in The Los Angeles Times, 7 February 1997.

McCarthy, Todd, 'Fast Food Nation', in Variety, 19 May 2006.

McCarthy, Todd, 'Me and Orson Welles', in Variety, 8 September 2008.

McCarthy, Todd, 'Waking Life', in Variety, 25 January 2001.

McCarthy, Tom, '"Formula" makes Newton Boys shine', in The Daily Beacon, 9 April 1998.

McGurk, Margaret A., 'subUrbia turns out to be desolate destination', in The Cincinnati Enquirer, 2 May 1997.

Millar, Jeff, 'Linklater's subUrbia not worth a visit', in The Houston Chronicle, 19 March 1997.

Millar, Jeff, 'Newton Boys cautious and bland', in The Houston Chronicle, 25 March 1998.

Miller, Laura, 'The Mild Bunch: Richard Linklater takes a stab at a stale genre with The Newton Boys', in Salon, 27 March 1998.

Miranda, Carolina A., 'Slack is Back', in Time, 13 September 2004.

Moreno, Ashley, 'Zen and the Art of Winning Championships: Richard Linklater profiles living legend Augie Garrido in Inning by Inning', in The Austin Chronicle, 30 May 2008.

Muller, Bill, 'Bad News Bears', in The Arizona Republic, 22 July 2005.

Murray, Noel, 'Richard Linklater', in The Onion A.V. Club, 14 June 2006. <http://www.avclub.com/content/node/49451/>

Nelson, Rob, 'Double Vision: The same-but-different philosophies of Richard Linklater's Cannes twofer', in The Village Voice, 30 May 2006.

Nelson, Rob, 'Richard Linklater: Grazed and Abused', in Mother Jones, November-December 2006.

Noh, David, 'Fast Food Nation', in Film Journal, 17 November 2006.

Norton, Glen, 'The Seductive Slack of Before Sunrise', in Post Script: Essays in Film and the Humanities, 19, no.2, Winter-Spring 2000.

Null, Christopher, 'It's Impossible to Learn to Plow by Reading Books', in FilmCritic.com, 2004. <http://filmcritic.com/misc/emporium.nsf/84dbbfa4d710144986256c29 0016f76e/54304a02c3c6 849088256f050001d05a?OpenDocument>

O'Hehir, Andrew, 'School of Rock', in Salon, 3 October 2003.

O'Sullivan, Charlotte, 'Julie, Madly, Deeply', in The Independent, 23 July 2004.

O'Sullivan, Michael, 'Tape Eventually Unravels', in The Washington Post, 16 November 2001.

Ottenhoff, John, 'Movie Reviews', in *Christian Century*, 15 June 1994.

Pearlman, Cindy, 'Billy Bob's *Bears*', in *The Chicago Sun-Times*, 17 July 2005.

Perry, Tim, 'City Slicker: Austin', in *The Independent*, 11 March 1996.

Persall, Steve, '*Bears* hibernation ends', in *The St. Petersburg Times*, 21 July 2005.

Persall, Steve, 'The Perfect *Sunset*', in *The St. Petersburg Times*, 22 July 2004.

Phelan, Stephen, 'Auteur State: *Tape*', in *The Sunday Herald*, 9 June 2002.

Phillips, Michael, '*Fast Food Nation*', in *The Chicago Tribune*, 17 November 2006.

Phipps, Keith, '*A Scanner Darkly*', in *The Onion A.V. Club*, 5 July 2006. <http://www.avclub.com/content/node/50156/>

Phipps, Keith, '*subUrbia*', in *The Onion A.V. Club*, 29 March 2002. <http://www.avclub.com/content/node/2968/>

Pols, Mary F., '*Fast Food* film opens eyes while tenderizing message', in *The Oakland Tribune*, 17 November 2006.

Poyser, Bryan, 'The Revolution Will be Animated: Is *Waking Life* a Wake-Up Call for Indie Animators?', in *Independent Film and Video Monthly*, 24, no.3, April 2001.

Price, Brian, 'Richard Linklater', in *Senses of Cinema*, June 2003. <http://www.sensesofcinema.com/contents/directors/03/linklater.html>

Quinn, Anthony, 'Hail, hail, rock 'n' roll!', in *The Independent*, 6 February 2004.

Radman, Jon, 'Generation X and Postmodern Cinema: *Slacker*', in *Post Script: Essays in Film and the Humanities*, 19, no.2, Winter-Spring 2000.

Raftery, Brian, '*Slacker*: 15 years later', in *Salon*, 5 July 2006.

Rainer, Peter, '*Before Sunrise*', in *The Los Angeles Times*, 6 April 1996.

Rainer, Peter, 'Dreams Work', in *New York Magazine*, 29 October 2001.

Rainer, Peter, 'Grudge Report', in *New York Magazine*, 12 November 2001.

Rea, Steven, 'A mind trip of talk in a surreal world', in *The Philadelphia Inquirer*, 26 October 2001.

Rea, Steven, 'The kids are all right, and so is the teacher', in *The Philadelphia Inquirer*, 3 October 2003.

Rea, Steven, 'Three-way volley of mind games, in just one room', in *The Philadelphia Inquirer*, 16 November 2001.

Rechtshaffen, Michael, '*Bad News Bears*', in *The Hollywood Reporter*, 18 July 2005.

Relyea, Lane, 'What, me work? Interview with director Richard

Linklater', in *ArtForum*, April 1993.

Richardson, Daniel C., 'Idea-dropping', in *Christian Century*, 21 November 2001.

Rickey, Carrie, 'New *Bad News Bears* whiffs, but bawdy Billy Bob makes contact', in *The Philadelphia Enquirer*, 22 July 2005.

Robey, Tim, 'The Best Years in the Life of Richard Linklater', in *Sight and Sound*, April 2007.

Rocchi, James, 'TIFF Review: *Me and Orson Welles*', in *Cinematical*, 11 September 2008.

<http://www.cinematical.com/2008/09/11/tiff-review-meand-orson-welles/>

Rodriguez, Rene, 'Talking heads fill *Waking Life*', in *The Miami Herald*, 9 November 2001.

Romney, Jonathan, 'Dude, I'm not feeling myself', in *The Independent on Sunday*, 20 August 2006.

Romney, Jonathan, 'Haven't I seen you somewhere before?', in *The Independent on Sunday*, 25 July 2004.

Romney, Jonathan, '*Slacker* doodles', in *The Independent on Sunday*, 21 April 2002.

Rosenberg, Scott, 'Post Teenage Waste Land: For the dead-end kids in *Suburbia*, a rock star's return offers a chance at escape', in *Salon*, 7 February 1997.

Russell, Mike, 'The *CulturePulp* Q&A: Richard Linklater', in *CulturePulp*, 54, 16 July 2006.

<http://homepage.mac.com/merussell/iblog/B835531044/C1592678312/E20060701140745/index.html>

Russell, Mike, 'The Richard Linklater Interview', in *CulturePulp*, 54, 16 July 2006.

<http://homepage.mac.com/merussell/iblog/B835531044/C1162162177/E20060717001411/index.html>

Ryhs, Tim, 'Hanging Out with Richard Linklater', in *MovieMaker*, February 1997.

<http://www.industrycentral.net/director_interviews/RL04.htm>

Savlov, Marc, '*Bad News Bears*', in *The Austin Chronicle*, 22 July 2005.

Savlov, Marc, '*Fast Food Nation*', in *The Austin Chronicle*, 17 November 2006.

Savlov, Marc, 'Securing the Substance: Richard Linklater on his adaptation of *A Scanner Darkly*', in *The Austin Chronicle*, 7 July 2006.

Schwarzbaum, Lisa, '*Bad News Bears*', in *Entertainment Weekly*, 20 July 2005.

Seymour, Gene, '*Fast Food* takes guts to watch', in *Newsday*, 17 November

2006.

Shoard, Catherine, 'Zac Efron is a revelation in Richard Linklater's *Me and Orson Welles*', in *The Guardian*, 18 September 2009.

Shulgasser, Barbara, 'Modern *Roman Holiday* alive and well in Vienna', in *The San Francisco Examiner*, 27 January 1995.

Simon, John, *'Before Sunrise'*, in *National Review*, 6 March 1995.

Simon, John, *'SubUrbia'*, in *National Review*, 10 March 1997.

Slonin, Jeffrey, 'A Thousand Words', in *ArtForum*, December 1993.

Slonin, Jeffrey, 'Rocky Mountain High Points', in *ArtForum*, April 1995.

Smith, Bec, 'Richard Linklater on *Waking Life*', in *Inside Film*, 15 December 2001.

Smith, Gavin, 'Gavin Smith on Richard Linklater's *Waking Life*', in *Film Comment*, March 2001.

Smith, Gavin, 'Lost in America', in *Film Comment*, July/August 2006.

Smith, Kyle, 'Stick it in your bun', in *The New York Post*, 17 November 2006.

Stack, Peter, 'Bank-Robbing *Newton* Brothers Show Boys Will Be Boys', in *The San Francisco Chronicle*, 27 March 1998.

Stein, Joel, 'He's Having a Ball', in *Time*, 11 July 2005.

Stein, Ruthe, 'A plentiful serving of diet don'ts', in *The San Francisco Chronicle*, 17 November 2006.

Stuart, Jan, *'Bad News Bears'*, in *Newsday*, 22 July 2005.

Stack, Peter, 'Bank-Robbing *Newton* Brothers Show Boys Will Be Boys', in *The San Francisco Chronicle*, 27 March 1998.

Stack, Peter, 'Grim Message of *subUrbia*: Linklater's latest takes bleak view', in *The San Francisco Chronicle*, 14 February 1997.

Sublett, Jesse, 'Another Day, Another Dollar', in *Texas Monthly*, 1 April 1998.

Taubin, Amy, 'Cannes 2006: Help Me Make It Through The Night', in *Sight and Sound*, July 2006.

Thomas, Dana, *'Slacker'*, in *The Washington Post*, 23 August 1991.

Thomas, Kevin, *'Tape*: Tense reunion showcases strong acting', in *The Los Angeles Times*, 2 November 2001.

Thomas, Kevin, *'Waking Life'*, in *The Los Angeles Times*, 19 October 2001.

Thompson, Anne, 'Catching Up With Richard Linklater', in *Premiere*, 19:9, June 2006.

Thompson, Ben, 'The Return of the Talkies', in *The Independent*, 22 January 1996.

Thompson, Gary, *'Waking Life'*, in *The Philadelphia Daily News*, 26 October 2001.

Tobias, Scott, *'Bad News Bears'*, in *The Onion A.V. Club*, 19 July 2005.

<http://www.avclub.com/content/node/24938/>

Tobias, Scott, 'Before Sunset', in *The Onion A.V. Club*, 29 June 2004.

<http://www.avclub.com/content/node/17850/>

Tobias, Scott, 'Fast Food Nation', in *The Onion A.V. Club*, 16 November 2006.

<http://www.avclub.com/content/node/55385/>

Tobias, Scott, 'Inning By Inning: A Portrait Of A Coach', in *The Onion A.V. Club*, 17 June 2009.

<http://www.avclub.com/articles/inning-by-inning-a-portraitof-a-coach,29316/>

Tobias, Scott, 'School of Rock', in *The Onion A.V. Club*, 30 September 2003.

<http://www.avclub.com/content/node/17226/>

Travers, Peter, 'A Scanner Darkly', in *Rolling Stone*, 23 June 2006.

Travers, Peter, 'Bad News Bears', in *Rolling Stone*, 22 July 2005.

Travers, Peter, 'Before Sunset', in *Rolling Stone*, 16 June 2004.

Travers, Peter, 'Dazed and Confused', in *Rolling Stone*, 14 October 1993.

Travers, Peter, 'Fast Food Nation', in *Rolling Stone*, 13 November 2006.

Travers, Peter, 'Slacker', in *Rolling Stone*, 11 July 1991.

Travers, Peter, 'subUrbia', in *Rolling Stone*, 20 February 1997.

Travers, Peter, 'Tape', in *Rolling Stone*, 8 November 2001.

Travers, Peter, 'Waking Life', in *Rolling Stone*, 8 November 2001.

Turan, Kenneth, ' School of Rock: An electric Jack Black blows out the amp as a musicianturned-teacher in *School of Rock*', in *The Los Angeles Times*, 3 October 2003.

Vice, Jeff, 'Author insisted on fictionalized *Fast Food*', in *Deseret News*, 19 November 2006.

Vice, Jeff, 'Bears is funny, but it's not for all', in *Deseret News*, 22 July 2005.

Vice, Jeff, 'Before Sunset talky but romantic', in *Deseret News*, 23 July 2004.

Vice, Jeff, 'Lose appetite at *Food*', in *Deseret News*, 17 November 2006.

Vice, Jeff, 'Scanner faithful to the book', in *Deseret News*, 14 July 2006.

Vice, Jeff, 'subUrbia', in *Deseret News*, 14 February 1997.

Vice, Jeff, 'The Newton Boys', in *Deseret News*, 27 March 1998.

Vice, Jeff, 'The School of Rock is messy, but hilarious', in *Deseret News*, 3 October 2003.

Villarreal, Phil, 'Before Sunrise: Soulmate warmth gives *Before Sunrise* its luster', in *The Arizona Daily Star*, 16 June 2006.

Villarreal, Phil, 'Dazed and Confused: Sprawling ensemble lifts *Dazed*', in *The Arizona Daily Star*, 4 November 2005.

Vognar, Chris, 'Bad News Bears', in *The Dallas Morning News*, 22 July

2005.

Vourvoulias, Bill, 'Fast Food Nation', in Interview, November 2006.

Walsh, David, 'An interview with Richard Linklater: You can't hold back the human spirit', in World Socialist Web Site, 27 March 1998. <http://www.wsws.org/arts/1998/mar1998/link-m27.shtml>

Walters, Barry, 'Deadbeats inhabit a verbose subUrbia', in The San Francisco Examiner, 14 February 1997.

Walters, Chris, 'Slacker', in The Austin Chronicle, 5 July 1991.

Westbrook, Bruce, 'School of Rock', in The Houston Chronicle, 12 May 2004.

Whipp, Glenn, 'Subtle shades of genius in each minute of Before Sunset', in The Oakland Tribune, 2 July 2004.

White, Jerry, 'Nouveau and Improved: The Montreal International Festival of Film, Video and the New Technologies', in Afterimage, September/October 1996.

Wilmington, Michael, 'A Scanner Darkly', in The Chicago Tribune, 7 July 2006.

Wilmington, Michael, 'Bad News Bears', in The Chicago Tribune, 14 July 2005.

Wilmington, Michael, 'Before Sunset', in The Chicago Tribune, 28 June 2004.

Wineke, Andrew, 'Fast Food Nation author notes change, good and bad, since book', in The Colorado Springs Gazette, 19 July 2006.

Winters, Rebecca, 'Q&A: Richard Linklater', in Time, 13 October 2003.

PICTURE CREDITS

IT'S IMPOSSIBLE TO LEARN TO PLOW BY READING BOOKS
Detour Filmproduction
SLACKER
Detour Filmproduction
DAZED AND CONFUSED
Detour Filmproduction / Alphaville Films
BEFORE SUNRISE
Detour Filmproduction / Castle Rock Entertainment / Columbia Pictures Filmhaus Wien Universa Filmpro / Sunrise Production
SUBURBIA
Detour Filmproduction / Castle Rock Entertainment
THE NEWTON BOYS
Detour Filmproduction / Twentieth Century Fox /Newton Boys Ventures Inc.
WAKING LIFE
Detour Filmproduction / Fox Searchlight Pictures / Independent Film Channel / Thousand Words / Flat Black Films / Line Research
TAPE
Detour Filmproduction / IFC Productions / InDigEnt / The Independent Film Channel Productions / Tape Productions Inc.
SCHOOL OF ROCK
Paramount Pictures / Scott Rudin Productions / MFP Munich Film Partners GmbH & Company I. Produktions KG.
BEFORE SUNSET
Detour Filmproduction / Castle Rock Entertainment
BAD NEWS BEARS
Detour Filmproduction / Geyer Kosinski / Media Talent Group
A SCANNER DARKLY
Detour Filmproduction / Warner Independent Pictures / Thousand Words / 3 Arts Entertainment / Section Eight Ltd.

FAST FOOD NATION
BBC Films / HanWay Films / Recorded Picture Company /
Participant Productions
INNING BY INNING
Detour Filmproduction
ME AND ORSON WELLES
Detour Filmproduction / CinemaNX / Cinetic Media / Framestore /
Fuzzy Bunny Films

BFI Posters, Stills and Designs. Roland Grant Archive.

CRESCENT MOON PUBLISHING

ARTS, PAINTING, SCULPTURE

The Art of Andy Goldsworthy: Complete Works
Andy Goldsworthy: Touching Nature
Andy Goldsworthy in Close-Up
Andy Goldsworthy: Pocket Guide
Andy Goldsworthy In America

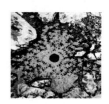

Land Art: A Complete Guide
Richard Long: The Art of Walking
The Art of Richard Long: Complete Works
Richard Long in Close-Up
Richard Long: Pocket Guide
Land Art In the UK
Land Art in Close-Up

Land Art In the U.S.A.
Land Art: Pocket Guide
Installation Art in Close-Up
Minimal Art and Artists In the 1960s and After
Colourfield Painting

Land Art DVD, TV documentary
Andy Goldsworthy DVD, TV documentary
The Erotic Object: Sexuality in Sculpture From Prehistory to the Present Day
Sex in Art: Pornography and Pleasure in Painting and Sculpture
Postwar Art
Sacred Gardens: The Garden in Myth, Religion and Art
Glorification: Religious Abstraction in Renaissance and 20th Century Art
Early Netherlandish Painting
Leonardo da Vinci
Piero della Francesca
Giovanni Bellini

Fra Angelico: Art and Religion in the Renaissance
Mark Rothko: The Art of Transcendence
Frank Stella: American Abstract Artist

Jasper Johns: Painting By Numbers
Brice Marden
Alison Wilding: The Embrace of Sculpture
Vincent van Gogh: Visionary Landscapes
Eric Gill: Nuptials of God
Constantin Brancusi: Sculpting the Essence of Things
Max Beckmann
Caravaggio

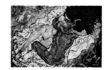

Gustave Moreau
Egon Schiele: Sex and Death In Purple Stockings
Delizioso Fotografico Fervore: Works In Process 1
Sacro Cuore: Works In Process 2
The Light Eternal: J.M.W. Turner
The Madonna Glorified: Karen Arthurs

LITERATURE

J.R.R. Tolkien: The Books, The Films, The Whole Cultural Phenomenon
J.R.R. Tolkien: Pocket Guide
Tolkien's Heroic Quest
The *Earthsea* Books of Ursula Le Guin
Beauties, Beasts and Enchantment: Classic French Fairy Tales
Sexing Hardy: Thomas Hardy and Feminism
Thomas Hardy's *Tess of the d'Urbervilles*
Thomas Hardy's *Jude the Obscure*
Thomas Hardy: The Tragic Novels
Love and Tragedy: Thomas Hardy
The Poetry of Landscape in Hardy
Wessex Revisited: Thomas Hardy and John Cowper Powys
Wolfgang Iser: Essays and Interviews
Petrarch, Dante and the Troubadours
Maurice Sendak and the Art of Children's Book Illustration
Andrea Dworkin
Cixous, Irigaray, Kristeva: The *Jouissance* of French Feminism
Julia Kristeva: Art, Love, Melancholy, Philosophy, Semiotics and Psychoanalysis
Hélene Cixous I Love You: The *Jouissance* of Writing
Luce Irigaray: Lips, Kissing, and the Politics of Sexual Difference
Peter Redgrove: Here Comes the Flood
Peter Redgrove: Sex-Magic-Poetry-Cornwall
Lawrence Durrell: Between Love and Death, East and West
Love, Culture & Poetry: Lawrence Durrell
Cavafy: Anatomy of a Soul
German Romantic Poetry: Goethe, Novalis, Heine, Hölderlin
Feminism and Shakespeare
Shakespeare: Love, Poetry & Magic
The Passion of D.H. Lawrence
D.H. Lawrence: Symbolic Landscapes
D.H. Lawrence: Infinite Sensual Violence
Rimbaud: Arthur Rimbaud and the Magic of Poetry
The Ecstasies of John Cowper Powys
Sensualism and Mythology: The Wessex Novels of John Cowper Powys
Amorous Life: John Cowper Powys and the Manifestation of Affectivity (H.W. Fawkner)
Postmodern Powys: New Essays on John Cowper Powys (Joe Boulter)
Rethinking Powys: Critical Essays on John Cowper Powys
Paul Bowles & Bernardo Bertolucci
Rainer Maria Rilke
Joseph Conrad: *Heart of Darkness*
In the Dim Void: Samuel Beckett
Samuel Beckett Goes into the Silence
André Gide: Fiction and Fervour
Jackie Collins and the Blockbuster Novel
Blinded By Her Light: The Love-Poetry of Robert Graves
The Passion of Colours: Travels In Mediterranean Lands
Poetic Forms

POETRY

Ursula Le Guin: Walking In Cornwall
Peter Redgrove: Here Comes The Flood
Peter Redgrove: Sex-Magic-Poetry-Cornwall
Dante: Selections From the *Vita Nuova*
Petrarch, Dante and the Troubadours
William Shakespeare: *The Sonnets*
William Shakespeare: Complete Poems
Blinded By Her Light: The Love-Poetry of Robert Graves
Emily Dickinson: Selected Poems
Emily Brontë: Poems
Thomas Hardy: Selected Poems
Percy Bysshe Shelley: Poems
John Keats: Selected Poems
D.H. Lawrence: Selected Poems
Edmund Spenser: Poems
Edmund Spenser: *Amoretti*
John Donne: Poems
Henry Vaughan: Poems
Sir Thomas Wyatt: Poems
Robert Herrick: Selected Poems
Rilke: Space, Essence and Angels in the Poetry of Rainer Maria Rilke
Rainer Maria Rilke: Selected Poems
Friedrich Hölderlin: Selected Poems
Arseny Tarkovsky: Selected Poems
Novalis: *Hymns To the Night*
Paul Verlaine: Selected Poems
Arthur Rimbaud: Selected Poems
Arthur Rimbaud: *A Season in Hell*
Arthur Rimbaud and the Magic of Poetry
D.J. Enright: By-Blows
Jeremy Reed: Brigitte's Blue Heart
Jeremy Reed: Claudia Schiffer's Red Shoes
Gorgeous Little Orpheus
Radiance: New Poems
Crescent Moon Book of Nature Poetry
Crescent Moon Book of Love Poetry
Crescent Moon Book of Mystical Poetry
Crescent Moon Book of Elizabethan Love Poetry
Crescent Moon Book of Metaphysical Poetry
Crescent Moon Book of Romantic Poetry
Pagan America: New American Poetry

MEDIA, CINEMA, FEMINISM and CULTURAL STUDIES

J.R.R. Tolkien: The Books, The Films, The Whole Cultural Phenomenon
J.R.R. Tolkien: Pocket Guide
The *Lord of the Rings* Movies: Pocket Guide
The Ghost Dance: The Origins of Religion
Cixous, Irigaray, Kristeva: The *Jouissance* of French Feminism
Julia Kristeva: Art, Love, Melancholy, Philosophy, Semiotics and Psychoanalysis
Luce Irigaray: Lips, Kissing, and the Politics of Sexual Difference
Hélene Cixous I Love You: The *Jouissance* of Writing
Andrea Dworkin
'Cosmo Woman': The World of Women's Magazines
Women in Pop Music
Discovering the Goddess (Geoffrey Ashe)
The Poetry of Cinema
The Sacred Cinema of Andrei Tarkovsky
Andrei Tarkovsky: Pocket Guide
Andrei Tarkovsky: *Mirror*: Pocket Movie Guide
Andrei Tarkovsky: *The Sacrifice*: Pocket Movie Guide
Walerian Borowczyk: Cinema of Erotic Dreams
Jean-Luc Godard: The Passion of Cinema
John Hughes and Eighties Cinema
Ferris Bueller's Day Off: Pocket Movie Guide
Jean-Luc Godard: Pocket Guide
The Cinema of Richard Linklater
Liv Tyler: Star In Ascendance
Blade Runner and the Films of Philip K. Dick
Paul Bowles and Bernardo Bertolucci
Media Hell: Radio, TV and the Press
An Open Letter to the BBC
Detonation Britain: Nuclear War in the UK
Feminism and Shakespeare
Wild Zones: Pornography, Art and Feminism
Sex in Art: Pornography and Pleasure in Painting and Sculpture
Sexing Hardy: Thomas Hardy and Feminism

In my view *The Light Eternal* is among the very best of all the material I read on Turner. (Douglas Graham, director of the Turner Museum, Denver, Colorado)

The Light Eternal is a model monograph, an exemplary job. The subject matter of the book is beautifully organised and dead on beam. (Lawrence Durrell)

It is amazing for me to see my work treated with such passion and respect. (Andrea Dworkin)

Sex-Magic-Poetry-Cornwall is a very rich essay... It is like a brightly-lighted box. (Peter Redgrove)

CRESCENT MOON PUBLISHING
P.O. Box 393, Maidstone, Kent, ME14 5XU, United Kingdom. www.crmoon.com

Lightning Source UK Ltd.
Milton Keynes UK
UKOW04f2053251014

240628UK00003B/141/P